The Producer's Medium

The Producer's Medium

CONVERSATIONS WITH CREATORS
OF AMERICAN TV

Horace Newcomb / Robert S. Alley

New York   Oxford
OXFORD UNIVERSITY PRESS
1983

Copyright © 1983 by Oxford University Press, Inc.

Library of Congress Cataloging in Publication Data

The Producer's Medium

   1. Television producers and directors—United States—
Interviews.   2. Television broadcasting—United States.
I. Newcomb, Horace, 1942–   .   II. Alley, Robert S., 1932–
PN1992.75.A4   1983   791.45′0232   83-10991
ISBN 0-19-503347-7

Printing (last digit): 9 8 7 6 5 4 3 2 1

Printed in the United States of America

For Our Children

Kate Newcomb	John Alley
Bob Alley	Jud Newcomb

Acknowledgments

We gratefully acknowledge the assistance extended to us by many friends as we developed this book. Professor of English, Irby B. Brown, colleague at the University of Richmond, participated in a number of the interview sessions and has made several significant suggestions. Martin Kasindorf, West Coast Editor of *Newsweek* during the preparation of the book, was extremely helpful in arranging introductions. The secretaries to the executive producers, unheralded powers in the television business, made all our work a good bit easier.

And as we sought to explore the TV industry through the eyes of producers, many persons in the creative community, in addition to the producers included in this volume, offered invaluable aid, among whom we mention those who were particularly generous with their time: Harry Ackerman, Alan Alda, Peter Andrews, James A. Brown, Al Burton, Virginia Carter, Robin Chambers, Elinor Donahue, Nancy Malone, Philip Mandelker, Delbert Mann, Liam O'Brien, Gene Roddenberry, Robert Rosen, Jay Sandrich, Norbert Simmons, Van Gordon Sauter, David Sontag, and Paul Junger Witt.

A special word of thanks is extended to the John and Mary R. Markle Foundation which supplied important funding during the period of research.

In the preparation of the manuscript we were aided constantly by three sterling typists: Jane Crum, Helene Jainchell, and Diane Swinney. In the difficult task of editing we were ably guided by Curtis Church. And a particular word of appreciation goes to John Wright of

Oxford who brought us together, persevered with us, and continually and gently reminded us of deadlines.

Finally, to our wives, Sara and Norma, thank you for pretending that extended stays in California were genuine vacations for all of us.

Austin, Texas   H.N.
Richmond, Virginia   R.A.
June 15, 1983

Contents

Introduction, xi

The Television Producer: An Introduction, 3

The Producer's Medium, 3
Television in American Culture, 18
Creativity in Television, 34

Quinn Martin, 46

Interview with Quinn Martin, 56

David Victor, 74

Interview with David Victor, 82

John Mantley, 96

Interview with John Mantley, 104

Richard Levinson and William Link, 128

Interview with Richard Levinson and William Link, 139

Earl Hamner, 154

> *Interview with Earl Hamner, 161*

Norman Lear, 173

> *Interview with Norman Lear, 183*

James L. Brooks, Allan Burns, and Grant Tinker, 196

> *Interview with James L. Brooks and Allan Burns, 208*
> *Interview with Grant Tinker, 224*

Garry Marshall, 230

> *Interview with Garry Marshall, 238*

Index, 255

Introduction

Most of us still discuss television as a generalized force let loose in the home and in society. It is unpredictable and worrisome because of its large effects on our lives, yet is paradoxically familiar and comfortable within individual experience. And, above all, television is anonymous.

When we want to assign responsibility for errors or evils, we speak of "the networks." We speak of "broadcasting" as if it were unmanned, undirected, an airy, invisible layer of technology and business, remote, beyond our inspection. We attribute motive, and assign decision-making ability, but fail to identify human agents.

The people who make television prefer the designation of "the industry," or, if success is more recent than setback, it is "our" industry. Like the general public, television professionals are quick to cite "the structure of the industry," or "network executives" as limitations on creativity. The network officials, on the other hand, argue that they are misunderstood by members of "the creative community."

There are obvious short-term advantages in such attitudes. The public need not discriminate when talking about "television." Network officials can enjoy their relative obscurity and operate at a safe remove from public inspection. The creators of television content can use the vague generalizations to avoid responsibility for poor work. And when everything else fails each party can assume that the viewers have only mediocre taste and justify its actions in the name of "giving the audience what it wants."

This book is designed to shatter the anonymity of television. Because we are interested in prime-time, commercial, fictional television we introduce readers not to institutions, but to the *people* who are the primary makers of *Happy Days, The Fugitive, Gunsmoke, All in the Family,* and other massively popular television programs.* The people are the focus of this book, and have described their work in personal, individual terms. They have been willing to say "I," "we," "my decision," "my role," and "my responsibility." Through it all they have been willing to speak of failures as well as successes.

In focusing so precisely on certain individuals, however, it may be argued that we err in an opposite direction, giving more credit than is due to privileged participants in a complex system. We hope to avoid such a narrow view. Television is a highly collaborative medium, a sophisticated industrial process in which hundreds of individuals contribute to every show. Our concern with the role of the producer is based on several factors. First, given the structures of the industry's economic organization the producer is often assigned legal and financial responsibility for the final television product. A commonplace within the entertainment industry is that television is a "producer's medium." Second, in series television, several episodes or even several series are under production at any given moment, and the producer is the person who must oversee entire projects. The producer must hire or fire other members of the production team, including line producers who often see to day-to-day activities. Directors, writers, editors, and guest stars may work only in a single episode of a series. The producer, involved with the project from beginning to end, sees to it that continuity is maintained, that peace is kept among other members of the team, and, most importantly, that the series concept remains secure. Even in productions that are not part of a series, the same formal and informal authority and responsibility belong to the producer.

These skills, of course, can be described as "creative" only in the broadest sense, the sense that is often intended in speaking of "cre-

---

*No fewer than twenty-six separate television series produced by the men dealt with in this volume have been placed in the Nielsen top ten annual ratings between the years 1960 and 1980.

ative businessmen,'' or ''creative politicians.'' It is in this sense alone that many Hollywood producers are the ''creative'' centers of their endeavors. They can bring in projects on time, within budget, and without rancor within the production team. They are highly prized and highly rewarded within the industry, and they can do their work, in some cases, without involving themselves in the minute details of their productions. Many of them avoid that sort of total involvement.

Yet it is this further involvement that we feel is necessary to support our definition of the ''self-conscious, creative producer.'' The individuals we focus on in this study go beyond the basic ''creativity of competence'' we've described here. They also establish the creative vision of the projects they control. The term vision exceeds ''content,'' or ''ideas,'' exceeds the notion of a ''message.'' The vision encompasses all these things and recognizes the best ways to express them *as television*. On the successful combination of these components the producer gains the recognition of his peers, the confidence of network officials, and the bedrock on which these measures are grounded—the response of a mass audience.

For similar reasons members of that audience can, in many cases, recognize immediately the style of a particular producer, may even be able to recognize other shows as copies of that style. This may be true even when the producer is working deeply within one of television's strong traditional forms such as the situation comedy or the crime-adventure show. The creative producer is well aware of the strengths and weaknesses of the tradition and is able to make his own expression distinct within it. Or the producer may be known as a true innovator, one who takes the traditions in new directions or creates new forms that are closely identified with his work alone.

We have no wish to be restrictive in our view. Good, important, even great television is not always the result of the creative producer's controlling hand, eye, and ear. Quite obviously, many television productions rest on the ability of a central actor or an ensemble cast, and such productions would be successful so long as attention were paid to the minimal administrative detail required of a competent executive. In other cases television has been able to attract some of the most skillful writers in America to bring us comedy and high drama equal to that produced for any other medium. We do argue, in spite of these qualifications, that a self-conscious creative producer may be able to take what appears to be a mundane idea, a cast of no distinction, or writing that seems to be ordinary and conventional, and transform it into a better sort of television. When the happy circumstance arises in which the producer is able to assemble the best writers, actors, directors, and film editors, and is able to impress upon them a central concept that speaks his vision, then the potential is present for exceptional work. It can be created because art is mastery, discipline, and vision. It is the ability to mold constraint into creative contour. This book allows producers to speak for themselves about the making of television art.

The book is based on interviews with the producers who are its subject. The interviews were begun in 1975 by Robert Alley and continued by him on several subsequent trips to California. In January and July of 1979 Alley and Horace Newcomb returned to California for more interviews. In some cases, then, we have worked with several interviews from a single individual, gathered over a period of time. In other cases all the material selected was obtained in a single extended session. In formal settings, in restaurants, over coffee, in homes and offices, these interviews ranged over many topics, experiences, and examples, not all of them related directly to the subject.

The interviews have been edited to remove common tics of speech, interruptions, repetitions, and so on. We have also edited to focus the comments on television, the creative process, and the role of the producer. We have rearranged material from original sequences in some cases in order to gather dispersed comments on specific topics. But we have in no case altered the sense or meaning of any statement.

Our intention is to allow some of the people who make television to speak for themselves, explaining what it is they want to do and how they do it. They have talked about art, about business, about the ways in which these things go together. They have talked about how they use television as a medium of personal expression and social commentary. At times they have chafed at our questions, thinking them the wrong ones, but with good will have gone on to follow our interests. At other times, we have found ourselves following their leads, and in both instances some happy discoveries have been made.

Like most people they have found it difficult at times to articulate ideas and describe processes which they exercise daily almost by second nature. When we have asked them to consider alternative views, to express things in ways that would be understandable to someone who is not "in the business," they have generally been willing to do so. But they have also insisted that those not initiated into the mysteries of television production have a responsibility to try and understand the special references, the language, the sense of technique and the forms of commitment and personal expression that are the defining characteristics of the medium. We agree with that view. We think all viewers will be better off knowing more about the medium than is now generally the case. To that extent, then, the book is designed to take the television viewer "behind the scenes."

But our book is not only a set of interviews. Because we think these producers have been responsible for the creation of important works of television art, we also want to explore those works. Our own view, then, is that the interviews constitute a new body of material that must be studied in its own right, must be interpreted and applied. The interviews comment on the works themselves, offering the interpretation and intention of the creators. But we do not always agree with what is said or accept it as the final, accurate explanation of how programs have become important objects of enjoyment and analysis. At times we think our questions have led producers into saying what they assumed we wanted to hear. At times we think they have led to genuine, previously unconsidered insight. At times we think the producers have provided us with sparkling judgments of their own works. At other times we do not think they see nearly enough in that work. Sometimes we think they overrate their work. As often we think they underrate it.

The commentary that surrounds the interviews, then, is designed to supplement the perspectives of the producers. We offer further analysis, using their views as a new source for our own critical judgment. Ideally, any reader who is familiar with the television programs discussed can do the same thing, can compare the comments of the producers with private experience and critical interpretation. The producers who comment here do so freely and with good intentions; reader-viewers owe them the same intention and effort.

Finally, we wish to make it clear that we do not think we have in any way totally defined or even surveyed the ranks of the self-conscious creative television producers. There are glaring omissions in this collection. In some cases they are ours, the results of limited time, money, opportunity, and appropriate introductions—limitations that will be readily acknowledged by any producer. In other cases certain producers whom we approached with proper introductions, notably Aaron Spelling and the late Jack Webb, chose not to be included. It should be clear to any readers that many of their favorite programs, programs that they feel must be the result of great creativity, are not represented here in the person of the creator.

Some of the omissions also occur because we have focused on people who have made a mark on television that extends over time, who have established, maintained, and modified style, content, and form. Doubtless there are many producers who have created important, high-quality programs, who have not yet gained the reputation, backing, or authority to go on and sustain their creativity through many productions. Among them, it will be quickly noticed, are most women and minority producers. There are, to our regret, no women and no minority members in this book because the structure of the television industry, like the structure of American society, has been dominated by white males.

That same domination has effectively blocked, with a few notable exceptions, genuine representation of minority groups on television. Norbert Simmons, as president of MCA New Ventures, one of a very few blacks in a top executive position, fears that even though there "were a few marked successes in the seventies," a "retrenchment" in black roles is now in evidence. He is convinced that until blacks in greater numbers fill senior administrative posts, the situation will not improve. He views the current situation as not so much a result of overt race prejudice as simply a reflection of the entertainment production system at work. That system is based upon hiring those you know and meet socially. The Hollywood social scene, shaped by forces at work elsewhere in American society, separates along racial lines and there is, therefore, "very little social contact between the races."

Similarly, the representation of women has been accomplished through traditional male perceptions. Hence, men are careful, women picky; men are firm, women stubborn; men exercise authority, women are tyrannical; men are stern taskmasters, women are difficult to work with. Not only are these images conveyed on the screen, they often determine actions behind camera. In spite of some recent progress, serious barriers remain for women directors and producers. To be sure, this is partly explained by the long years in which the television business offered no access to beginning jobs for females. But we would be naive if we failed to recognize that much of the continued white male dominance in television stems from an observable, intractable bias.

In spite of these difficulties the representation of minority groups and women is not all presented from a single perspective in television. The very problems outlined here have often become the subject of television fiction, sometimes in the work of the individuals interviewed. Because television is a highly charged, symbolic, fictional system, these issues become central in what we call "television's internal dialogue." The limited numbers of women and minority members in the production community indicate to us that that dialogue is flawed, narrowed, in ways that must be corrected if social inequity is to be rectified not only in the television industry, but in American society at large.

What all the omissions say to us is that there should and will be other versions of this book, other books that explore the creative process in television. Some of them will focus on producers and, we hope, in the future will include representatives of every group in our society. Those books will find other subjects as young producers create the successes that will gain for them the kind of control that has made the men discussed here dominant in their profession at a particular time. Among them will be men and women of great talent who choose television as their medium of expression. Television depends on their creative vision, on their abilities to gather and marshal the talents of others who contribute to the television process. These persons of vision and control are the creative producers. They are the television makers. And television will be *their* medium.

The Producer's Medium

The Television Producer:
An Introduction

THE PRODUCER'S MEDIUM

We offer these studies of television producers knowing that even as we write the television industry is in a thorough-going process of real flux. Once again, technology has revolutionized thinking—about the future of networks, the future of those responsible for television content, and the ways in which audiences will deal with the new opportunities for entertainment in the coming decades. Our presentation is predicated on the form of American television which prevailed from its beginnings to the successful development of cable technologies. Essentially this history has been the story of three commercial networks and, since the late 1960s, the Public Broadcasting Service.

Discussions of cable and satellite technologies now consume nearly as much media space as the great debate over color systems did in the fifties. No certain future appears, but it seems that the decade of the eighties is beginning to offer significant new production alternatives. Already the environment of television production in Los Angeles is experiencing important change. Our observations, then, need to be understood against the background of the height of independent television producers' power. We have chosen to focus on the mid-seventies because research and observation support the conclusion that the zenith of creative production power was reached at about that time. While another cycle of equal importance may develop at any time, it will inevitably be within the context of the new technologies, and will be measured against that earlier time. It will be measured against the brightest glow of the network era.

A visitor to the Hollywood scene in 1975 would have witnessed nearly limitless excitement and activity surrounding the personalities who bore the title of ''producer,'' particularly around those who are featured in this study. The cumulative Nielsen ratings for 1975–76 reveal that of the top twenty-five TV series, Norman Lear was responsible for six, Brooks and Burns two, Garry Marshall two, and Earl Hamner one. In the previous year Quinn Martin claimed two series in the same listing. John Mantley was then producing the final year of *Gunsmoke,* television's longest-running western series. David Victor was producing the final year of *Marcus Welby, M.D.*, ABC's first number-one show. And Link and Levinson were in the midst of their successful run with *Columbo*. The two giants in independent production were Tandem/TAT and MTM.

At the old Republic Studios on Radford Avenue in Studio City the space occupied by MTM suggested a near melding of CBS and its prize independent production supplier, Grant Tinker, president of MTM. The marriage was duplicated across town at CBS Studio Center where Norman Lear still used the office space once reserved as an apartment for Danny Thomas at the Tandem/TAT headquarters. Boasting fifteen of the top twenty-five series in the previous year, CBS executives seemed confident that its two comedy sources were capable of supplying an endless collection of critically acclaimed episodes in series such as *The Mary Tyler Moore Show, Rhoda, The Bob Newhart Show, Phyllis,* and *Doc* from MTM; *All in the Family, Maude, Good Times, One Day at a Time,* and *The Jeffersons* from Tandem/TAT. With the addition of *M*A*S*H*, filmed at Twentieth Century Fox, the network could hardly have written a better script for its future. This confidence was certainly shared by the production companies as they experienced growing respect from their colleagues in film. They were doing something to fill the ''vast wasteland'' with respectable popular art.

Against a backdrop of recent Watergate revelations, a general unrest spawned by the Vietnam War, and a rising interest in consumer protection, liberal-minded creators like Lear, Alda, Gelbart, and Burns and Brooks plied their trade assured of public acceptance of their best work. Scripts addressed controversial subjects in a way never before thought possible for TV comedy. Tom Swafford, CBS vice president of program practices, openly predicted that within a few years his job would no longer be required of a maturing industry. Sensitive treatments of a long list of public issues provided comedy with a new image, one that prompted Brooks, half in jest, to ask in 1976, "How dare these little half-hour comedies take themselves so seriously?"

The busy studios were peopled with large numbers of young and enthusiastic writers, producers, and directors, a large percentage of whom had been reared on the TV comedies of the fifties. Some, like Brooks, were self-consciously reacting to the images of family life portrayed on shows like *Father Knows Best* and *Leave It to Beaver*. Of course financial control still lay, for the most part, with men whose childhoods had not been influenced by television. In the area of comedy it is fair to say, however, that these were television's "Golden Years."

The long lines that trailed every afternoon along Radford Avenue, in the warm rays of Southern California summer sun, were content to be herded slowly, very slowly, into cool studios after a wait of two or more hours. The shepherds were a group of immaculately clad, somewhat self-impressed, young ushers. The ritual was repeated daily by thousands of tourists eager to experience at first hand the families that entered their living rooms each week during the winter. CBS feverishly supplied free tickets that often created disappointment because, as the small print warned, "Ticket distribution is at times in excess of studio capacity—therefore a ticket does not guarantee admittance."

Through the chain-link fences that separated the crowds from the studio grounds, one could read colorful signs heralding MTM properties then in production, festooning the clear white exteriors of sound stages where the fortunate would see the play. Once the "tape and save" seats, reserved for dignitaries known to cast and production staff, were filled, the show would begin, often presided over by a writer or producer.

The carnival atmosphere was enhanced by a live band and constant banter among the various persons on the stage that stretched left and right far beyond the 300-seat stands. The film process employed by MTM required at least two hours for the completion of each episode, much of that time consumed in set changes and commentary by writers and actors on the progress of the twenty-three minute play.

The band played, actors talked in a leisurely fashion to the audience, and the mood was positive. The audience's positive response enhanced the producers' feeling of well-being, a constant show of affection for fictitious characters that represented the millions of their fellow citizens who would be watching the results in a few weeks.

Strategically placed in a rambling old building just inside the CBS lot, MTM producers, staff writers, and business executives generated a family-like atmosphere in the summer of 1975. Jim Brooks and Allan Burns, creators of the *Mary* Show, naturally occupied a central position in the offices, but each series had its own area, in easy proximity to all the others. Oversized pictures of the cast of each series decorated the walls, with the image of Mary hovering over the whole collection of activities. Across the driveway the new CBS executive office building, looking strangely like its counterpart in New York, was a corporate presence among the pastels. Grant Tinker's office in a top-floor corner overlooked the home of the production staff. It was difficult not to feel a contagious optimism as one made the rounds of offices and stages. One could sense a sincere family pride exhibited by most of the creative staff. Mary would appear at a filming of *Phyllis* to wish Cloris Leachman well in the spinoff. It was a time of tinsel, glamour, creativity, and familial enthusiasm.

Certainly the set was not always tranquil and the battles among creative forces often exploded just out of view of the public. But even in those moments of tension and anger there appeared to be space for multiple career successes that allowed ample room for the extremely large egos that are stock in trade of the Hollywood world.

Yet even as MTM and Tandem/TAT found gratification in the successes of 1975 and 1976, the seeds of change were planted. Robert Wood, president of CBS, who had been responsible for placing these shows on the schedule, left the network; violence on TV became a public concern once again, and found detractors in the House of Representatives; Family Viewing Time emerged as a self-righteous effort by the networks and the FCC to placate pressure groups that seemed to reflect a new national mood regarding "traditional morality." This last, the effort to restrict the content of shows appearing before 9 P.M. (in the East; varying times elsewhere) caused a serious breach in relationships between networks and independent producers. A lawsuit ended FVT, but the nearly successful effort to keep *Soap* off the ABC schedule in 1977 warned of alternative programs of censorship. Even though it had a monopoly on MTM and Lear, CBS tumbled from the top in the ratings, its supremacy in TV comedy undermined by ABC.

MTM remains in the same buildings and there are still a few audience series to attract the lines, but the future of MTM has shifted to its brilliant non-audience successes with *Lou Grant* and *Hill Street Blues,* and the potential of *St. Elsewhere.* Allan Burns noted some of the difference in a 1980 interview.

> It was ten years ago and the three years from then were tremendously exciting times in television comedy. There was a great deal of competition that we felt. We needed to do better than Norman and his shows and we respected them and watched them and we watched *M*A*S*H* and we watched *Maude* and we watched *All in the Family.* There was an enormous amount of respect that I think was mutual. Even within our own company—with the *Newhart Show* and *Rhoda*—there was a certain amount of competition there that was really good for us all. We were always trying to do a little better show than the other guy. You didn't want to rub anybody's nose in it, but it was nice to feel like you had, in a given week, a better show than they did. I don't feel that today. There are a couple of shows that are still head and shoulders above the others, and nothing much else.

The crackly fresh sparkle of MTM and Tandem/TAT seems quite distant. The mood has changed. The 1980 strikes of SAG and AFTRA demanding a large share of profits pointed to a new and uncertain future for the independent producer at the very time when talk of cable and cassette complicated the situation.

But the work goes on. The producer still sets out to develop a concept that will attract the attention of the networks, that will, just maybe, collect a vast audience. The day-to-day work is the same, work that puts the producer in the controlling seat in the making of television.

Les Brown offers a useful, if brief, description of a television producer in *The New York Times Encyclopedia of Television* that provides an excellent departure.

The producer is the person in charge of a TV production, who establishes the working spirit and dictates the standards to be met. Ideally, as head of the creative team; the producer is both businessman and artist, caring about administration and budgetary details while nurturing the talent and providing the vision for the project.

In the more than thirty-five years of commercial television history in America, this wedding of creativity and ledger has been a major determining factor in the measure of programming quality available to the public. The harnessing of a new technology early became the responsibility of the TV producer. To accomplish this task while allowing scope for an artistic vision, the producer must work within a complex system.

Network executives at the three New York headquarters determine the nature of projected prime-time schedules months in advance. While more and more network executive power is being located in the west—NBC's Grant Tinker has offices on both coasts—corporate control and final authority still remain on the Avenue of the Americas and in Rockefeller Center. Final decisions about the airing of specific series come after examination of pilots or, in some cases, elaborate descriptions developed by producers. In large part, the submissions of proposals to networks follow the guidelines adopted by each network respecting the nature of programming to be featured in the coming season, though it should be pointed out that network executives are making their own decisions by choosing from among what they realize are the creations of producers, new ones in a few cases, familiar faces and styles in most. For the producer, creativity is understood, maintained, and fostered within these constraints.

As the word spreads about what the networks may be buying for the fall, independent producers may still find themselves in sharp disagreement over issues of content and focus, issues that may cause serious conflict with a producer's sense of artistic quality. If the producer who submits a successful proposal has a ''track record,'' if he has developed ''clout,'' then the network will likely offer greater latitude in the future development of scripts and content. But, as Gene Roddenberry aptly noted, ''God help you if you are just hanging on.''

In the actual process of making programs it should be understood that TV producers, unlike their counterparts in films or theatre, are not primarily fund raisers. They must still have reasonable financial backing, however, either through private funding or studio support. Once the network programmers have settled on a particular series, a contract is drawn usually calling for thirteen episodes to be supplied by the producer. The network pays 80 percent of the cost of production, the producer supplies the remaining 20 percent. Through judicious budgeting this arrangement may mean that the producer spends very little cash. For its investment the network obtains the exclusive right to air each episode twice on a day and at a time of its choice. Although producers may receive a handsome fee for this work, in Hollywood and New York terms, they make no real money from these first two airings of the shows in series. They may even lose. It is the network that recovers its outlay at that point through sale of commercials.

Once the first two appearances occur on the network, all rights revert to the producer. If the series has received good ratings and is renewed for a second season, the opportunity for the producer to make large profits arises. As the producer builds a library of episodes of a popular series, the potential income from syndication may exceed $100 million. Since each commercial television station in the country purchases old programs to fill time during the day and early evening or very late evening hours, the demand for popular series, of at least fifty episodes, is high. So too is the price to be paid for a *Barney Miller* or a *M*A*S*H* or an *All in the Family*.

If the producer has not sold an idea or a pilot for a series, but instead has sold a made-for TV movie, the rules of this process change. The producer is given a "license fee" which is to cover all costs of production. In 1982 that fee averaged $2 million for a two-hour production. From this amount the producer must pay all costs, including his own fee, and attempt to salvage some profit. Again, the network has two guaranteed showings, after which the producer is free to sell the work to cable television, in foreign markets, and in theatres if that is at all possible. In this way the producer seeks to maximize profit.

Once the license fee is granted, the producer of the "made-for" must care for the same matters as his series counterpart. The costs are greater here, and the creative discretion allowed is wider than that for series. For the network, of course, this is a single business transaction rather than a long-term investment, and therefore less problematic in terms of content. Nevertheless, there are guidelines and they frequently amount to what William Link refers to as "prior censorship." The producer of the movie made for television knows the bounds and works his own way through them, establishing personal vision within the restraints imposed by network censors. Failure to heed the restraints might result in less opportunity for another contract. An excellent description of the day-to-day activities of the producers of movies made for television is to be found in Link and Levinson's book *Stay Tuned: An Inside Look at the Making of Prime-Time Television* (New York: St. Martin's Press, 1981).

Once the producer of the series or the made-for has sold his or her product to the network the massive work of production begins. The producer must assemble a staff of line-producers, directors, writers. He must also hire "below the line"* professionals: sound and camera specialists, lighting technicians, and so on. And all of this must be done within strict budgetary limitations.

Depending on the various working styles of individual producers, they may attend to such details as the style of the lighting, the wardrobe planning, the set design, and the make-up of the actors. Some producers are far more concerned with these details than others. Some will delegate a great deal of authority, others retain final word on all decisions. The producer must deal with tender egos of actors and skilled specialists. While casting may continue to be a knotty issue, particularly if the network exercises a peremptory right in this area, the producer must see to it that the group works toward the goal of a successful show. If the series becomes a hit, of course, the producer is inevitably involved in the renegotiation of salary contracts with stars and central characters who demand higher pay commensurate with ratings success.

All of this work must be accomplished within the incredibly tight schedules necessary for producing large amounts of material in relatively short times. In comedy production, for example, most series are shot on film or tape before a live audience. Here again styles vary. Norman Lear effected a major change in the habits of many half-hour

---

*Below the line is a phrase that refers to those craftspeople who perform the technical functions associated with cameras and lighting, as well as many other essential activities in a TV production.

comedy producers when he instituted the video taping of *All in the Family* before an audience. The episodes were performed as one-act plays taking no more than an hour to complete. This allowed for two separate tapings each week, which could then be edited into the "best" single performance for network airing. By contrast, MTM and Garry Marshall employ three-camera filming before an audience, a technique that requires a different type of direction and consumes perhaps two and a half hours for each week's performance. A few half-hour comedies such as *M*A*S*H* used a single film camera and no audience, a procedure almost universal among producers of hour-long dramatic series and made-for-TV movies.

In comedy a minimum of four days of preparation is needed for final taping. This includes script consultations, rewrites, rehearsals, and late night "fixes." This schedule would be approximately doubled for an hour-long dramatic production. The producer must be constantly aware of the flow toward the shooting days and final taping, and the pace of the editing and dubbing. The "post-production" work that follows must also be supervised closely in order to bring the finished product to the network on time.

To the producer, then, falls the overall task of caring for continuity, consistency in character, and the orderliness of plots within the series. The fictional characters must become real to the producer who searches for appropriate behavior for a Mary Richards, an Inspector Erskine, a Columbo, or a Fonzie. If a producer desires, as in the case of Grant Tinker, to assemble other creative producers to undertake artistic tasks—writing, for instance—it still remains his responsibility to see that the activities outlined here are attended to.

Obviously the producer has a major stake in the ratings success of the series or the movie. Artistic considerations and personal statements may well be paramount to the producer who cares for the work, but without ratings there is no market for the creativity. The affirmation of mass audiences in the form of ratings is often cited as evidence that there is no art, no personal vision involved in television. But that judgment is not one we would make. The audience is a constraint which the television producer, bound both to the ledger and to a dream, must recognize. It is a disagreeable, but accepted condition.

As Garry Marshall puts it, with a clearly reasoned perspective:

> I'm an artist in a business and since television is the biggest
> business it's harder to be an artist. . . . I'm an artist as often
> as I can be. The craftsman is the stopgap of not letting it be
> really bad. I have to be a craftsman too. On the weeks when
> you don't have time for the art, your craft has to keep it up to
> a certain quality.

Even as we develop the thesis that the television producer is the creative center who shapes, through choices big and small, works of television art that speak of personal values and decisions, we are mindful
of this plight, a plight that is as old as television, and perhaps as old
as art itself.

In its infancy television possessed an immediacy that was lacking in
the cinema. Hence, while the new medium was destined to be compared primarily with the motion pictures with which it was early in
competition, in fact early TV had far more in common with the legitimate stage in production quality and with radio in technology. It was
only in the sixties, with the appearance of quality color and picture
definition and the demise of live TV drama, that television and film
drew closer together as art forms. But these later developments should
not cloud our understanding of the roots of television. In its early days
TV was neither as slick nor, as David Sontag observed, always as
"golden" as it appears sometimes in retrospect. Early critics of the
medium were more than a little aware of this, and using standards
established for other forms their comments were harsh and often invid-
ious. Most critics recruited to comment on television failed to envision
it as a new form, but rather saw it as a poor imitation of more traditional entertainment forms.

In those first years, then, no one was talking about a "producer's
medium." The nature of the entire production structure was often cha-
otic. Sontag, who has identified himself as the "youngest living sur-
vivor of the 'Golden Age' of television," has described the turbulent
beginnings.

> In the early fifties there was a strange advertising control mix.
> Some advertisers bought time periods and had absolute control
> over programming during that period. Program and time costs

were relatively inexpensive . . . allowing the networks the option of accepting or turning down programs which adverstisers
had bought directly and were attempting to place on the network or developing programs that they, the network, believed
in . . . feeling that there were sufficient advertising dollars
available to insure the sale of the program if not to one sponsor, then surely to another. . . . The Program Departments of
the networks then were populated with executives whose train-
ing had been in the theatre, motion pictures, or on the production side of radio. An air of creativity prevailed throughout the
medium. It was a time for experiment . . . a time for new
ideas . . . a time for gambling.

By the mid-fifties television production began an exodus to California and with that move came the steady decline in the number of
live anthological dramas, such as *Playhouse 90,* available on the air.
As early as 1953 Pat Weaver, president of NBC, had argued for a
"magazine" concept in advertising that would mean the licensing of
programs by the networks and then their sale to sponsors. Only two
significant innovations came of this idea, the *Today* and *Tonight* shows,
and when Weaver left NBC in 1955, sponsor identification with series
continued as the rule. Two factors spelled doom for this old order.
Sponsor interference and censorship continued, causing great unease
at the networks. And in 1959 the quiz scandals broke, implicating
sponsors in rigged programs. It was then that Frank Stanton of CBS
vowed, "We will be masters in our own house."
    At this juncture the networks began a wholesale encouragement of
independent producers, now for the most part located in Hollywood.
With costs beginning to spiral, the networks determined upon developing what Sontag described as a "partnership with the independents." With the power of advertisers eroded by the new format, the
networks encouraged speculative activity on the part of producers, who
thus emerged as the third force. Meanwhile, the creative core of writers and producers at the networks dispersed, and these new independent producers were no longer dealing with men and women who were
similar to themselves in background. Now "a new type of program
department emerged, one made up of sales and research men." For
practical purposes the networks became middlemen, purchasing pro-

grams and selling them. At times, to be sure, Sontag noted, "the producer needed to lock the network in with a financial commitment. . . . Surely his chance of having the new show go to series was increased if the network was his partner."

This type of partnership, between producer and network, coupled with the business-dominated network structure, meant that whatever creative control remained in television would lie with the independent producers. They became purveyors of concept and content within guidelines established by network programming departments. Certainly this dynamic was totally different from the order of the earlier days. The very existence of three parties—network, producer, sponsor—made pressure a more successful tactic, and it did not mean freedom from interference for the creative community. To be sure, not all producers have been in conflict with the varying temper of network programmers, but for the individuals examined in this study, network interference has often been a serious impediment, and one that poses unique creative challenges.

Before an episode can be aired the independent producer must deal the network's office of "broadcast standards" or "program practices," the internal censors of each organization. Since the mid-sixties these departments have exercised near absolute control over final scripts, examining language, violence, and sex. The present role of this network department is clearly defined by Alan Alda.

> On the whole I would say that most of what appears to be values on television is the result of not wanting to offend the people who are watching and not wanting to offend the advertisers. The censorship department at the network probably has more effect on promoting what seem to be a set of values than anybody's conscious design.

Ironically, these severe restrictions upon producers have contributed immeasurably to the emergence of the producer as the shaper of television art, as the voice of social commentary. For the producer must parry the network thrusts and translate these defenses into rational instructions for writers, directors, actors and other personnel who strive for a sense of creativity, at the same time as the producer maintains his enormous fiscal responsibility.

The emergence after 1960 of the strong independent producer did not uniformly replace earlier sponsor and network productions. As profits increased and ratings became ever more important, the intense competition for the sale of ideas to the three outlets caused several patterns to evolve. We have identified three general categories into one or more of which most modern producers appear to fit. Often the lines are not clear and there are producers who move easily from one category to another.

The Independent Producer. For our purposes here we would define the independent as a person committed to a single project or series who receives a network license fee directly. William Link and Richard Levinson acted in this capacity in 1979 when they produced *Murder by Natural Causes,* a two-hour film starring Hal Holbrook and Katheryn Ross, for CBS. On occasion, as in this case, writers who wish to gain greater creative control will strike out as independents to achieve it. Indeed, at present the production ranks are being filled more and more by the new "hyphenate," writer-producer. Many of the most able producers have traveled this road, but seldom have any remained in the category for extended periods. This status is seldom held by many persons at one time because networks are unwilling to risk the license fee on an independent without strong evidence of prior and continuing success. For related reasons most producers do not work exclusively as independents. They usually move rapidly to the second alternative that we suggest.

The Production Company. Talented producers have two choices relative to the production company. They may form a company to undertake multiple activities as did Quinn Martin, Danny Thomas, and Sheldon Leonard in the earlier days of the medium. These individuals successfully developed clout in the industry, and Martin, a writer, focused the entire QM company on his personal creative approach. In the seventies Norman Lear and Garry Marshall, both originally writers, structured operations of massive power, in Lear's case rivaling a small studio. Aaron Spelling and Leonard Goldberg began production in 1960 and now are major suppliers to ABC. Significantly, each of these producers has been identified almost exclusively with a single network: Marshall and Martin with ABC, Lear with CBS. In each case the company productions were identified as distinctively the work of the individual in charge of the company. When one thinks of *All in the Family* one thinks only of Norman Lear. Similar identification emerges with Garry Marshall and *Happy Days* or Quinn Martin and *The Streets of San Francisco*.

But not all individuals are so bold as to form a personal company. As an alternative the writer-producer may find it wiser to seek out a company such as MTM or Lorimar in which the chief executive happens to function primarily as a business executive. This was the case with Grant Tinker during his direction of MTM and remains the case of Lee Rich at Lorimar. Neither Rich nor Tinker lacks the sensitivity necessary for creative productivity, but they have generally chosen to turn over to other persons the responsibility exercised by a Marshall or a Lear. The classic case of this type of activity is the MTM company that has produced an exceptional list of major successes. None of them is credited to Grant Tinker as creator; rather a number of writer-producers worked for MTM to initiate and oversee these projects. The chief advantage of this type of arrangement appears to lie in the willingness of a Rich or a Tinker to assume the burdensome business responsibilities, relieving creators such as Hamner or Brooks or Burns from that day-to-day financial involvement.

The Studio Producer. This is the most traditional form of production, harking back to the major studios of earlier Hollywood days. Universal Studios is possibly the largest operation in this grouping and has been the most consistently successful. NBC in particular has made large use of Universal over the years. Other highly successful studios include MGM, Twentieth Century-Fox, and Warners. The concept of a major film studio moving its system into television production had a certain logic once film became the dominant television technology and the industry was housed primarily in Los Angeles. These huge businesses had no central guiding creative figure or director, no Lear or Tinker or Martin, but they developed a large collection of respected producers who were given considerable latitude in their exclusive arrangements with the studio. Notable among Universal producers were Link and Levinson who developed, wrote, and produced *Columbo* for the studio, and David Victor who was responsible for *Dr. Kildare* and *Marcus Welby, M.D.* All the studio producers were the creative center of the productions of which they were in charge.

These three types are in no way restrictive. Yet most of the producers with whom we talked were prepared to agree that the industry's array of producers do seem to fit into the patterns we have delineated, and that the producer is central in the creative process of television. When one considers the complexities of the medium—complexities complicated by the presence of the Federal Communications Commission, the three-network structure, the advertisers, the mammoth audience attracted even by failures—the problems faced by these individuals assume overwhelming proportions. When we then impose time restraints involved in almost continual production, the logistics of readying twenty hours or more of film or tape for viewing within six months, the composure of the most sanguine creative talent could be shattered. But it would be foolish and illogical to assume that creativity must be thwarted by these factors.

In our examination of television producers as artists, as the creative voices expressing personal visions of culture and society, then, we assume quality and value in a good number of instances. Alan Alda's remarks are appropriate in this context.

> I don't think people are mainly involved in the production of television shows or the creation of television shows in order to express good values, or what they think are good values. But values do get expressed. There are some people who really care enough about their own existence and the part they have to play in the culture, they care enough about not pouring poison into the reservoir, that they will not take part in things they feel represent bad values. They care enough to try, if they are going to do something in the business, to do something that reflects a responsible set of values.

Clearly, definitions of "good" and "responsible" will vary. We do not always agree that a particular vision is "good," even when we recognize that it is clearly defined and consciously developed. But the men we have selected as subjects for this volume all appear to us to have determined to take responsibility for their actions, albeit in significantly different ways. Each has demonstrated artistic talent, and each has attained a high degree of success in the medium, both in terms of ratings and in peer evaluation.

In the course of our study we have occasion to identify some of the differences among producers with regard to matters of style, freedom, responsibility, power, and expressing values. But to the extent that freedom exists or values are expressed, it is the producer who is the catalyst, the one responsible for the decisions. It is the producer who meets network demands, or fights them, faces the consequences of time restrictions, and, in the end, owns some of the property. One may detect, on occasion, the skilled hand of a director of the calibre of Jay Sandrich or Jack Shea, the quality of a writer like Susan Harris, yet the final artistic decisions rest with the producer. The writer or director with some share of the artistic clout on a regular basis must assume the title of producer as well. The talent of producers may best be perceived in the ability to identify able creators in several fields and to use those abilities in combination with their own. As facilitator, the producer is striving for the highest number of those moments when one "flirts with the edges of art" while addressing the nobler sentiments of humanity. The single most telling complication, one we will have occasion to discuss with each of the producers interviewed, is that the producer must achieve these "noble" goals while tightly bound to the profit motive.

What we have described in this section is the context in which that motive has led to the structure of an industrial system devoted to the creation of entertainment that can, at times, be referred to as art. In the next section we discuss the role of television in the context of culture rather than that of industry and economics. For it is in drawing on and contributing to the development of cultural meaning, symbol, and significance that the television producer more closely resembles the *artists* of traditional, pre-industrial societies than the solitary creative individuals to whom we have given that title in modern times.

TELEVISION IN AMERICAN CULTURE

Television is now central to American society. Our primary means of public communication, it is that rare factor in a world as complex as ours—the element most commonly shared. As an interwoven net of institutions and individuals it can be approached from a variety of perspectives. It is big business, and for many who seek to understand it, the economics of television, the drive for profit, the "business behind the box," determines and directs everything else about it and is thus the best means of explaining it. Decisions regarding content, style, programming schedules, are all determined by the reach for greater revenue and the subsequent freedom to reproduce previously success-ful patterns. To others, however, television is an example of a com-plex social institution, best understood in terms of its internal socio-logical structures and its sociological connections to other aspects of American life. Analysis focuses on the structure of the industrial hi-erarchy, on the social backgrounds of principal individuals and groups, or on decision-making processes at various stages of production and programming. Another branch of sociological analysis, frequently in-volved with questions of the effects of television violence, regards the audience as the most important factor, and seeks to establish links between television content and social behavior.

For still other groups, these first two approaches to understanding television, even in combination, must be subordinated to the larger political functions of the medium. This view does not, for the most part, focus on alterations of the American political process resulting from the presence of television, or on the content of specific political presentations. It is concerned, rather, with the entire organization of the television industry and with the substructures of television content as they reflect a particular set of political assumptions. From this per-spective television is the most powerful and the most pervasive repli-cation of captialism yet developed in American society. As a result, in its form and content it guards the values underlying its own success, reflects those assumptions that make ''the system'' a natural, taken-for-granted thing, rather than the construction of individuals whose interests it protects.

None of these approaches provides, in our view, the best, most comprehensive explanation of the medium. For us, television is most centrally a set of stories, a body of fiction. In this book we focus on those parts of television designed specifically as fictions that entertain, the primary content of television series and movies made for tele-vision. But in our larger view these stories are closely related to stories that inform—news stories—and stories that persuade—commercials. More importantly, for our purposes here, television fictions are closely related to those stories that have entertained Americans throughout our cultural history. They have appeared in every medium. They have emerged as popular, formulaic patterns and as complex works unique in design and presentation. Audiences are, therefore, familiar with the plots, the character types, the caricatures, the settings, the actions, and the value structures of these stories even before their constant repetitions on television. So, too, are writers, directors, actors, purchasers, programmers, and network censors. So, too, most centrally for our concerns here, are the producers of television.

Somehow, the stories seem taken for granted, dismissed as trivial, even by those who make them and those who enjoy them night after night. Yet it should not seem strange that these same stories should be taken as the organizing principle for a study of the medium, for around them all the other actions and choices revolve. From the economic standpoint the stories must attract and hold mass audiences which can be "delivered" to advertisers, for on this all the other economic decisions hang. The most cynical, least appreciative view of television content, that which suggests that television stories are "merely" commercials for the commercials, overlooks the significance of that insight. What is it that draws the millions to this gigantic billboard? One must assume a massive addiction to anything appearing on the screen, and combine that assumption with the view that all television presents a total, exhausting worthlessness of content, to avoid the premise of a certain power and importance within the stories themselves. The copying of successful television formats and motifs is hardly a thoughtless lurch of economic desire. It is a purposeful grasp at meaning, at the elusive elements that have structured the "new" program and shifted the ratings count a narrow, crucial, percentage. So, too, the choices of sponsors to support shows, and of advertisers to design those commercials, are choices focused on content. Even the enormous financial waste of the television industry can best be explained as a terribly inefficient, trial-and-error means of selecting appropriate stories with which to attempt to capture that ever larger audience, the audience that is always on the verge of leaving the channel, turning off the set, ignoring the program.

From the sociological perspective all questions are directed toward the functions of groups and individuals who, for whatever ends and from whatever backgrounds, must make choices related to the stories on which they base their careers. That those choices are constrained in particular ways by structures of the industry reflects on the ways in which the stories are actually made and eventually placed before the viewers. The stories may even be secondary in the minds of those who make and place them, superseded by far more specific goals regarding career enhancement, profit taking, competition among industrial giants, and the like. But none of these aims can be achieved without attending to the centrality of the stories, for on the successes of the stories hangs all that these individuals seek.

For those whose aim is the measurement of behavioral change and the establishment of the causes of that change, the stories should be even more important, though this is not always the case. Often the assumption is that the stories do not count as much as do discreet bits of information within the stories. While this is undoubtedly true for some viewers, our contention here is that most individuals experience television fiction in the patterns of narrative structure. Studies that seek to measure the effects of television are, in our view, most sound when they consider the total impact of fiction on the lives of individuals rather than the effects of isolated moments of fictional action. It is also our view that a narrative pattern contains a great deal of information that does indeed "get into" society and influence behavior in ways far more complex than can be easily studied in simple analysis. A fertile field waits for complex analysis of the role of television fiction in American society.

The more sophisticated political analyses of television move in this direction. They take the fictions into account far more quickly than do other beginning points. Rarely do they crudely suggest that the political power of television is located in the attitudes of the few individuals who have sought and gained control of the industry. It is, rather, in the consistent patterns of reward and punishment, heroism and villainy, success and failure, that these critics discover political significance. In this view, society, political structures, and personal attitudes are relatively frozen. As the culture reproduces itself in these repetitive stories, change, and the desire for change, are immobilized. Like all bodies of culturally based fiction, television legitimates the social order that exists. Among those who wish to maintain this status quo are many individuals who create and program television stories. Often they also participate in the varied interlocked ownership structures of American business, industry, and politics. And they wish to see their own way of life validated, their own interests protected.

Many analyses of television from this perspective are unnecessarily flawed by an excessive rigidity and a focus on the exclusively negative aspects of social maintenance. As a result, the appropriate focus on television fictions is distorted and, in its worst form, becomes a thinly veiled diatribe on American society and politics rather than a careful examination of how television functions in relation to them.

None of these approaches entirely fails. Each of them tells us something important about television, and taken together they offer an overview that might explain television's place in American culture and provide a potentially useful understanding of the role of the producer within television. But the combined descriptions would be rather different from what we propose here. It would be different because all of the previous approaches to television rest on a view of the medium and of mass communication that is fundamentally at odds with what we intend to suggest. These distinctions between what television is and does, and the subsequent definitions of how producers (or any other group, for that matter) function, rest on the now familiar distinction between "transportation" and "ritual" views of communication. The economic, sociological, and political models described and summarized all too briefly above rest most thoroughly on the transportation view, although other views exist in those fields. As articulated by James Carey, this model holds that communication is "a process of transmitting messages at a distance for purposes of control. The archetypal case of communication then, is persuasion, attitude change, behavior modification, socialization through the transmission of information, influence, or conditioning."[1] The relationship between this view of communication and the methods of study outlined above should be readily apparent. All of those methods expect communication to result in control of one sort or another, and the direction of the control is uni-directional, from the creator-owners to the viewer audience.

Against this view, however, Carey poses the "ritual" view of communication. Here communication is "not directed toward the extension of messages in space, but the maintenance of society in time; not the act of imparting information, but the representation of shared beliefs."[2] He amplifies these descriptions with a definition of his own. "Communication is a symbolic process whereby reality is produced, maintained, repaired and transformed."[3]

Clearly, any study of television or any group crucial to television proceeding from such a definition will be fundamentally different from those preceeding from the transportation view. Our aim, then, is to clarify what a ritual view of communication tells us about television generally, and subsequently, to demonstrate how this view illuminates the role of the television producer.

When we speak of ritual we do not mean the patterned, repetitive viewing of television. While the ritualistic nature of the viewing experience is essential to a full understanding of the significance of television in culture, our interest here is with the transmitted content of popular commercial television. Insofar as we approach questions of audience in this book those questions have to do with producers' conceptions of audience understanding rather than with actual audience behavior.

In order to place the content of television within the context of the study of ritual we turn to the work of anthropologists who have examined the role of ritual in traditional, pre-industrial, pre-literate societies. In recent years some anthropologists, with colleagues in the fields of literary, linguistic, and film analysis, have applied these observations to the study of complex, technologically advanced societies.

Victor Turner, for example, suggests that a primary function of ritual is to serve as a commentator on society.[4] It is in the practice of ritual that individuals and groups are taught of the worlds in which they live. Roger Silverstone[5] turns to the work of anthropologists and indicates a similar function when he suggests that television "articulates" the culture in which it appears. Clearly, such a function tends to suggest the maintenance of structure, of boundaries, guidelines, and well-defined roles as a result of ritual. This conservative function has often been cited by critics who regard ritual as a device central to the retardation of social change. But Turner, while admitting this feature, suggests that ritual, properly understood, is far more complex. He calls attention to the fact that ritual is a *process* rather than a static product, and argues that we must read that process as part of a symbolic cultural fabric. Central to the processual understanding is the "liminal" stage of the ritual process. The liminal stage is the "in-between" stage, when one is neither totally in nor out of the structures of society. It is a stage of license, when rules may be broken or bent, when roles may be reversed, when categories and restrictions may be overturned. Its essence, suggests Turner, is in its "release from normal constraints." It tears apart our notions of common sense, and suggests that the things we take for granted, or take as meaningful, are arbitrary, constructed notions. In the liminal realm we can reconstruct basic cultural units "in novel ways, some of them bizarre to the point of monstrosity." The liminal, then, is the arena of "interesting" or "uncommon" sense. This sense of ritual freedom has as its purpose and function no mere diversion from the more serious aspects of sociocultural life. Rather, it is a teaching tool, a mechanism with which to explore the given and to examine alternatives to what we accept as "natural." As Turner says, the liminal experience reveals to those who participate in it the "building blocks from which their hitherto taken-for-granted world has been constructed." These experiences "reveal the freedom, the indeterminacy underlying all culturally constructed worlds, the free play of mankind's cognitive and imaginative capacities." It is precisely these "cognitive" and "imaginative" capacities that enable human societies to create alternative modes of thought and action, to accomplish change as well as to maintain stability. The function of liminality, in Turner's view, is nothing short of a contribution to cultural survival.

For us, the significance of Turner's recent work is his suggestion that these views of ritual may apply equally well to post-industrial, complex societies such as our own. The analogy to traditional ritual liminality is to be found in modern societies in the arts. All of them, from the most sophisticated theatre in "high culture" to carnival at the level of "folk culture," provide a space and a time for imaginative freedom, the release from constraint. Between these forms of entertainment and the biological and ecological aspects of life, Turner finds a "reflexive or dialectical relationship." We "think about" the more mundane survival-oriented aspects of existence by means of the performative genres and forms which we often think of as unimportant aspects of our lives. "Entertainment," Turner reminds us, is a term "which literally means 'holding between,' that is, 'liminalizing.' " With entertainment, then, we "make statements" about our societies, we "monitor" those societies. And we do so with forms "at least as bizarre as those of tribal liminality." These notions of observing, and commenting on our society through entertainment forms, remind us of Carey's definition of communication itself as a "symbolic process whereby reality is produced, maintained, repaired, and transformed.'' With these views in mind, the implications for the study of television are most significant. For now we can consider the relationship of the world of television to the world of experience as a very special one, one that is perhaps *not* best understood by seeking to praise or criticize television programs for their relative match to reality.

That special nature of fiction, the creation of a kind of liminal arena, helps us to understand the presence of forms as bizarre as a story about Ozark mountaineers who take their money and their traditional values to Beverly Hills, and there encounter and overcome the flimsier values of another, more modern world. We can better appreciate the presence of monstrous hulks and bionic men, twilight zones of unreality, the popularity of space exploration as a fictional device, and the importance of traditional character types with whom most viewers never come into personal contact: detectives, cowboys, and undercover policemen. In soap operas, in fantasy programs such as *Love Boat* and *Fantasy Island,* in worlds of extreme adventure where heroes always win and worlds of zany illogic where comediennes are never hurt by their mistakes, television creates a realm of its own. It is a realm that perpetually comments upon the nature of our day-to-day existence and experience. The question of whether or not the medium reflects or creates attitudes, behaviors, and values, becomes secondary. Like other forms of entertainment, other forms of education and influence, television "talks and thinks" about these aspects of our lives. As members of a culture, we approach the entertainments with information about their form, content, and history. We have ideas of our own. We have values established by other influences and individuals in our lives. With varying degrees of education and varying ability to implement our beliefs in the realms of work and play, we use television for a range of purposes. We enter its imaginative worlds and return from them. While there is no question that television has changed behavior in America, it is also the case that this process is not so different from other forms of change in our past and the past of human experience. To the degree that television, by its sameness and massive applications, enters the lives of more individuals in the same manner, it does differ from previous technologies. It is nevertheless still drawing on our history and its own history, and thereby becoming a part of our shared experiences, of what Carey[6] refers to as "public thought.'' While it surely contributes to all aspects of that thought, it would be a mistake to assume that it drives all other forms of public thought out of existence. As Newcomb and Hirsch have put it,

> . . . television is both a part of this larger cultural pluralism and currently its central component in American life. In its role as central cultural medium it presents us with its own multiplicity of meanings rather than with a monolithic presentation of a dominant point of view. Because it is, to a great extent, culturally written, television presents us with our most prevalent concerns, our deepest dilemmas. Our most traditional views, those which are repressive and reactionary, as well as those which are subversive and emancipatory, are upheld, examined, maintained, and transformed. The emphasis is on process rather than product, on discussion rather than on indoctrination, on contradiction and confusion rather than on coherence.[7]

This is not a hidden process. The cultural roots of television are much on the surface. We need only cite a few examples of different types to illustrate the constant processing of important cultural material. It is material that derives from our past and our present and, in the blending, television offers us an imaginative space in which to assess what we are and what we shall be.

If we take traditional cultural material, such as the representation of a region and its people, we can observe transformations in the meaning of that material over time. We could easily discuss the depiction of New Yorkers, or Texans, but one of the most consistently presented groups provides an even better example. Rural southerners from the Appalachians to the Ozarks have populated television series in almost every decade. From the *Beverly Hillbillies* and *The Real McCoys*, through *Petticoat Junction*, *The Andy Griffith Show*, and *Green Acres*, to *The Waltons* and *The Dukes of Hazzard*, this group has provided a set of televised images that range from caricature to character. The shows include the strange, the silly, the humorous, and the melodramatic. Our list itself makes clear the possibility of multiple meanings. In all these shows, however, the rural South and the people who live there form a repository of traditional American values. Jed

Clampett, Andy Taylor, and Zeb Walton always have an appropriate answer for the problems that trouble the youngsters and not-too-bright adults. Older women, like Aunt Bee and Granny Clampett, express wisdom that transcends generations, stands for an ongoing strain of folk knowledge that echoes with deep significance. The young people, the children, and the simple-minded seem to express a kind of gentleness not often found in other parts of the world of television.

These shows use the characters and settings to ring changes on the themes of innocence and corruption, truth and deception, integrity and duplicity. Again and again the plots demonstrate the worth of the positive qualities in these pairs. In California, the world of sleazy, get-rich-quick schemes, the Clampetts, in all their gullibility, outwit with their deeper values the swindlers and the con men. Andy is able to demonstrate to city slickers the richness of small-town life. The Waltons take in outsiders, heal their spiritual and physical wounds, and send them on their way, gladdened by the experience. Even the Duke family, the "almost outlaws," deal with the more vicious members of their own community in a fashion that teaches rather than punishes.

But these similarities of theme and content should not obscure the fact that the shows are very different from one another, that the representation of the South and its meaning to larger America has shifted over time. It is used by the makers and programmers of television for different purposes in different contexts. The typical *Beverly Hillbillies* treatment, while comically sympathetic, perpetuates deeper cultural patterns of ridicule and discrimination. It reminds us that television, in turning to the South, merely extended the use of these images and types. In fiction and in film, the "hillbilly" had come to stand for something less than admirable. In its more virulent representations the image stood for the shiftless, the ignorant, the primitive, the crude root from which "we" had emerged and which we now find embarrassing. It was the image of the dirty savage that almost all cultures seem to need in their repertoire of images, the screen against which to project their nobility. Something of these negative meanings remains in the television shows. The Clampetts, for example, for all their wisdom, for their expression of what is noble and pure in the economy of American values, are clearly not to be taken too seriously. The representation removes them from a world of true adult responsibility. They are, when all is done, depicted as delightfully bizarre children. Their innocence is the innocence of children, or of the child-like caricatures of primitive people.

The Andy Griffith Show moves its characters closer to actual adulthood. While Barney and Gomer and Goober seem equal to the Clampetts in simplicity, Andy is far more related to the world of the viewer. His wisdom is not presented as some sort of arcane, unearned, genetic folk-wisdom. Rather it seems to be the product of careful observation, experience, application, and testing. Especially in his dealings with his son, Opie, this sense of adulthood comes to the fore. In effect, Andy is the father of the entire town, and the fact that he is the sheriff comments on the nature of authority and power as much as on the function of fathers. If all towns were run with the sagacity of Mayberry's leader, most of us would enjoy life more. Clearly, this too is an idealization.

With *The Waltons* some of these same topics are addressed and actually become the focus of the show's continuing story. There are obvious liberties taken with historical reality. We never experience the depths of America's Great Depression, nor do we see the breadth of rural American life. With the historical frame, however, we do have a strong sense that the show is more directly based in experience than is *The Beverly Hillbillies*. The intriguing thing for the cultural analysis and comparison of these shows is that they use the same basic imagery to make forays into American ideas and ideology. The generational differences, the presence of folk wisdom, the contrast with another value system, all these are common to both productions. The significant difference is that in *The Waltons* the very issue that clouds *Hillbillies* is addressed repeatedly. If the Clampetts are never allowed to grow up, the Waltons explore the process of maturation as the major theme of the show. In tracing the family's history through almost two decades the series has had to focus on the growth of the children. We have observed the lessons that are painfully necessary to the transition, felt the difficulties of both parent and child, felt relieved when mistakes are recognized and responsibility is accepted on both sides. The fictional process has been enhanced by the complexities related to the real development among the cast members. The exit of Richard Thomas as John Boy, the death of Will Geer, and Ellen Corby's stroke added to the sense that here was a deeper reality, one that transcended fiction and sentimentality, even while it traded in fictional images and themes often cloying in their ''noble mountaineer'' expressions.

Paralleling this shift, is a much more complex social process, one that has centered on shifting attitudes toward the American South. With the presidencies of Lyndon Johnson and Jimmy Carter, with the population shift and economic advantages in the Sunbelt, with the increasing popularity of country-western music, has come a change that allows a positive image of the region in fiction. The older attitudes, those that suggested that true American values might reside in those rural hills, have now come to the surface. *The Waltons* did not provide us with a set of unrealistic values, ideals useless in a world filled with complexity and strain. Rather, the show suggested, quite intentionally, that the values it expressed were a vigorous alternative to other mainstream values flourishing at the same time. It provided an explicit suggestion that the values which had sustained the culture in other troubled times could be appropriated by the world of the 1970s. *The Beverly Hillbillies* offered an escape into a silly world where real values proved a running undercurrent of social criticism. *The Waltons* raised that current to the surface and made the criticism direct. The images, so similar, spoke a different language. Both in our view were understood by the viewing audience because both were tied to American images and patterns of fiction that had long been mainstays of popular entertainment.

But it is not only in the shifts over time that we read television's processing of cultural information. We can see similar variations even within a single night's viewing. In the 1980–81 program season, for example, *The Waltons* led the CBS Thursday night program line-up. For a good part of that season the show was followed by *Magnum, P.I.,* an action-adventure series set in contemporary Hawaii. The contrast in historical and geographical settings, values, and attitudes was marked. The shows were related, however, by the fact that *Magnum* involved a search for meaning in a post-Vietnam world. Its central character is plagued by flashbacks to the war. He needs something to get him through, just as America did in the Depression. An even stronger comparison is provided by the final show in the Thursday offerings, *Knots Landing*. Created by the producers of *The Waltons* and *Dallas,* the Lorimar company, *Knots Landing* is also a show about families. Its setting is contemporary southern California, and the show focuses on the problems faced by families in that milieu.

In some ways *Knots Landing* is truly reminiscent of *The Waltons.* The central family, the Fairgates, fight many of the same battles fought in the hills of Virginia. They want the best for their children. They want them to be strong, to be able to fend for themselves, to behave reasonably with other members of society. In short, they want them to grow into healthy adults. Many of the plots revolve around the assumption of adult responsibility, the gaining of experience, maturation in all its forms.

But if the core of the story is similar, the surrounding layers of text differ from the world of the Waltons. For now the children are explicitly concerned with first sexual experience, with drug use, with the problems of the divorced and divorcing adults who live around them. None of this is cloaked in poetic symbolism, in gentle rural mystery and wonder. Mother and daughter discuss sexual activity and birth control. Daughter and boyfriend experiment and come to their own conclusions. Drug abuse is condemned, but drug use is acknowledged.

These shifts in personal problems are surrounded by even greater changes. The real distinction between *The Waltons* and *Knots Landing* is found in the community surrounding the families. Gone is the reassuring sense that the children are learning values and behaviors shared by most of the adult members of the community which they will enter. There is, instead, the possibility that adults are equally promiscuous, equally abusers of drugs, equally "immature" in their behavior. More poignantly, there is the clear sense that the adults are equally unable to make the proper choices by which to control their lives. There is alcoholism, violence, and confusion in the world of these adults. We want them to succeed, to revise their lives somehow, to avoid pain for themselves and their neighbors. We admire the ways in which friends stick up for one another. But we anticipate, because we have evidence that tells us to, that we will see one neighbor slipping quietly across his back lawn to spend the night with the divorced sister of one of his friends. We fear that a divorced husband will return and kidnap his children from their mother, who has custody. We care for these individuals, but our care is matched with the sense that this world has somehow gone awry.

If *The Waltons* is skewed in favor of a time too gentle, a more sentimental society, and a deep, working morality, *Knots Landing* is equally skewed. The people here have more than their share of drastic problems. Like the characters of *The Waltons* they have a sense of what is right, but our sense as viewers is that it is infinitely more difficult to make that sense into reality. The family is as potent a core-symbol in the later show as in the earlier. But its meaning is determined by the fragility of this new world.

All this sense of flux and negotiation is possible, we suggest, because of the ritualistic nature of television. It provides that in-between space in which our own culture can "entertain" such important matters. This is Turner's liminality. For television scholars John Fiske and John Hartley, this is the "bardic function" of television.[8] In our own terms, this central cultural function is best described by the "choric" nature of television. We take the term from the role of the chorus in Greek drama. The chorus expresses the ideas and emotions of the group, as opposed to those of individuals. Its focus is on the widely shared, the remembered, the conventional responses that take into account the notions of socially approved—because socially tested—notions of heroism, epic event, and collective memory. Dependent on widely recognized "types" rather than on the unique, the choric forms render for their audiences patterns of experience within which to couch new problems and issues. They aid in the maintainence of society, but also, in the repair and renovation of that society.

Given the strength of these insights provided by a cultural approach to television, it is easier to understand why the roles of significant individuals have been minimized, why there is little discussion of the creative nature of much of the work that goes on in the medium. To date, television has drawn much of its formal quality from other media: vaudeville, radio, film, fiction. Its industrial structures also came from radio, complete with the schedule of commercial interruption and the approved time units for programming. On the other hand, much of the specific content of television comes from society at large, from recurring problems and topics or from current events. It is never surprising to discover a television program focusing on old unresolved cultural tension between the sexes or generations. And no longer is it unusual to see a television program treating in fictional form an item that we have seen on the news in recent weeks. This content must remain familiar and accessible. It cannot bear the radical interpretation and reshaping that we often associate with the "artist's vision."

Still, within these constraints it is the task of the successful producer to create a significant difference. This does not mean that the producer must define a new form in every individual case, although that sometimes occurs. It does mean that the producer must somehow see and present a set of relationships that call attention to his program or series, something that will attract a network buyer because it promises to attract a mass audience. The producer, then, presents inflections on common themes and patterns of representations. Even the writer of a choric strain in Greek drama was faced with the task of using that standard form with its rigid and repetitive patterns to say something that related to the topic under consideration.

Again, we emphasize the cultural function of such a role. We reject the notion of the producer as the network hack, the individual who restricts creativity by seeing that the work of writers and actors and directors is homogenized into the merely and massively acceptable. We also reject the notion of the producer as the representative of an industrial system that turns out product notable only for its lack of distinction. While this may describe what is often a result, it is not a necessary condition, nor does it define the creative role of the producer.

Instead, we see the producer as comparable to Marshall Sahlins's description of the role of the market researcher, advertiser, or fashion designer. "In the nervous system of the American economy," he says, "theirs is the synaptic function. It is their role to be sensitive to the latent correspondences in the cultural order whose conjunction in a product-symbol may spell mercantile success."[9] These creators are, as Sahlins suggests, true readers, true analysts of the cultures in which they live and work, the society in which they must seek and create an audience. They must be sensitive to many sorts of cultural change, technological as well as sociological, cognitive, or political. Just as they have dealt with shifts in the symbols of American culture, for example, so must television producers become sensitive to the meaning of the cable television revolution, a change that may alter their role in significant ways.

Sahlins's notion of the popular artist functioning in the synaptic space of society is a powerful one. With it we contend that such individuals, including television producers, are more than panderers. We note the complexity of their task, the utility of their work, the power of their perceptions. In the body of material that comprises popular entertainment, in its commercial nature, in the advertisements that surround it, the styles that shift within it, we can begin to delineate the fabric of contemporary culture. Those who create this significant body of texts must seek to remain ahead of their audiences, reading cultural shifts and making, reading, the sense of those events. We need not agree with their readings, or approve of their manipulation of that cultural raw material in order to recognize their centrality as cultural commentators. In television, then, the fears and failures of the society are written along with the dreams, desires, and successes. We see upheld the sinister and repressive alongside the honorable. The sinister and repressive can be seen to change, to shift over time toward the goals defined by the honorable.

All of this suggests that the role of the producer is an exceptionally complex one. Like his audiences, his critics, and his clients, he knows the history of the entertainment form in which he works. He realizes that it will be in his own interest to minimize shock and innovation. But he also realizes that it will do him no good to stay mired in convention, to practice only with careful copies of someone else's new ideas. He cannot afford to let new trends and social attitudes go unnoticed, nor can he easily accept every shift in the wind of opinion, follow every cult to its illogical conclusion. He walks a narrow bridge toward a dreamed-for success.

The result of this is similar to the result in any other form of expression. Much television is mundane. All of it is grist for the mill of cultural analysis, but little of it draws a mass audience over extended periods of time or attracts special attention to itself. Its very transparency is one of its virtues. It is no wonder then that we focus in this book on a handful of producers, on those who have established a place for themselves and their work by successfully reading and responding to the culture, criticizing it and creating new forms within it, using it to their own advantage and, in our view, to its own. In looking at their work and at their own understanding of that work, we examine those who create in the "bardic" center of our shared culture, those who give voice to our own "chorus."

CREATIVITY IN TELEVISION

In this section we explore the ways in which certain voices *within* the television "chorus" become distinct, and we relate this problem to questions of creativity. It would be simple to avoid the topic by suggesting that creativity in television is no different from creativity in any other form, that the concept is not medium specific. To a degree that is true. As a process of the human mind, creativity depends on individuals rather than on materials. But this observation, as basic as it may be, is of little help. In most instances it forces us back on hazy generalization. Without delving into cognitive psychology (and even there the notion of creativity is a vague one), our understanding of expressive creativity is terribly vexed.

The problem is obviously more acute in discussions of popular arts. The history of responses to popular entertainment is as intriguing as it is repetitive. Over and over, works which attract mass audiences have been dismissed as mere diversion. Their attraction is explained as evidence of the *lack* of creativity. Later, however, many of these same works have been cited as masterpieces, works embodying the deepest sense of humanity, culture, and society. In this later stage the questions focus on how the creator could, in the midst of crass commercialism or industrial constraint, produce works of such beauty, power, and grace. So we are forced to realize that our understanding of creativity is powerfully bound to the sociology of taste, to definitions of art prepared by various groups, and to ephemeral and sometimes arbitrary distinctions. Where, after all, did *Casablanca* come from, and why was it—how could it have been—thought of as merely another movie?

Television now occupies the social position formerly held by other massively popular forms and, as a result, our society does not make the assumption that creativity is central to the process of making television. We do not expect great or even important or significant works to emerge from it. We tend instead to expect the commonplace, the inferior, the repetitive, even the vulgar. We must examine the historical and social roots of our current definitions of art and the creative process in order to understand this.

With other Western societies we have, since the Renaissance, distinctly valorized the innovative, the daring, the non-traditional, the "unique." The presence of these qualities rests, in turn, on our willingness to grant to the artist something like "freedom" or "individuality." The autonomy of the artist is viewed as the source of creativity, and without it, "true" art is deemed impossible. All else is craft, or skill, or industry. Muriel Cantor's description of the television production process, for example, frequently focuses on this question.

> Though it is impossible to account for all controls, it is possible to examine how autonomy is enhanced or controlled by the legal system, industrial organizations, creative people working in the industry, and the various publics and clients who view the series. Autonomy and power are being used interchangeably in this study. The question most often asked is, "Who controls television?" (Seiden, 1974) The Answer is those groups and creators who have the most power or discretion to make independent decisions concerning the content and dissemination of the program.[10]

Many of the producers examined here have reached a level of "autonomy" within the television industry that gives them a significant degree of control over the content of their programs. Still, their interviews are rife with comments and complaints about the lack of power that still restricts them. And even with their relative power they have not, generally, been accorded the status of "creative artist." In many cases, as we shall see, they have not even sought it. And the question is interesting not because the understanding of television depends on that label, but because it is important to understand how certain types of television get made and how individuals view themselves within that process of *creating* significant cultural meaning.

It is this same set of problem-questions that underlies John Ravage's study of television directors.[11] In Ravage's view it is not the producers, but the directors who, by definition, are the artists of the moving visual image. Perhaps because of mistaken notions of "auteurism," he, like many critics, wishes to identify the creative function with the director's role. The directors in Ravage's interviews complain about the lack of creativity *caused by* the role of the television producer. As he puts it, "Directors find that they must sacrifice a careful and insightful style in favor of satisfying the producer's wants."[12] The result is a woeful situation.

> The issue . . . is the perseverance of directors in a medium which restricts their talent by imposing demanding pressures of time and money and a narrow range of creative forms. Most directors have learned to cope by accepting the occupation for what it is, and they try to work within it. Many others sublimate their creativity into other considerations; they learn to "get involved" with the minimal human values present in the scripts on which they must work; they search for meanings not readily apparent in the original scripts; they attempt to create interest and vitality by an artful edit or a sly expression, tucked away where the producer's inquiring eye might miss it. The successes are minimal, but they tempt the director to try to make the form more malleable.[13]

Autonomy, then, or control, or power, or *creativity,* seems to mean in this view that the artist is essentially free to do whatever he or she desires without regard to systemic constraints that might thwart such personal designs. Indeed, in almost every study of the creative process, systemic constraints are understood as counter-creative forces. Thus, while Ravage is willing to grant that not all producers are "totally commercialized nor . . . simple Philistine," his final judgment is that producers (presumably unlike directors who will exclusively seek ways to exercise their personal visions) "have suppressed their sensibilities in order to survive in a highly competitive industry that rewards only one thing: public acclaim as reflected in Nielsen ratings and percentages of the viewing public."[14]

Cantor's position is similar, though without the simplistic error of seeking creative potential in a single profession. She cites the interaction of responsibility among groups, but places the major blame for a lack of creativity with the networks, where executives are trapped by the economic system into undermining creative power. They, in turn, trap most television producers in the same manner, and the result is much like that described by Ravage.

These perspectives bring us closer to the central questions of this chapter. Generally, our cultural vision of the "creative artist" is closely bound to the image of the solitary, hungry, alienated genius. His works are unappreciated by the masses because his vision—also frequently having to do with alienation and isolation—is too "profound" for mass understanding. Economic success, dependent on mass acceptance, comes to be understood as clear evidence for the *absence* of creativity.

As an ideal, this concept of the isolated creator may be manageable. In practice, even the most solitary artist will discover barriers to full autonomy and the necessity of dependence on other individuals and support systems which impose certain restraints on private desires. Yet so pervasive is our cultural bias against popular entertainment that even the most outstanding members of television's creative community speak of "art" in hushed tones, with a reluctance born of embarrassment. They talk of craft and skill, but in many cases would disparage their own work rather than risk the burden of defining and referring to it as art. Many of the interviews recorded here indicate a struggle for autonomy, freedom, power. They indicate definitions of success measured primarily in terms of radically individual distinction and they lament the necessity for resemblance and repetition. The more a show approaches the "mass" in the views of some producers, the less successful it becomes.

The historically grounded class-bias of such a view should be evident. The innovative work is valued not only for its innovative vision, but for its sheer difference. The two are vitally intertwined in what Walter Benjamin refers to as the "aura" of a work of art.[15] That sharp and startling artistic perception, embodied in an experimental or innovative form, runs counter to the norm, the accepted, the confirming and conforming. It is available, then, to those who are so privileged as to be able to "understand" and "appreciate" such visions. In some cases this means that the vision is accessible to those who are fortunate enough to receive an education that values the kind of vision produced by the artists. In others, however, it simply indicates sufficient wealth to acquire a work of art on the advice of someone else in order to be a member of the "proper" group in one's community, to be above or beyond the more generally accepted boundaries of one's society. The true power, then, the sense of freedom, is often to be found in the autonomy of the *purchasers,* the users, of the work of art. The artist, possessed of intellectual or aesthetic power, of skills of a certain order, is finally dependent on recognition, acceptance, purchase, patronage of one sort or another. His "autonomy" results in a freedom to accept or reject the patronage of one group over another.

Like other analyses, our own have often emphasized similar concerns. We have been very careful to point out the ways in which individual producers have broken new ground in form and content. Our goal is to select a group of subjects who *have* distinguished themselves by creating a "distinctive" or "recognizable" style. In that regard, then, we agree with John Cawelti's generalization linking popular art to conventional notions of creativity.

> . . . there are a number of distinctive problems and techniques characteristic of formulaic art. In general, the most significant formulaic artists are those who effectively solve those problems in a way that balances the claims of escapism and the fulfillment of a conventional experience with the artistic interests of revitalized stereotypes, some degree of originality, and as much plausibility as the boundaries of the formula will permit.[16]

This project, however, has required us to re-think some of the more conventional notions with which we began. The very depth of the belief in innovation and originality as definitions of art is startling, especially as it is expressed by television producers whose more "conventional" works we find immensely powerful and compelling. Our task has become one of explaining the true excellence we often sense in works which are disdained by critic and producer alike, "patronized" not by wealthy collectors searching for the unique but by massive numbers of viewers who "buy" the works with their time and attention and thus make possible the producer's success and increase his autonomy within the structures of corporate decision-making. Instead of seeking to define creative television production in terms of distinction alone, then, we seek to define creativity in the context of the choric.

In order to clarify our own point of view we turn to a work by Larry Gelbart, a producer not included in our study. Gelbart is noted as the creator of *M*A*S*H*, but it is to his more distinctive *United States* that we now look. This series appeared in the early, heady days of Fred Silverman's ascendancy to the presidency of NBC. Silverman called for "quality" productions, and promised a new degree of freedom for the creators of innovative television artists. On the strength of *M*A*S*H* and in light of his publicized disdain for conventional television and conventional television production processes, Gelbart was one of the first producers to whom Silverman turned.

He was given extraordinary freedom, including a surprising lack of network control and a contract for thirteen episodes sight unseen. He used the freedom and his own skill to create a television show which we also consider extraordinary. It looked different; it played differently; it dealt with old topics in new ways. The show failed. Audiences and critics agreed in this case, and it was removed from the air soon after its beginning. In part the failure was due to programming decisions, the exercise of the network's final, powerful stage of control. Scheduled at 9:30 in the evening because of its mature treatment of sometimes controversial topics, it was always doubtful that audiences would turn away from a continuing hour-long production in order to catch this new, strange comedy. But there are other reasons as well for the failure of *United States*. And in spite of our own view that it deserved a far better response, its presence and its trial and failure speak to the issues of creative control that are central to a thorough understanding of the role of the television producer.

Gelbart made it clear that the show was a "personal" one. This was more than a matter of style. In published interviews he stated that the show, focused on the marital problems and joys of a young, upper-middle-class couple, was based on his own marriage. While the title, *United States,* refers to the way its characters function *in* the "state" of matrimony, it is equally important that we were concerned with the characters' states of mind, their emotional states, as expressed in their endless stream of words. These characters were hardly *in* a series of events or actions. They certainly were not *in* a familiar formulaic pattern or genre. They were truly in a state. There were aspects of situation comedy in the show, and elements of soap opera, but finally the series created its own sense of time and place and character, a world unlike most of the enclosed worlds we experience on television.

Visually, the show was more complex than many television productions. High-angle shots, floor-level shots, strange perspectives and points of view, all added to the unfamiliar tone. Stylistically the production reflected the tastes of its central characters rather than the "middle ground" decorative styles common to most shows. There was no laugh track. The titles were "hand-written" notations that added a distinct sense of personality.

It drew on the tradition of soap opera in that it was deeply concerned with "what happens to people," with events in the lives of individuals. In Gelbart's show we were not only concerned with what happened to the people, but even more so with "what people *say* about what happened to them." These exceptionally articulate, witty, educated individuals lived at the conceptual level. They drew out complex arguments with which to explain to one another the consequences of actions and beliefs. Their conversations were like small treatises couched in the emotions, guidebooks to psychic response. The few "actions" we witnessed were almost exclusively erotic. There was little in the show that heightened the sense of everyday, ordinary life for these two strikingly individualized characters. Far more than in even the most thoroughly process-oriented soap opera, *United States* flattened events in life so that almost everything became equal, equally "interesting," equally "important," equally "particular."

We were dropped into a stream of lived events. Presumably life went on when we were not "there," for the characters were thoroughly unpredictable. Something, viewers assumed, must have gone on in "the meantime." Even more importantly, the characters changed during the individual episodes. We were given occasion to observe the characters in the processes of their lives, making decisions, thinking aloud, being unique. In a very real sense viewers were voyeurs, treated to a view that almost no socially involved individual would ever have of another family's life. And this, apparently, is not what viewers and critics wished to see.

In spite of its failure with critics, the show did offer many of the things that they most often bemoan the lack of. Its pace was much slower than the usual. Gone was the frantic sense of "something happening" in every scene that so annoys some critics. Its content was inevitably about serious topics. The people themselves were treated seriously. Ideas were dealt with in a complex manner rather than as simplifications of complex problems. There was no laugh track cuing us to predicted responses. Yet the reaction was that the show was *too* slow. The "plots" were *too* thin. The characters were judged variously to be boring or excessively witty, as if no one could imagine a ''real'' couple with such quick-draw vocabularies. In short, these people were too highly individualized, too realistically particular, too unique. They were the opposite of conventional, generalized, formulaic television, but that was not what the critics had meant, not what they had wanted to see.

Our own point here is hardly to debate the merits of a particular television program, or even the merits of different kinds of television. Instead, we suggest that the freedom given to Gelbart, and the work that he produced, sheds light on the larger problem of creativity in television and popular entertainment in all its various forms.

Gelbart's *United States* can serve as an example of a distinct type of television more akin to conventional notions of ''art'' than to the television we have defined as ''choric.'' Because it appears in the context of the choric, and is recognized as relating to but differing from it, we prefer to identify it as *''lyric television.''* Indeed, this style draws on qualities associated with the lyric from its context in Greek drama, through the history of poetry, to the twentieth-century novel and the art film. The lyric is rooted in subjective response. It is dependent for its force on the acute perceptions of the sensitive individual, and on that individual's ability to reconstruct subjective experience in a way that evokes a similar response in the reader-viewer. Like the song as contrasted to the sonata, its voice is personal rather than social. It is intense, pointed, often brief. It frequently turns to the common and everyday for its focus, certainly since the nineteenth century. It shuns the exaggerated, the heroic, the widely shared social event.

Clearly the more personal, the more subjective, the more lyrical television is, the more limited is its ability to attract a mass audience. It must depend on the excellence and power of its formal qualities to attract mass attention for it does *not* rely on elements that already relate us to one another or to the history of popular forms of expression. *United States* in our view presented an extreme example of lyric television. Early live drama may have worked in much the same manner, presenting us with the personal visions of sensitive writers and directors, catering to a smaller, more thoroughly and conventionally educated audience.

But these historical distinctions hardly exhaust the benefits of marking the differences between the choric and the lyric. It is perhaps an even more useful measure of the variations within the work of individual producers. Indeed, we can find elements of both in the productions of all the subjects of this book.

The producer who, in some ways, is closest to the lyric pole suggested by Gelbart, is Norman Lear. There is a definable, discernable Lear style even in those shows that are built on traditional forms of comedy. More importantly, there is a clear subjective perspective, variously described as moral, ethical, or political. It is a perspective that offends some members of the viewing community and some critics, a response common to the lyric. Yet Lear escapes some of the subjectivism found in Gelbart by focusing his attention on primary social issues. While concerned with the responses of his individual characters, he is equally concerned that his presentations be considered as contributions to a wider social discourse. He is injecting his own ideas, via his television shows, into the national debates on general problems: racism, sexism, class conflict, and personal rights. His very ability to include controversial social commentary *within* the context of conventional domestic comedy is a powerful contribution. This blend of the lyric and the choric not only protects him in the responses of the mass audience, but indicates that the two forms are not mutually exclusive and that when combined in powerful forms they can attract even larger audiences than either in isolation.

There is another body of Lear's work that bears on our definition. This work is more exclusively lyrical. The varied successes of shows such as *Mary Hartman, Mary Hartman* and *All That Glitters* indicate that our basic distinction is a sound one. These shows were perceived by network executives as too narrowly focused, too reflective of the personal (too lyrical in our view), to attract a mass audience. Programmed in syndication, they were able to attract small but loyal audiences, *segments* of the mass able or willing to respond to the more subjective style and content of these shows.

Lear's prominence should not obscure the fact that the other producers discussed here also create special blends of style and content in their own work. The inclusion of controversial socio-medical-personal problems in the work of David Victor, the use of the western and the period piece by John Mantley and Earl Hamner, and the personalization of the crime-adventure story by Quinn Martin, all indicate that these producers are masters of the choric forms. The same could be argued for Marshall and the Brooks-Burns-Tinker coalition in comedy.

The distinctions we will make between two forms of expression by Richard Levinson and William Link can also be better explained in terms of the lyric-choric contrast. While Levinson and Link often point to their made-for-TV movies as their more innovative contributions to television, it is quite possible to see most of those stories as rather conventional social-problem plays. They break important ground thematically, and are able to do so because the formal conventions remain intact. With *Columbo,* however, they vary both form and content of the detective formula, and, in our view, present us with their more lyrical expressions in that production.

In what follows we focus on the major traditions in choric television and on the artists who have created significant versions of our most public art. Once again we are made conscious of the fact that technological changes are pushing at the edges of our definitions. Cable television, with its ability to survive with smaller audiences, segmented and targeted according to interests, values, and tastes, pulls away from the choric center. Inevitably it will be possible for producers to speak more precisely from their personal experience. No longer will their task be to speak in terms of the common, to express differing opinions about the shared, to help in the continuing definition of cultural meanings. They will be able to address those who already agree with them, to locate those audiences of a few hundred thousand individuals who can even now create a "best seller" in the literary market place.

Such a development is often hailed as a grand new possibility. Television will not need to be "dragged down" into the mire of the mass. Writers, actors, directors, and producers, as well as critics and cultural commentators, eagerly await the market fragmentation.

But we are not so certain of these benefits. We suggest, somewhat iconoclastically, that the limitations of the present system, the constraints on autonomy, have their virtues. Not the least of these may be that artists find it impossible to attain the consummate freedom they so often seem to desire. The artistry that we find in commercial television is an art that explores the central regions of the American mind. In recognizing its value we realize that television production in our own advanced, post-industrial culture is not so different finally from the production of central, significant artistic expressions in more traditional societies. The more familiar choric forms *and* the more innovative lyric ones must relate to the shared systems of meaning and symbol that form our cultural life. Our television producers are, then, not very much like the solitary romantic artist. Rather, they resemble the artists who carve ritual masks for the Ndembu of Zambia. Victor Turner describes their work:

> The woodcarvers who create the masks, though they portray a limited range of types (the Foolish Young Woman, the Crazy One, the Wise Old Chief, the Fertility Binder, etc.), display a wide range of personal aesthetic initiative in generating variant forms.[17]

The television producer, creating the "ritual masks" of contemporary America, performs a task of equal significance, and with equal creativity.

NOTES

1. James Carey, "Communication and Culture," *Communication Research,* April, 1975, p. 177.
2. *Ibid.*
3. James Carey, "A Cultural Approach to Communication," *Communication,* 1975, vol. 2, p. 6.
4. Victor Turner, "Process, System, and Symbol: A New Anthropological Synthesis," *Daedalus,* Summer, 1977.
5. Roger Silverstone, *The Message of Television: Myth and Narrative in Modern Society* (London: Heinemann Educational Books. 1981).
6. Carey, "A Cultural Approach to Communication," p. 15.
7. Horace Newcomb and Paul Hirsch, "Television as a Cultural Forum: Implications for Research," *Quarterly Review of Film Studies,* Summer, 1983.
8. John Fiske and John Hartley, *Reading Television* (London: Methuen, 1978), pp. 85ff.
9. Marshall Sahlins, *Culture and Practical Reason* (Chicago: University of Chicago Press, 1976), p. 117.
10. Muriel Cantor, *Prime-Time Television: Content and Control* (Beverly Hills: Sage, 1980), p. 6, referring to M. H. Seiden, *Who Controls the Mass Media? Popular Myths and Economic Realities* (New York: Basic Books, 1974).

11. John Ravage, *Television: The Director's Viewpoint* (Boulder: Westwood Press, 1978).

12. *Ibid.*, p. 9.

13. *Ibid.*, p. 10.

14. *Ibid.*, p. 11.

15. Walter Benjamin, "The Work of Art in the Age of Mechanical Reproduction," *Illuminations* (New York: Knopf, 1968), trans. Harry Zohn.

16. John Cawelti, *Adventure, Mystery, and Romance* (Chicago: University of Chicago Press, 1976), p. 20.

17. Victor Turner, "Process, System, and Symbol: Toward a New Anthropological Synthesis," *Daedalus,* Summer, 1977, p. 68.

Quinn Martin

Quinn Martin began his career in film editing, and later served in numerous other behind-the-scenes jobs before he turned to writing. He was working for Desilu when he was given responsibility for the production of *The Untouchables*, first telecast in 1959. Within a year the series was ranked in the top ten programs by Nielsen. From that success Martin was able to found his own company, QM Productions. There followed a collection of dramatic hour-long productions beginning with *The Fugitive* (1963) and continuing with *Twelve O'Clock High* (1964), *The FBI* (1965), *Dan August* (1970), *Cannon* (1971), *The Streets of San Francisco* (1972), and *Barnaby Jones* (1973). All of these productions received excellent ratings and lasted for several seasons. Martin was also responsible for several other dramatic hours that had a brief stay in prime time including *The New Breed, The Invaders, The Manhunt, Most Wanted,* and *Tales of the Unexpected*. In addition, Martin has produced several films for television.

In 1978 Martin sold his company to Taft Broadcasting and agreed to leave television for five years during which Taft was to have exclusive rights to his QM company name and Martin was not to compete with Taft. The covenant expired in 1983 and Martin, who had been teaching in theatre at the University of San Diego at La Jolla, began exploring new television ventures.

Martin is a native of Los Angeles and an alumnus of the University of California at Berkeley.

Quinn Martin's television dramas have, for the most part, been dismissed as prime examples of slick, violent, "action-adventure" formula shows, although sometimes praised as the best of their type. His shows bear clear and distinctive stylistic traits, often marked for viewers by such obvious features as the "Epilogue" common to many QM productions. *The Fugitive,* moreover, is remembered as a landmark of Hollywood television entertainment for capturing and imaginatively involving an audience with its character studies and its grinding threat of passionately misguided justice.

But Martin's work also bears the brunt of two forms of negative television criticism. The social attack on TV's fictional violence often centered on *The Untouchables, The F.B.I.,* or *The Streets of San Francisco.* Perhaps because of their high sense of style and their easily recognized structures, these shows became examples of problematic television even when violence was not a prime ingredient of their makeup. The second criticism is sometimes more subtle, though not always more complex in argument. It suggests that Martin's shows are powerful examples of television's social and political repression, its defense of the status quo, its ability to thwart radical or even moderate forms of change. Television, it is argued, maintains old values and traditional power structures, and Martin's work dramatically reinforces right-wing attitudes. In this argument violence is no vague "social problem;" it is a tool with which aberrant and system-threatening individuals are brought into line.

Martin has never shied away from recognizing or discussing the political and social content of his television dramas. Openly he has discussed his idealization of authority structures and individual authority figures such as policemen and federal agents. When fully presented, as it is in our interviews, his position is more adequately argued than it often has been in brief quotations. It is also more thoroughly placed with regard to other elements in a television show, in the formula of action-adventure-crime drama, and in the overall context of the medium. His comments on the content, values, and meanings of his series offer material for a new perspective on Martin's work. It goes beyond simplistic political analysis of the crime shows and leaves behind easy cultural and literary analysis that lumps him with other creators of "adventure" formulas. It does this because it is able to identify and apply the distinguishing characteristics of his series.

A television show for Martin is a structure of three layers, each with its own significance. Every element within the show is assigned to one layer, its placement indicating a priority, a sign of its meaning and value. In this process of sorting out we begin to understand more clearly the reasons for various judgments, decisions, and choices made by the producer.

The constituents, or layers, of television drama are, in Martin's terms, Melodrama, Emotion, and Theme. Melodrama should be equated with plot, or action. Emotion is a collective shorthand term that includes motivation, characterization, and the universal dimensions of human response to extreme situations. Theme indicates specific social or political significance or lesser moral "lessons" that can be drawn from the dramatic events. These aspects of television drama are ordered in the sequence given here. Melodrama is the surface, Theme the substructure. The central quality of any QM production, the quality Martin uses to evaluate shows by other producers, and the element that he works most for in his own shows, is Emotion. The relationship among these factors is crucial, so much so that one of the producer's primary responsibilities is to work with them, manipulate them, until the successful mix is achieved.

Shows that focus on melodrama, on plot, are those that offer the sizzle without the steak. They are the "go, go, go" shows. Although Martin recognizes that such shows can be very successful, and even cites examples from works produced by friends and acquaintances, they are, for him, best defined as "bubble-gum" television. They represent much that is wrong with the content of the medium. The clear impression is that this layer of TV is the most formulaic, the most easily accomplished and copied. Although it is an essential element, it is as likely to lead to trouble as to success. Martin often demonstrates this troublesome aspect of melodrama, and the problems of maintaining balance, when he discusses network interference in program design. In one example network program executives, eager to grasp every rating point, keyed on high audience responses to a villain in one of Martin's pilots. Insisting that the villain be kept in the series, they made him a side-kick to the central character instead of an antagonist, yet they were dismayed at the show's failure. To Martin, the

Quinn Martin

explanation was simple. The network choice ignored the dramatic function of the character, and with a thoughtless and uninformed decision, the balance of the show was wrecked.

On the other end of the spectrum of internal elements is Theme. This is the realm of journalistic currency, of hot news topics molded into the series formula. This factor, too, is secondary. The thoughtful producer "teaches a little" in all shows. He has a theme that is "making a statement about something." Still, "it doesn't have to be heavy." It is possible to have "a little substance in what you are doing." These apparently condescending descriptions should not be taken to indicate that the issues are not significant ones for Martin. They do indicate, however, that he avoids turning the shows into explicit, immediate statements about current social problems. Above all, at this level, one must avoid the "polemic." When this element overwhelms the others, the production becomes a tract instead of real drama, real entertainment.

With these distinctions it is easier to see why the idea of "violence" has never been a vital issue for Martin except as it affects the design and programming of shows he has constructed. As part of any action-adventure, police, or law enforcement series, violence, in his view, is technique. It is clearly relegated to the realm of the melodrama, the action, the formula, the go, go, go, used there to attract and hold audiences, upon entry from other shows, past the commercials and above the distractions that surround viewers in the home. Given the fact that it is part of every show of this type, in Martin's view part of every one-hour format, it should hardly be taken with undue seriousness or isolated from its context. In response to pressure, of course, one can merely change the nature of the representation of violence. Violence can occur offscreen. It can be shown with or without physical results, depending on what critics think is more effective as a deterrent. Car crashes can be substituted for more direct interpersonal violence. These technical changes can be quickly and easily accomplished because the violence is not directly related to the essential content of anything that Martin is trying to present to his viewers.

If, on the other hand, violence is to be treated in and of itself as a subject, it should not be treated as a "theme," as a social statement. That would require a precise sort of political position statement and Martin would then enter the ballgame of opposing views surrounding the "topic" of television violence. Even more to the point, the thematic or polemical response to violence would not be the truest, most significant response that could be offered. That best response comes in the realm of emotion, where truth, for Martin, always resides.

It is in the properly motivated human response of strong characters that one must deal with such issues. Thus we have episodes in which policemen anguish over the violence they encounter and in which they must indulge. Most likely these characters respond to these situations ambiguously, for there are few easy answers in their fictional worlds. In spite of the charges that Martin's characters are one-dimensional, that all of them represent the same point of view, this is not often the case. Although stories are resolved in terms of repeated reaffirmations of roles and values, the characters are most frequently men capable of being profoundly troubled by the worlds in which they live. If, finally, they must act in ways that are predictable, ways that can be classified socially or politically, they must do so as a decision central to the drama, and not merely as a matter of formula. To do otherwise would actually undercut the power of the values and reduce them to mere thematics, to polemics. In Martin's view such a choice is a sure step toward losing the audience.

Emotion, then, in Martin's view, is the layer in any television show which must govern the ratio of melodrama and theme. Emotion, the universality of human response, is crucial in building a successful show. Located here is the honesty that cuts across socio-economic lines and builds the mass, general audience.

Still, this is not an honesty patterned on reality as we experience it. Even emotion as a dramatic element, is governed by Martin's concern for idealization. A translation of this term makes apparent his intention to present things as they "should be" rather than as they are. Such a view is part of a strong tradition, one always open to the artist. The swerve toward "realism," so prevalent in the history of modern fiction, and the "realistic" nature of visual media, tend to distort the historical importance of the tradition of idealism. But such a perspective is strong within the popular arts. Martin's work is tied directly to heroic American types, to the heroes of popular westerns and to the protagonists of detective fiction. And, as astounding as it may first appear, there are equally direct links to the strong central figures created by Hemingway or Stephen Crane, to John Ford and Howard

Hawkes, to a wide range of "respected" American artists in fiction and film. They, too, idealized characters who face danger, who are able to participate in violent acts without flinching. Theirs are, in important ways, characters defined by Martin as "bigger than life." Yet they are ordinary, flawed, romantic, pressured individuals like his.

All these creators draw on a similar vein in American cultural thought. Their characters ultimately affirm some of the values of "the system," and say that whatever needs doing can be done by individuals if not by society. Always, explicit political or social notions are subordinated to specific human response. Always, the brave, compassionate hero stands central, and in his actions we affirm our universal ties.

In Martin's fictional worlds, then, two ratios are at work. As creative controller he must establish the relationship among his three layers within each show and he must regulate all of them toward a presentation of his own idealizations. Each show becomes a variation of this ideal world. The details of each world highlight the distinctions among his programs.

The world as it *should be* is presented as a world in order. When order is disturbed, those in positions of traditional authority are sometimes called upon to set it right. The characters, policemen and detectives for the most part, are in fact symbolic representations of "the system," by which Martin means the American system of society, government, and justice. Threats to the system also come in the form of individuals, but they, too, are representative. They may stand for those who do not abide by the system, those who choose to place themselves above authority. Or they may simply be indicative of larger forces, "the forces of the big city," for example. In a show such as *The Streets of San Francisco*, it is the city itself which is the villain, which is out of order, and thus causes confusion, pressure, distortion, violence, and crime, situations in which humans must test themselves, their systems of order, and the compassion that must reside in that order.

The system can demand respect, but it must be tempered with human warmth and compassion, human expectations and failures. The people who represent the system are most honest when their own weaknesses show. There is, in *The Untouchables, The FBI*, and *Twelve O'Clock High*, a weighting in favor of strong authority. Rarely do the central figures of these shows display weakness or vulnerability. The human factors are most obvious in *The Fugitive* and *The Streets of San Francisco,* where questions of human frailty repeatedly emerge.

But the system itself has weaknesses, as demonstrated both in *The Fugitive* and its weaker imitation, *The Invaders.* In such cases ordinary citizens find themselves called upon, in almost Hitchcockian fashion, to try to correct the distortion. Interestingly the disorder in those shows results in large part from a refusal on the part of official authority to accept compassion as part of its role. Over and over Lt. Gerard comes up against Richard Kimble's humanity only to reject it in favor of an abstract, *disordering,* reliance on the law.

Again, this is a matter of ratio, of balance, of controlling point of view. Martin's decisions in shaping these shows offer some of the clearest examples of the making of television art. His discussions of *The FBI* and *The Fugitive* illuminate his theories of television and his own sense of the idealized nature of his worlds.

In very early episodes of *The FBI,* for example, Inspector Lewis Erskine is remarkably open and vulnerable. In one episode from the first season he is clearly relieved when a sympathetic bank robber outruns him and escapes into Mexico. Like Erskine, the man is a Korean War veteran. Also like Erskine, he has lost a deeply loved wife and has only a single child left to him as family. His life, however, unlike Erskine's has not gone according to plan, has not moved toward success and self-definition. Erskine says to his assistant that he can envision himself in the man's position. He even questions his job, a job that forces him into strong, potentially violent confrontation with such a man. In spite of these doubts he arranges for the man to learn that his son is still in this country, knowing that the loving father will return for him. When he does, he is captured. Justice prevails, but it is justice confused, cognizant of the weaknesses in "the system."

Such a perspective is quite in keeping with many of Martin's other shows, but in this case it was not judged a success. Martin describes those early days of the show by pointing out that Erskine was portrayed as very like the typical member of the audience in "human" terms, a portrayal unacceptable to some members of the audience.

I really thought a general consensus from my mail was that people got uptight that the FBI guy had the same kind of problems that they might have . . . . the people wanted to relate to the FBI as a super-protector and to get their emotion from the guest star. And I switched to that direction and it was immediately successful. So that didn't come from the FBI. That came from the people.

In one particular episode where Inspector Erskine identifies with a criminal, about the third one I shot, the FBI liaison asked, "Is it good?" They were not dramatists—he was asking, "Is it good to have the FBI guy question his job?" And I said, "It's good." And then they said, "Fine." But it wasn't fine. The audience didn't want it.

The most interesting result of this change, of course, is that it created an emotional tie to the guest star. Most often these stars portray a criminal or a member of a criminal's family. Such a structure would seem to be dangerous. But Martin clearly trusted the outcome of his stories to stand as affirmations of appropriate American attitudes.

By contrast, *The Fugitive* seems to be pointed in another direction, one that more obviously seems to cut across the aim of idealizing the system. Here, drastic mistakes are made, and an innocent man is threatened. When questioned, however, Martin's answer again demonstrates the values that determine the structure of his fictional worlds.

If a man has done everything ethical he has a right to protect himself. That was my justification. I thought long and hard about whether I was really doing something wrong in making a show that says a man is living outside the law. We made it very clear that he had all the appeals. He had tried to do everything, and now he escapes. He tries to clear himself. He didn't go out and play around; he's not a jet-setter. He worked beneath his station. He did a lot of things to try and find out who killed his wife. And he did.

The idealization then includes both justice and mercy, strong authority and temperate compassion. Ultimately, it comes down on the side of "the system" because Martin believes that an appropriate range of varied responses can actually be found there. The system works, though not always in harmony.

This is precisely the point at which a larger question emerges. The question is posed by Martin himself at one point.

Well, then you say, What right do I have to take this attitude?
Well, it's my belief. I think in general things are better. I'm a glass-is-half-full guy rather than half-empty. I believe in the positive attitude. I've always wanted to tell a more idealized version of things in an honest manner.

It is at this level, we would suggest, that large political statements are made. Martin cites the smaller "theme," the "message" underlying his shows as the principle political content. But it is in this other choice, this choice of world view, that the more potent, because more pervasive, political comment is made. There is no polemic here. Instead there is the far more powerful undercurrent, the substructure of assumptions which orders and governs the mix of other factors.

Again, this view, like the aesthetic one, mines a strong American tradition and one could ask the same questions of Hemingway and Crane that one asks of Martin. They are moral and political questions. Harshly put, they go like this. How far can the idealization go and remain honest? For whom are things really better? Is this particular idealization the only one, the best one, the appropriate one? Is it too closely related to visions that involved us in moments of failure, such as Watergate, that have lead to the negativism that Martin deplores? Do too many of us accept too easily the idealized versions of authority? These are questions often asked in political analysis of television, from the right and the left. Martin's productions are cited as evidence of television's strong support for the conservative right, for the political status quo. By attending to Martin's own views, to the undercurrent of basic assumptions, the harshest judgment becomes much too simple.

The easy political indictment of television and television content is moderated by a closer look both at the medium and at those who create for it. The intermix of elements within shows clearly makes multiple interpretation possible for viewers. In Martin's case, in spite of the definable political assumptions, emotion is always central. We are asked to involve ourselves in the lives of believable characters from many sides of the political spectrum, and this cushions the idealizations whether the cushion is intended or not. Even when characters with opposing views are presented negatively, when those views are oversimplified or ridiculed, the element of fictional choice is present. On a more elementary level we often experience an understanding of the criminal, and sympathize even more directly with those who, as family and friends, are touched by his actions. We feel something of lived experience in the best shows, of victimization, frustration, even anger at "the system."

It is possible to make qualitative distinctions among Martin's shows on such a basis. The sense of humanity is strongest in *The Fugitive* where the system itself is questioned. This show, for us, remains Martin's central achievement. The same sort of sympathy is powerfully present in *The Streets of San Francisco,* a show originally planned as a story of newspaper reporters rather than of detectives. *The FBI,* by contrast, is weakened in its insistence on the role of authority at the cost of compassion. In *Cannon* and *Barnaby Jones,* while an attempt is made to create character interaction, there is ultimately little to work with and the shows, while moderately successful, have little of the rich texture of earlier work. There is simply too little room for emotion to develop and we are left with a residue of melodrama and a touch of theme.

These distinctions within Martin's work demonstrate for us the strength of television's internal variety, a variety clarified by close attention to the producer's understanding of his own work. Neither the clearest intention nor the most extensive control can bring about homogeneity, even if it were desired.

INTERVIEW WITH QUINN MARTIN

THE PRODUCER'S PERSONAL STYLE

[MARTIN] I began my career as a film editor, but I'm an English major. I've studied the art of screenplay writing and creative writing till it comes out my ears. I don't think a producer is a producer if he can't write or fix a script by himself. But I was a film editor and I was the head of an editorial department. I was still in my twenties and I was in motion pictures, holding one of six jobs in town as head of an editorial department, and I decided I wanted to produce. The only way that I could produce, prove that I was creative, was to write. So I started writing for television. And then I began to sell so when a producer was fired on a show for which I was writing, I took over. It was in 1957 on the *Jane Wyman Show*. After that I put material together to help Desi Arnaz get the Westinghouse-Desilu Playhouse anthology. Desi then hired me to produce on the Playhouse and one of my shows was the two-hour special *The Untouchables*. I went on to executive produce *The Untouchables* as a series, it exploded, and from that I developed a big career and formed my own company.

People compare me to the old moguls of the movies. And I am really a controller. I believe in control. When I say I am a benevolent dictator I really mean that. I was always brought up that the guy at the top had the responsibility of control. Now that is an offshoot of my environment. We're all products of our environment. I grew up in this town and grew up seeing strong father-figure images: Mayer, Cohen, Warner, Zukor. So I patterned my style without even thinking about it. To me, coming out of films, it was just natural for me that that's the way you did it.

Q. *Will you comment on the thesis that television is a producer's medium?*

I don't think there's any question that in television the medium is a producer's medium. I very strongly controlled the creative content of everything that came out of this shop. We laughed when I used the term benevolent dictator but I do believe that it's necessary to have a single focus or point of view. Once that is established I give people a lot of freedom. But there is a stamp that is placed on each show. You create a point of view in terms of story, look, casting, everything else. Then people can go do as much as they want. But I still OK'd every idea for every show before it started.

Q. *How do you project a series?*

We literally lay out an entire season. I always sat down with the producer, and the story editors to talk about the entire season and to write up maybe fifty "notions" [story ideas]. Then, out of that collection of notions we would pick the twenty-two or twenty-four that we would plan to do. We would then assign these to writers. Now this doesn't mean that if a writer came in and had a marvelous idea we wouldn't use it. But we feel the best way to control our own destiny is to assign the point of view and then work with the people. Then when the scripts would come in our staff would take our notes, combine them with theirs and rewrite to fit our point of view.

We've always prided ourselves on maintaining a high degree of quality in our writing. We insisted that things make sense, be structured right, be properly motivated with theme, character, plot. I don't know how else you do it when you are mass-producing quality. I've had years when we've turned out 120 epsiodes. If you don't have an organizational point of view, how do you operate? I don't know that everybody does it that way, but that's how we have always operated here.

Q. *Did you read every script?*

Absolutely. And not only that, I have a sidekick. I've always had a head story man who would write notes in addition to my notes, and we would correlate to see that we didn't miss anything. You don't feel that you are just alone. If I go to London, to Hawaii, I want to make sure I have a backstop who's OK, knows what's going on with the writers.

Q. *Did you match writers with in-house story ideas?*

Yes, we try to. First of all, the writing pool is hard. And I created my own monster because I started making producers out of writers thereby creaming off the best to begin with. We really take who's available, who's the best writer, and when the producer has a stack of ideas he matches the ideas to the man who most relates to them. You always have a couple of guys that each producer has a working relationship with, works well with.

There's something else with this kind of system. We never send the networks the long outline that most people do. We send them a notion, a story idea. My deal is, they OK the story, and we deliver the script that follows it. The network does not have any more control. I don't think there is anything wrong with showing them something, but you can't make shows by committee. If the network were in on every step of what you are doing, then there's not going to be any point of view.

Through the years that position has been chipped away a little and I even gave up a little. Because I didn't have to show them anything. How do I know whether they're doing another show with another company that may be exactly the same. And we do not have actors approved or directors or writers. Other companies do. I would never have networks approve actors. Now again, each to his own. There seems to be a new breed of guy coming in and it doesn't bother him. But Norman Lear and I, you know, and Herb Brodkin and Link and Levinson, the guys that were in my era, we were all fairly strong-minded. I don't mean nasty or anything, but we had a point of view that the responsibility of the show was ours—either buy us or don't buy us. And it's gotten to be more of a group think sort of thing in TV today; committees on both sides. That's the way it is. Things happen; things change. This is not the reason I have sold my company but it didn't make it painful to sell when the industry is going through a period of group think. It's a bore to me to have to sit and talk to twenty people. I wouldn't do it that way.

Q. *Everything is laid out to the degree that your entire staff knows what is required on a QM show?*

Right. I can always get a good director to come do a pilot or something, where I can give him extra money. But I've gotten the best mechanics, the assistant directors, the script clerks. Two of my best directors are former script clerks. We lay out the style of the show, whether it's low angle, or it's moody, and these people get the coverage. We cast it, we do the script. The director comes in and shoots the show and we get the pace, the angles, whatever, and we put it together. And we come back to the end. The director gets the credit and goes off to do something else. It may sound mechanical, but I don't know how else to do it. I'd rather have that kind of guy than some great artist.

We had one director who did a *Streets of San Francisco* and all of a sudden the lights come on and the producer is asking didn't I think this was great. There was a sixteen and a half minute scene and it was based on a half-page. I said, "No. That's not good. There are two lines in there that are important and we've got to get on with the story.'' And we went in and got them. The director did a very bad job. Now he's gone into pictures and he's become a good director.

Q. *As producer, what relation did you develop with the actors?*

With Karl Malden, with Bob Stack, anybody, I would sit down for hours before I ever started a series and find out everything about that guy. Just as you're doing, we'd get a tape going and I know what he eats for breakfast, his hobbies, whatever. I tried to get that man's emotional attitudes involved in the character because I feel that the character in a show should only be about 15 percent off the person. If you're playing a college professor, I've got to play it as you, because you're going to play it better. Especially in television, you're not trying to create something different every two minutes.

On top of that, though, that's the way stars were made when I grew up. Clark Gable played Clark Gable whether he was playing Rhett Butler or anyone else. I believe in that, the star system. If you look at the history of stars, there have been only a couple, maybe Jack Nicholson and Marlon Brando, who'll give you something different every time they play it. You get Bob Redford whether he's in *The Way We Were* or *Butch Cassidy,* as you'll get Paul Newman as Hud or Cool Hand Luke and so on and on. I think that's what makes stars. But for you to be able to do that right you've got to learn as much about that guy as possible.

So we would work according to that perspective. We'd give the actors the scripts ahead of time. An actor comes in and wants to talk about his role, I gave my permission, carte blanche, if there's anything within reason, rewrite it for them if it makes them more comfortable. But when we get on the set, you shoot the script. That's the rule. We give you all the leeway ahead of time, but once we're in agreement you don't start playing games because we don't make shows like that.

I'm a big believer in organization. I think you get as loose as you have to before you start. But once you get in there the only way you can manufacture quality, I think, is to have control. It's a word I use a lot. I believe in control.

I don't mean to sound like a braggart when I say control. You've got to relate it to the period and, as I say, the whole reason I formed my own company was to get away from all the bureaucracy. I was given total control by a network which was looking desperately to get on the boards and I really pulled it off. I was the only one who did in those days. I had four shows in the top ten for ABC at the time when it was really tough because we used to start off with fifty stations short the first of every year and have to prove ourselves. Be tougher than anybody. I earned my spurs in a very tough market.

I've set up a system where, honestly, once a script is done and everything's been talked out, you can put it into the system and it will get made. It will look as if I did everything because I've got a head casting guy, a head editorial guy, a head production guy. I mean we all worked together to a point where the company is the producer. I'm the executive producer and the producer is really the story editor. There's nothing wrong with that. I think it's good. I think it's the only way you can have mass-produced quality. My producers have always liked it.

During the twenty-year phase just closing they did not have to bother with wardrobe, locations, all the stuff that makes guys groan about twenty-four-hour days—Because I split the responsibility. I was the producer, and the producer on the credits was a high-class story editor making a lot of money and getting a credit.

I've always been a believer in fighting for what you believe in. In the final analysis, if you're working for someone you say what you believe in. If they still want it the other way, you state your position, and if he wants it that way you do it the best way you know how or you get out.

I formed my own company twenty years ago because I didn't want to play that game. I wanted to have the responsibility. If I wanted to say, "Screw it" to the network, "I don't agree with you," or whatever, I was doing it on my own and there wasn't a board of directors. That really propelled me into being successful on my own and I always fought them if I thought they were wrong. Of course, you give in to them if you think they're right. Without that give and take I don't know what you have. You might just as well be an order taker and just report in. But I'm not.

Q. *Is there a Martin style on every show?*

Yes, I always try to put a stamp on every show so that you viscerally know what show it is just by seeing it and feeling it. *The Fugitive,* if you will, is more John Ford in that it's the great country and wide open and a little more straightforward, eye-level camera and forty millimeter. Whereas *The Streets of San Francisco* was getting inside the city with a low-key twenty-five millimeter, desk-level camera; a little distorted emotionally, being inside the melodrama. So in every show I would try to pick a camera style and a photographic style and have it be something recognizable. And I get letters from people saying, ''I knew it was your show the minute I saw the first scene because of the style.'' It happens enough that the audience must get a definite feeling from them. I really care about what people write in—very informative.

Q. *Have you changed the way in which you shape the ideas in your shows? Is there something different in the way you did* The Fugitive *because of* when *you did it?*

Absolutely. I believe you have to keep up every day of your life because things change. I used to shoot fifty-page scripts on *The Fugitive* for fifty minutes. And I shoot sixty-four-page scripts now for fifty minutes. So we used to play everything out; the exit walk, the long dissolve. I mean, people were very literal fifteen to eighteen years ago—1963—where they couldn't absorb if you moved quickly. Well, as commercials got people so used to absorbing information quickly, I had to change my style to give them more jump cuts or they'd be bored or I'd be bored watching. And one of the good, and bad, things of American television is that it's speeded up people's reactions mentally. People interrupt each other. When we have a commercial now, we tell them in twenty seconds what we used to tell them in a minute. The whole art form has speeded up.

Another thing that's happened; we used to say it and say it again and say it one more time, if it was a very important story point. People did not, on a smaller tube in a newer medium, didn't get it. My epilogue used to really reinforce a point. Well, again, I get 800 to 900 letters a month—that's been fairly standard on a successful film. Well, I read them. Or I have people read the letters and I look at the different parts. And you should keep aware of what people's reactions are and when people wrote, ''I don't have to be told twice,'' we stopped telling them twice. Part of that you get from the feeling, part from input. I would say the major change has been the speed with which we tell a story—which also makes it more costly. If I now have 40 percent more setups to tell that story than I used to, because we're not having the long walks, the exit, etc., then every time you move a camera it's more money; but more exciting.

Again, we are less heroic in television today. I've always had a point of view of telling an idealized version of life in that you can show a bad cop but don't show a bad police department. In other words, I don't think it's wrong to show a corrupt police officer but have the police department straighten out the problem. I believe that we have too much power in our hands, and if we're going to make everybody feel uncomfortable all the time, then we're doing a negative thing. Well, then you say, what right do I have to take this attitude? Well, it's my belief. I think in general things are better. I'm a glass is half-full guy rather than half-empty. I believe in the positive attitude. I've always wanted to tell a more idealized version of things in an honest manner. But today, I wouldn't be as heroic as I was fifteen years ago because people, young people especially, say you gotta be more laid back, you gotta be cooler. You still have a hero and you still have winners and so on, but you don't make as much out of it. I'd say, just in general, we're talking about the same kind of thing, but we're telling you faster and we're telling it in a more sophisticated manner.

Q. *Is there a difference among conceptions of your various series?*

There is a definite difference, but it's based on the nature of the show. *The Streets of San Francisco* is based on a situation that exists. There *is* a police department in San Francisco, and there are teams of homicide detectives. So that right out of the newspaper, thematically, you deal every day with the mores of society. Art should reflect life, and you should be right up to date. It's almost journalistic reporting, whether it be the Zebra killer or the fact that women's groups are forming to combat the attitude about rape—whatever you read in *Time* magazine. I try to be as up to date as possible, reflecting the mores of society told through the two guys on the show.

When you *create* a private eye, as in *Barnaby Jones,* who is a senior citizen who comes out of retirement to look into the death of his son who has taken over the private detective agency, and finds the culprit and then says, "Gee, I was bored being retired," and goes back into practice and uses the wife of his son as his secretary . . . that's different.

Barnaby and Cannon were fictitious characters doing stories we had to make up and then make seem real. The other is based on real stories that we had to fictionalize. In both cases you're trying to make a statement thematically, in every show, about something underneath the entertainment. But one is based on reality and one is completely made up. There aren't private eyes that carry guns and do the kind of things that Cannon and Barnaby do, so that you're in a whole different bag.

You still should try to do good characterizations. Your character should push the plot rather than vice versa. You should have a theme underneath every entertainment. To try to correlate it with a movie, a movie like Clint Eastwood's *Escape from Alcatraz* is going to be totally different than a Bond picture. They're both done well. They're both entertaining. But one is really based on a true story taken out of life—the Alcatraz thing. And the other is made out of whole cloth—big entertainment, pretty girls, bigger than life. It's like trying to compare apples and oranges, I think.

The only thing that you can look for is a continuum of style. Is there attention to detail? Was it cast well? All of these things. And I think all those things stand up. But one is more superficial than the other because it's made up rather than coming out of reality.

I happen to like *Streets of San Francisco*. My taste personally goes more toward that than the other. Not that I don't like Barnaby, and you can't only do one kind of thing, but the more I can deal with the truth and then dramatize it, then I like it.

Q. *What is your conception of the audience for which you create?*

Well, first of all, you can't work in a vacuum. I think initially you have to believe in what you do. Then I truly believe that I related to a general audience. I think if you do things that are emotionally solid that it doesn't matter whether the guy is under-educated or in a lower socio-economic area. I think you can hit a very broad spectrum of audience because you're hitting people where they live. If things are emotionally correct, then they hit everybody. So I always try to make sure that the characters are motivated properly, that people understand, that they get a feeling of what's going on. So I've always been rather proud that my shows have really hit a very broad section. I get the college kids and I get the truck drivers. I've always gotten a very broad selection of audience.

Q. *What is an example of a show that is emotionally incorrect?*

I think that many shows, today, rather than be specific, are superficial in that they're based on plot and not character. Go, go, go. No point of view. No depth. I think more television is that way than less.

I'd rather give you a show that I think is the epitome of what I'm talking about positively. That's *Lou Grant,* a show that I fought for. A vice president in programming at CBS tried to get me to tell MTM how to make the show. They wanted to turn it into a glorified cop show with more action and with Lou Grant in on everything beginning to end. I looked at several episodes one day in my projection room, saw what MTM was striving for, and loved it. I told the network it would succeed if the girl was changed* and they let MTM do their style. I also called my friend Grant Tinker and tipped him off. Anyway the show emerged mid-season and was a hit—would have been taken off though if MTM didn't have a full season deal with CBS, who wanted a series with Ed Asner after the *Mary Tyler Moore Show* went off the air. Good shop. I respect them.

To me, for the best television, you go back to *The Fugitive* days, the *Naked City* days, *Streets of San Francisco* days, the *Defenders* days, the *Ben Casey* days. Things had more depth. Now it's almost impossible because you can't build honest characters and honest emotion in three weeks. If they didn't have a full year deal because of Ed Asner on *Lou Grant,* it never would have stayed on the air. That's again what's wrong with television today, on and off, on and off. They don't give enough time, so people are selling anything that's got sizzle and there's not much steak underneath, and that's why there's so much of what I think is a kind of bubblegum television.

CREATIVE CONTROL

Q. *How did the anti-violence campaign affect television content?*

Well, first of all, I've always felt it was a political football. It *never* had a reason for being. Historically, the Surgeon General's report came out, and I know for a fact, because I did a lot of work in

---

*In the first season Rebecca Balding played the part of Carla Mardigian in the newsroom. That character was dropped and Linda Kelsey was added to the cast as Billie Newman.

Washington on *The F.B.I.,* that those people were on orders from the White House to try to blacken television. They couldn't. They're honest men and they went as far as they could and never proved any one-to-one relationship. There have been tons of studies and everybody agrees that there is no one-to-one relationship of TV action and real-life violence.

What happened is that there has been a strong minority voice, the PTA, and AMA, the Moral Majority, that finally made the networks give up because the networks care more about money than they do about what they're really doing up there. They always have and they always will. So we were forced.

I lost a couple of shows. Strangely enough I lost one of them because I was arguing just the opposite. Fred Silverman, when he came to ABC, tried to force me to make the fifth year of *The Streets of San Francisco* more violent. He thought the characters talked too much. And I said, "That's what the show is. You can't change a show when it has a certain tone." I said, "You're going to bring the tent down on you."

I actually saw *Most Wanted* as a cerebral kind of puzzle, where he wanted that to be *The Untouchables.* And I said to Silverman, "Alright, we've just started that show. I can creatively do that."

As an interesting historical footnote Fred also made me drop Tom Selleck, who played a computer expert. He said, "Where did you get that guy? He stinks. Get rid of him." Networks have control of who plays running roles in series. So I was stuck, if I didn't drop Selleck the show would have been dropped. I called Tom personally to tell him what had happened and he was shaken. I said your day will come. It did and could not have happened to a nicer guy.*

I lost both those shows, *Streets* because I wouldn't give Silverman more violence, *Most Wanted* because I gave him all he asked for and the tent did come down with a consumer boycott. And they both were in the top ten. Well, so be it.

Overall I'm not unhappy because we had twenty-four cops on TV and that's too much. But within the framework of that, if you're going to do a cop show there should be a certain amount of action-violence.

---

*Tom Selleck is now the highly acclaimed leading man on the CBS series *Magnum, P.I.*

There should have been then and there should be now. The interesting part of it is that I'm selling *The Streets of San Francisco* in syndication and I'm doing very well. They are dumping *Kojak* and they're dumping *Mannix*. They can't sell them. And that's because I've always done every show for what it is. I don't mean to sound holier than thou, but *The Untouchables* was supposed to be violent, damn it, it was supposed to be violent. *The Streets of San Francisco* to me was always a show of ideas, of pressures on people in the big city. It had a minimum of violence. The same with *Barnaby*. Again, Cannon was a guy bigger than life who walked through walls—a little more violence. You have to tailor each show for what it is.

What has happened is that when you have it now you're forced to do it in a way that to me is so antiseptic that I think the negative effect is that the audience may be brainwashed, desensitized. This is a medium that affects a lot of people. The networks may be brainwashing young people not to respect the problems of violence enough. When you get shot it's really ugly, or when you get a knife wound. That to me is violent. My only concern is whether or not they're going too far in being antiseptic about it and not making young people understand that it's a no-no. Other than that I could care less. You play with what the game is.

Within that game you cannot do any law enforcement—of course I don't think you can do *any* hour show—without three beats of action. An opening action to start the show, a middle action to get you through two minutes of commercials, a closing action to wrap up the show.

I think all the failures that have been had in the late seventies are because the networks did not understand that whether you're doing *James at 15* or some other bland thing like *The Class of '65*, you have to follow the same formula—because you've got people trained in an art form. You totally violate the art form and the audience is going to be bored. I have never done that.

Q. *Will you discuss any recent dealing with the networks?*

Fred Silverman called me over the weekend. I had created a show called *Sloan* and he was having a problem in a certain area and his order had literally changed one of the most important things in the show. Now because of his order there was a whole chain effect he didn't understand. I explained it to him. He said, "My God, you're right." But yet nobody on the company side—I'm leaving to go into other things—challenged him. They had to know it was wrong too. I mean it was so simplistic.

In a meeting a year ago Fred said, "I think a James Bond type show would work on television." I said, "Of course it would, an American version. Just take the genre, with bigger than life heavies, bigger than life problems, but a credible lead who's got a lot of style. You get your warmth and your honesty and your believability out of him. You get the big gimmickry, the machinery, and so on, externally."

Well, in the pilot that I wrote with the writer, we used a seven-foot black man who had a kind of Cuisinart for a hand. It could make drinks, cut through things, really a gimmick, a very Bondian gimmick. That man was killed in the pilot, as was the boss heavy, playing a Donald Pleasance kind of character. At the testing I mean the needle went up. They bought it.

But the black man tested very highly. By this time I've sold the company. Somebody says, "That black guy with the hand tested so high, make him the good guy's assistant." So the other day I'm talking to the new show's executive producer and he said, "You know, I'm really having a problem with the show. I love everything about it, but it's getting to be a comic strip because I can't get any warmth into the leading man."

And I said, "Well, you know, I created a show that had incredible heavies, incredible situations, and a credible leading man. You give the credible leading man the seven-foot man with the funny hand and now *he's* incredible. Now you can't get warm subtext."

He was bright. He said, "Jesus, you're right. But I'm too deep into it and I've got to figure out how to get around that." There again, there's a decision made, pure and simple. The meter said the black man tests well. Bring him back. Stick him somewhere. No thought given to it, and everybody falls in line. That's just one of the areas that really disgusted me with television. They just put the money in their pocket and aren't thinking through what they're doing. The show will fail.

I've left television because it got to the point that if you just fought for your point of view you were looked upon as a heavy, and it just got to be a bloody bore. All my life I had creative control and I fought for that before I fought for money. If you have an integrity about what you're doing you want to feel that you're going to be right or wrong and accept the responsibility. The people who put up the money always have the right to have some input, but in the final analysis it should be you. Then you rise or fall whether you're right or wrong. That's all changing. The networks want total creative control now.

SOCIAL RESPONSIBILITY AND EFFECTS

Q. *Tell us about some of your series in terms of social impact.*

Well, let me go back to square one. First, Warner Brothers made *The F.B.I. Story,* a feature, with Jimmy Stewart and Vera Miles, at which time Mr. Hoover said to Mr. Warner, who wanted to do a series—at the time Warner Brothers was very heavily involved in television with things like *77 Sunset Strip*—"I don't want a television series, but if we ever do it, we'll do it with Warner Brothers."

Dissolve. I get a phone call. This is now six, seven years later. Tom Moore, the president of ABC, called me at home on a Sunday saying, "Quinn, Warner Brothers owns the rights to *The F.B.I.* but I want you to do it and the FBI wants you to do it. I'll give you an on-the-air deal of thirty-two new shows and eighteen repeats and you can have complete control. You know, you can make your own deal and you'll be in charge and whatever."

I said, "I don't know if I want to do that." And he said, "What are you talking about?" I said, "Well, I am much more politically left of the FBI." I continued, "I think I'd have constant hassle." And he said, "Look, I want you, and Mr. Hoover wants you."

I really tried not to do the series because I felt that shows that had official seals on them turned out to be puff pieces. But I finally agreed. It's very difficult when the president of the network calls you ten times and you're offered something that is the kind of show you like and is monumentally good financially. I mean, it's big-budget action-adventure with a point of view. I did insist that I go to Washington to meet with them, talk to them, see if I could be on common ground with the Bureau. I spent several days in Washington, met Mr. Hoover, whom I liked in spite of not being politically in the same place. The day I got there he was ranting and raving about Martin Luther King being a bad guy, but we talked about horses, catching carp, Jack Warner, etc., not a word about the show. Two hours and I never saw him again for the ten years I did the show. I was turned over to his second in command, Cartha "Deke" DeLoach (known as Deke) who became my friend and confidant, and still is today. Deke wanted a show to show off the Bureau but promised to let me do whatever I wanted storywise as long as they could protect their image, i.e., we wouldn't name an informant, and so on. With that agreement they turned over four thousand files and I went to work not worrying if I were doing propaganda for the FBI because I knew I could make a good series. I avoided the hot story like the three civil rights workers who were killed in Mississippi in 1964 because I didn't feel in a weekly series I could do it correctly. I did the good action-adventure point of view stories, gray heavies, not black and white heavies. And the only change I made was taking the FBI guy away from being three-dimensional and making him two-dimensional because the audience didn't want it the other way. I later did the civil rights murders as a four-hour special and they received a 40 share two nights on CBS.

When I created the show I had the FBI man have a daughter who was in love with the inspector's assistant. Inspector Erskine [Efrem Zimbalist, Jr.] didn't want the daughter to be that involved with the guy because he had lost his fictional wife on a case when criminals were trying to shoot him.

I really thought a general consensus from my mail was that people got uptight that the FBI guy had the same kind of problems that they might have. And the show didn't start off that successful, so I took the daughter out because the people wanted to relate to the FBI as a super-protector and to get their emotion from the guest star. And I switched to that direction and it was immediately successful. So that didn't come from the FBI. That came from the people.

In one particular episode where Inspector Erskine identifies emotionally with a criminal, about the third one I shot, the FBI liaison asked, "Is it good?" They were not dramatists—he was asking, "Is it good to have the FBI guy question his job?" And I said, "It's good." And then they said, "Fine." But it wasn't fine. The audience didn't want it.

The FBI did not bother me ever about story content. They bothered the hell out of me in terms of procedure. They had the right to protect their image and they would say, "We would use cuffs there," or "We would do this there." And I didn't argue about that. I mean, I'm not an FBI guy; that's what you have technical advisors for. But I did shows about minutemen on the right wing that were caught by the FBI as well as left-wing spies. I happened to be fairly left of center politically then and I made it very clear that if I was going to have a hassle over that, not to ask me to do the show from the beginning. I didn't have a problem there.

Q. *What do you see as the morality issue in* The Fugitive?

If a man has done everything ethical he has a right to protect himself. That was my justification. I thought long and hard about whether I was really doing something wrong in making a show that says a man is living outside the law. We made it very clear that he had all the appeals. He had tried to do everything, and now he escapes. He tries to clear himself. He didn't go out and play around; he's not a jet-setter. He worked beneath his station. He did a lot of things to try and find out who killed his wife. And he did. To be fancy I think it's called Hobbes's Law.

Q. *Do your personal politics enter your series?*

I used to be ultra-liberal. Right now I'm a little left of center. I think part of that comes with age, part of it comes from success, part of it comes from getting smarter. I think every high I.Q. college person, I don't mean becomes a communist, but begins looking for a Utopian world. So you get into an ultra-liberal attitude and the welfare state and you have to help everybody. But as I've gotten to be a businessman, that's changed. This doesn't mean I'm voting my pocketbook or anything else. I still feel that the haves have to help the have-nots.

But on the other hand I understand about gross national product and about business and about a lot of things. So that I don't have simplistic answers like I used to, and while I might be very liberal about social issues, I'm very hard-nosed about not believing in détente, not trusting Russia and believing in a monetarist policy of controlling inflation. Where I used to think that there were simple answers under simple labels for everything, I think I've matured and my work reflects that.

Again, whether I was liberal, conservative, moderate, whatever—you can have an overall point of view, but you shouldn't use your vehicles to try to do a polemic. I've had some big fights with people down in the creative department. One writer—he's an ultra left-wing rich kid—is always trying to put a very close to communist point of view in shows. I'd just say, "Now stop already." He'd load it up figuring that if I changed part of it he'd still have part of it left.

I don't think that's what our business is. I do think you must have a point of view, first entertain, then make them think underneath. In fifteen hundred shows I tried to have a theme, whether it be as simple as "good conquers evil," or "live by the sword, die by the sword," even "nice guys don't have to finish last." It doesn't have to be heavy but I do think you can have a little substance in what you're doing as long as you entertain them along the way.

We start out saying, "Let's do an episode about old people, geriatrics, and how they're treated and what's the right way and the wrong way." Then, out of that you say, "How do you do that story in *Streets of San Francisco*?" And you do a crime that occurs because of the treatment of old people. So that we tried all the time to have a little more underneath shows than the average series, then we put the melodrama on top. I think I've gotten more sophisticated. I think I used to be a little more obvious about it than we are now.

Q. *Do you have any comments about the future of television?*

Yes, I have a lot of thought about the future of television. First, I feel privileged to have been part of the scene over the last twenty years. Second, I think the future will be the slow grinding down of commercial TV and the emergence of a new golden age in cable, direct broadcast satellite, subscription TV through the air, home video cassettes, and other things to boggle the imagination.

I recently saw a showing at CBS of an experimental Sony six-foot screen with all the works inside, 1200 lines, high resolution. I saw two shorts made on Sony experimental high resolution tape cameras. They were shot by Francis Copolla and the resolution was exquisite. The first tape I ever saw that looks like an emulsion film.

Well, I've endowed the Quinn Martin Chair in Drama at University of San Diego at La Jolla and when I lecture in class I say technology precedes creativity—that when this tape equipment gets into the home at a price people can afford you are going to see a renaissance of talent.

Just as in radio, movies, commercial TV, when guys like Norman Lear, Herb Brodkin, Link and Levinson, Bert Leonard, Quinn Martin, and others came forward to fill that box a new wave of talented newcomers will come forward to make their names in a medium that delivers movies into the home that bring back ten million dollars in today's money in one evening of viewing.

I don't know the delivery system but I know what it's going to look like in the home. I've seen it and so will you by 1985.

David Victor

David Victor began his career as a writer and worked on *Gunsmoke* in the early days of that popular series. His production tasks began in association with Universal Studios where he had a series of major successes, creating *The Rebel* (1959), *Dr. Kildare* (1961), *The Man from U.N.C.L.E.* (1964), *Marcus Welby, M.D.* (1969), *Owen Marshall, Counselor-at-Law* (1971), and *Lucas Tanner* (1974). In several instances he served as creator as well as producer. In the early eighties Victor left Universal and joined Paramount Pictures where his most recent venture was *Ryan's Four*.

Victor's career at Universal included several highly successful movies of the week including *Double Indemnity, Vanished, Women in White,* and *Little Women*.

Victor was born in Odessa, Russia, moving to the United States at the age of 12.

The work of David Victor, in familiar series such as *Dr. Kildare, Marcus Welby, M.D.,* and *Owen Marshall, Counselor-at-Law,* doubtless in the minds of many viewers stands for a kind of mainstream television. Contemporary in setting, unrestricted by the tightly defined codes of action-adventure formulas, focused on tense life-crisis moments, these works always return for their core to the emotional responses of realistic, threatened, perplexed central characters. In refining this pattern Victor has become one of television's supreme melodramatists, producing, in addition to series television, movies for TV and mini-series that reflect the same primary concerns.

In many ways Victor's definitions of television and descriptions of his own work are strikingly similar to Martin's, and the verbal similarities only seem to accentuate the obvious surface differences between the styles and content of the two producers' programs. This pattern of similarity and difference is repeated at a more complex level. Both producers exhibit and express abstract notions regarding the role of television in society that again appear almost identical. When we closely examine the television shows they have produced, however, we notice strong differences in the application of these ideas. In moving to this vantage point, then, we discover that Victor and Martin are creating television shows that contradict, as often as they complement, each other's approach.

Like Martin, Victor quickly acknowledges that any successful television production depends on a specific mixture of elements. If we look no deeper than at a basic list of those elements, described without commentary or analysis, either man could be happy with the other's recipe. Both agree, for example, that some sort of "hook" is necessary in beginning a dramatic presentation. They want their stories to begin on a note of excitement in order to focus audience attention on the plight of highly sympathetic characters. Both then work to have that excitement mount in tense gradations in order to maintain the numbers of viewers through commercial interruptions.

Imbedded in these melodramatic patterns of action there must be, for both producers, the "lessons." While these are, for the most part, small, generalized moral homilies in QM productions, Victor inserts far more factual material. Autism, breast cancer, homosexuality, mental retardation, impotence, senility: all of these and other subjects were topics in Victor's medical shows, and similar problems were faced by Owen Marshall in the legal sphere. Included with these subjects in every episode is specific information regarding incidence, treatment, legal implications, and social services available for those touched by the problems.

Still, for both producers the center of television is not the specific problem or even its specific solution. The aspect that not only holds an audience for a particular episode but brings it back week after week is the "human interest." They emphasize the necessity and the power of "character." If we are not made to care for the characters, if the central figures are not somehow believable, if we do not experience in these fictional creations some resonance with our own humanity, then the show will fail. Lessons or information will have no impact because there will be no audience.

These elements could easily be translated into Martin's basic three-part outline: plot, emotion, and lesson. But any one-to-one correspondence would be misleading. Because Victor's melodramas work on an entirely different basis from action-adventure formulas, the centrality of character and emotion takes on new significance. For Martin these factors provide a controlling tone, or key that relates and orders all other aspects of the show. Primarily they are used to balance the attention we pay to the violent actions that are necessary in his formulas and to point us toward the underlying lessons. In Victor's work, however, emotion spills out, flows through the action, pervades every other dramatic feature. He reduces the attention to plot, "because if I take interesting characters and put them into a stress situation, their peculiar interplay as those particular characters is what the plot's all about." What he does not go on to say is that whatever attention to plot remains is fraught with emotional significance. It is not merely that we care about what happens to these characters, but that we care about their reactions as well. We are concerned with *their* interpretations, *their* responses, with the ways in which they put their emotional as well as their social, economic, political, or physical lives back together. Emotion, the characters' as well as that generated in the viewer, is the key to evaluation. We judge individual characters by how honestly they allow their emotions to be the basis for their interactions with others in their fictional world.

Governing this difference between these producers, of course, is a personal choice of fictional context and central character. Martin's crime-adventure series remain greatly distanced from the viewer's world of experience. No matter how extreme the particular situation, how great or unusual the suffering of the characters, the worlds of hospitals, doctor's offices, and courtrooms are potentially familiar to the audience. Similarly, our interaction with doctors and lawyers is of a far different sort from our interaction with private detectives or police inspectors. While there must always be some tension in Victor's melo-

David Victor

dramas, a sense of real threat in the lives of the guest characters who enter each week's episode, there is also a strong sense of everyday life, the feeling that these things could and do occur in the experience of the ordinary viewer.

It was in order to heighten this sense of the familiar that Welby was developed as a type of mature extension of young Dr. Kildare. The hospital setting, with its constant sense of imminent crisis, had become repetitive. The family doctor, able to deal with all age-groups, at all points in the life cycle, presented an altogether different opportunity, one that expanded the possibility for plot and story. The success of that pattern, Victor realized, could be duplicated with the family lawyer. Instead of Perry Mason with his dramatic eleventh-hour solutions, Victor offered Owen Marshall, who focused his energies on private and personal encounters with legal complexities. No matter what the action or crisis in these shows, a given act is far more likely to end with a close-up of Robert Young's concerned frown than with a beat of action-violence, the preferred pattern in any QM production.

There is a quiet sense about Victor's stories, even when they conclude in frustration or tragedy. There is the feeling that problems will be solved with emotional responses as much as with physical action, with individual attention as well as through the efforts of official representatives of authority. Even the dispensation of factual information, the actual cure of the disease or the rescue from legal entanglement, is secondary to the assistance given by one human being concerned for another. More than doctors or lawyers, Welby and Marshall and their counterparts in other professions are emotional guides to the lost people who wander into their professional worlds.

Precisely on this point Victor is often taken to task by critics. Every aspect of realism, they suggest, is undercut by this fanciful depiction of an all-attentive professional, not only willing, but able to focus his energy and compassion on single cases or individuals. The shows are charged not merely with a lack of reality, but with a kind of perverse deception. Viewers' expectations, it is argued, are distorted, their own experiences denied, their ability to cope with their own problems weakened by attending to such programs. The charge may move from the particular show to the accusation that television, by definition, distorts, and that Victor's shows are only as false as the rest. The same argument would be applied to Martin's representation of the world of crime and law enforcement. Policemen no more thwart every criminal than doctors succeed in curing every disease or aiding the victims of disease to deal with their problems. This view is a corollary to the political indictment of television for presenting one side (either side) of the political spectrum to the exclusion of the other. Like that argument it is built on assumptions about the medium and about its producers, not about the content of television.

Victor's response to this attack echoes Martin's view. He, too, is an avowed idealist. He shares the sense that television as story-telling medium touches us deeply at the level of wish, fantasy, dream, and desire. To respond to these human and cultural needs is hardly to falsify or to lead a misguided audience away from social reality. As he puts it,

> Of course [*Marcus Welby*] is fictional. So maybe I err on the side of being optimistic, and glorifying, idealizing the medical or legal profession, but so be it. You know, on the other hand, I think that's one of the reasons why the shows are long-lived. People do want that assurance, and at ten o'clock at night, before the news and after all the other things, there's a little assurance in the fact that maybe somebody cares.

"Somebody cares." "There's some place to go to." With this type of comment we come to that sense of personal perspective that shapes individual works, formulas, and series. And it is here that we can distinguish most sharply, in spite of similar terms, between Martin and Victor. For ultimately their idealizations emphasize distinct aspects of the society that provides their model and their audience.

Idealization in Martin's works means essentially the idealization of a particular world-view affirming authority vested in established agencies of government. The reliance on order, the definition of particular actions as unacceptable threats to that order, the designation of criminal acts and individuals, all point to a maintenance of conventional political and social structures.

When Martin wishes to indicate the real possibility of error, of a flawed system, he creates an entire story-structure to accommodate what might be taken as criticism of the social order. In *The Fugitive* we sense the outsider's perspective. Even though Martin appeals to a "higher law" we recognize the possibility that mistakes can be made, even within our preferred social organization.

Victor's melodramas work in a different manner and point to a different social perspective. The melodramatic structure splits in two directions. On the one hand there is the inclusion of the specific informational content as a kind of didactic data bank. The information is selected and included with the intention of actually helping members of the audience cope better or know more about the problems that beset their lives. In the other direction there is the idealized emotional response. Again, our primary model here is the carefully designed central character. The doctors and the lawyers who treat their clients and patients with "unrealistic" degrees of personal attention serve as symbols of value structures. As audience members we are encouraged to respond to the plight of victims as they do, for the emotional responses of victims and oppressed individuals are legitimate here, and we can accept the problems. We are not dealing with persons castigated as social outcasts. Care is to be provided without concern for wealth, social status, race, or even for ability to pay. These "victims" are, in fact, like us. Potentially, we could face the problems that they face. This is perhaps why we respond so immediately and emotionally to these presentations. In such cases the "system" has done as much to create difficulty as to solve it. Identifying with the "victim," then, we are received and comforted by the professionals.

The didacticism and the emotional care are merged into an appropriate character, a spokesman who may appear to be a father figure, an individual with an almost religious sense of concern for us as individuals. Welby, Marshall, and even Kildare become perfect, ideal embodiments of the perspective from which Victor works. They are not representations of professional care as it is, but as it should be. Even the "should be" must not be taken literally. It is not that we need to have *individuals* who behave in precisely this manner, but that we should have health care, legal aid, hospital structures, and social agencies which put individuals at the center of their activities. Victor's work is an idealization of the values that should underlie our social structures but often do not, and when those values do support the structures, then the sense frequently is that they are not adequately expressed. The TV doctors and lawyers have become metaphors for social dreams, personifications of social spirit. To measure them by the letter of "reality" is to miss the point.

Inherent in this portrayal is a criticism of existing social services. At the informational level Victor is extremely proud of having treated a variety of controversial subjects in his medical and legal shows, of having been consciously critical of our ignorance of important topics. In some cases, such as homosexuality, the topics are perceived by the public as social threats. In many more, however, particularly in the medical context, the subject matters are merely those that have remained in social shadows because of ignorance. In bringing conditions such as impotence, sexual relations between retarded adults, epilepsy, and breast cancer into public discussion and dramatic, human context, Victor suggests that our prejudices may indeed be killing—ourselves and others.

At the emotional level his particular stylistic emphasis is on a skillful blending of social ideal and social reality that points simultaneously to failure and to possibility. Indeed, he measures our failures precisely in terms of our dreams. Where Martin questions the system with a fugitive outsider, Victor questions with mainstream "authority" figures, figures from respected professions. The dual thrust of his productions can be found in responses by those in the professions portrayed. On the one hand Victor has received awards for contributing to the image of the medical profession. On the other he has been scored, also by medical professionals, for creating "unrealistic" expectations on the part of patients.

Ultimately, of course, the points of view do not come together. Victor's productions hardly "challenge" Martin's in any direct manner. What does emerge is a range of alternatives. Questions are raised. If the "systems" of society were perfect, there would be little need for the nearly mythic characters of ideal doctors and lawyers or invincible policemen. Victor's productions indicate that we need as much protection and assistance when we deal with the socially approved institutions in our lives—medicine and the courts—as when we deal with lawless elements that threaten the system at large. This is hardly, in our view, a radical political statement. Victor does not challenge, implicitly or explicitly, the deeper forms of society that create and maintain these institutions. Rather he challenges individuals who, for various reasons, do not act with compassion and concern sufficient to respond to the stress, the pain, the stigma, of sickness, disease, and legal conflict. His alternatives, idealized individuals, correct the errors and go on to enlighten us, to create in us a sense of self-reliance and audacity with which to live responsibly and without threat. His final statement to us is to care for ourselves *and* for others rather than to invest too much in figures of authority or in systems approved by social forces. Social structures and service professionals built on this concern promise a kind of care too often missing in the worlds of our experience. As a result, viewers must somehow deal with conflicting representations and evaluations of the world in which they live. Victor's voice, one among many, offers one of those evaluations and one set of recommendations.

INTERVIEW WITH DAVID VICTOR

THE PRODUCER'S PERSONAL STYLE

[VICTOR] I was originally a writer and wrote for many years in radio and television and motion pictures. I wrote a book. About twenty years ago I decided I might be a good producer. And since the world is just not waiting for producers I knew that I'd have to have my first job as a story editor, or a glorified re-write man. So that's the way I started, in a little show called *The Rebel* with Nick Adams that lasted a couple of years. Then I began at Metro-Goldwyn-Mayer with a show called *Dr. Kildare* and after a couple of months I became a producer of that series and stayed with it for its five-year run. In addition to being the producer I was also at the beginning the story editor and I wrote a lot. At the same time I became very active at MGM, producing *The Man from U.N.C.L.E.*, among other shows.

We spun off *Dr. Kildare* a show called *The Eleventh Hour*, which became a psychiatric series. Then after that I came to Universal as a producer and the first thing I developed was one of the three segments of *The Name of the Game*, the Robert Stack segments, and that lasted a year. It was then that I created a pilot for *Marcus Welby*, which lasted for seven years. By then I was an executive producer which simply means that I was able to delegate authority and I was usually involved in more than one series. I also have done a lot of development for the studio and my own company. Since *Marcus Welby* I have done *Owen Marshall, Counselor-at-Law* which I co-created with Jerry McNeeley. That ran for three years.

David O'Connell and I produced the first of the long-form series, *Vanished*, which was the first four-hour dramatization of a novel, by Fletcher Knebel. Then we did a series called *Portraits* where we had interesting contemporary stories. We produced a film on the Duke and Duchess of Windsor with Richard Chamberlain and Faye Dunaway, one on Pope John XXIII with Raymond Burr, one on Harry Truman with Robert Vaughan, and one on Vince Lombardi with Ernie Borgnine.

I agree with you in many ways on the role of the producer in television. I'm a visiting professor at USC and I teach a seminar—I think it's probably the only course ever given before or after on television producing—and it's a graduate seminar, non-credit course. The reason for it is to focus on the producer as a combination of so many skills. Even when I go on speaking tours or publicity tours or whatever, even television editors don't quite know what a television producer does. They think that I risk money here, and that I'm an entrepreneur, and all that nonsense, which just isn't so.

My philosophy about producing is very simple and after many people asked me for a definition of a producer—which is, believe it or not a rather difficult definition to come to in a field as diversified as television where you have to be, not a master, but at least knowledgeable about a lot of disciplines—the only definition that I can think of is that the producer is the man with a vision.

If you don't want to be quite as pompous as that, call it the man with the concept. But somebody has to have the original concept, and it's usually the producer, setting out to do something, to see the *whole* picture. I knew what I wanted to do with four hours of *Little Women*. And even if you do a series, which I've done a lot of, then you've got a concept. What is *Marcus Welby* all about? Don't forget, there are a lot of transients in our business. Directors come and go. Writers come and go. Actors come and go. Who is the man with the original concept? Who is the man who has an overview of the entire project? So in *Marcus Welby,* Robert Young is not wise one week and a jerk the next. So the characters and a style and a concept of a project remain the same. And it's unlike motion pictures, where they're doing one at a time and a director has traditionally become the creator, or the man with the vision. At least the producers have let him become that. Some strong producers never would. I can't see Hal Wallace abdicating his authority, or some others. But traditionally directors have become auteurs and they became the guiding spirits. Not so in television because we have so much work to do, such a great output of material. And some of our series go on for so long and there's just so much to be done that you better have an overall head. And that is usually the producer, or should be.

When I work there isn't a story that goes into script, no matter how many, without my involvement. And I've been involved in six, seven hundred hours of television. At least not one script has ever become a script without my knowing the story.

When you become an executive producer there is less attention devoted to matters such as editing and dubbing, although some producers pay a lot of attention to that. I kind of husband my strength and my interest too, a lot of it concept, a lot of it story, because I'm pretty good by now in script and story. Casting is very important, and then the general humanity of producing a series. You deal with some very tender egos, you know. You deal with networks, you deal with management, you deal with large sums of money for which you are responsible.

But I, for instance, don't get involved as some people do in wardrobe, unless it's very important to the character. We did a ninety-minute picture, a biblical picture, for ABC, called *The Story of Esther: The Thirteenth Day.* Well, there, obviously, the wardrobe is very important because it's a big item in your pre-planning. There are certain things that I will concentrate on more, and some people scatter their talents so thinly that they have no time for anything else. I may miss an answer print, or let somebody else go to see that the color correction is right on it. It's more important to me to have a meeting with the writer.

So each producer, I think, specializes in his own mind in some things—although, as they say, to be a producer, you have to be a master, a small master, of many disciplines. For instance, I must know the minimum basic agreement of all the guilds, so I know what I'm entitled to when it comes to actors or writers. I have to know how to read a schematic from an art director, even though I don't know how to build a set. I have to know a little bit about how a camera works, although I really don't know. They can fool me with all sorts of details about lenses and all that. I don't know, nor will I ever know.

And I use my judgment as a producer. I go on the set. I'm there every morning before we start shooting even though it's eight in the morning. I take a look at a new set and if it's overdressed in my mind, too busy and all that, I'll call the set director, and maybe the light people and ask for what I want done. And, unfortunately, if it happens more than twice or three times that our taste doesn't agree, I win and he loses. Somebody has to make the final decision. And that's not fair. So, I mean, the producer has to know quite a few things about most of the areas in which he operates. He's somewhat of a creative man, we hope. He's also somewhat of a business man, even though it's Universal's money that's being spent. I have to be able to understand what a budget is all about, and that each department, as it submits its figures, is protecting itself, because there's nothing worse than for an art department to say it's going to cost $80,000 and then all of a sudden that's up to $120,000. So they'd rather play it a little safe. You have to go to each department in turn when you're a couple of thousand dollars over budget and see where you can get your money without hurting the picture.

I mean you know all the little details. But the one creative head that keeps control over all these things, hopefully, should be the producer.

CREATIVE CONTROL

Q. *How do you work with the networks? Does Universal stand between you and the networks and do some of the negotiating for you?*

Well, in the final analysis, the one thing that a producer hopefully learns early in his career is to be a diplomat—to be a minor Solomon, King Solomon, junior grade. He's got to be able, first of all, to create a feeling of enthusiasm for a project, a feeling of security that you're confident in what you're doing, the way you come in and talk to them—

because they're not secure. No, truly. And if you can convince them that you know what you're doing—I mean having a little track record helps, obviously. You know they can believe you when you're telling them but you really have to come and sell yourself each time. And in the final analysis, no matter how much of a buffer there is between the studio, it's on your shoulders, what you're doing.

Q. *In a show like* Marcus Welby, *did the image of Robert Young in* Father Knows Best, *reflecting earlier generations of television, affect the kind of scripts you could do?*

Probably subconsciously. You know, we did not write . . . I did not create the pilot for Robert Young. In other words, this was not designed for Robert Young, as such. The only series that was really tailor-made was *Lucas Tanner* for David Hartman. I knew David and wanted to get a project in which I thought he would be very good, and he was. But *Marcus Welby* could have been played by any one of three or four or five people. As a matter of fact, as you well know—it's a "well-known secret"—the network fought us tooth and nail about *not* putting Robert Young on it. They didn't want him; they didn't like him.

Partly this was because the network thought Young was an older man. The talk was that he was semi-retired and maybe he was too soft, you know, and it went on and on. We kept insisting that he was the one we felt should play it. And they pointed out something in the script which I wrote—but you described him as such and such. So I said, "I have a very sharp pencil, fellows, and now I'll cross that out and describe a man just like Robert Young, gray haired, a million-dollar smile." I mean the baby is mine, and that's what I mean by a producer operating as a producer-writer. It helps. It's my concept. Of course you compromise. Of course you do. With George C. Scott it would have been a different show.

Q. *Is* Marcus Welby *an extension of* Dr. Kildare?

Well, I thought it was more than that, but I came to the end of the fifth year of *Dr. Kildare,* and I suggested that everything was done then and the man should get the hell out of the hospital and go into private practice where he could offer a different kind of series for me to go on with. The network didn't feel that was the right idea. It didn't appeal to anybody. So I quietly licked my wounds and after an appropriate amount of time said, let me do *Welby,* because I've always believed that a family physician was as rich a character as you can find. Once you hang out the shingle you can do all the things that you can do because you touch people at the hot points of their lives legitimately: birth, illnesses, weddings, and death, trials and tribulations, the highs of the human spirit, the bottom of depression. So, on our dramatic pallet of doctors I thought that would be a good idea, and it proved to be.

Q. *Is there a major point of view in those two shows that might differ from something like* Medical Story *which dealt in its first episodes with problems of medical ethics?*

I'll tell you in honest truth how I feel about this. First of all, I am a little impatient with people who tell me that *Marcus Welby* was always soft and we had happy endings, that we never charged for rooms in hospitals, that we ignored medical economics. It's not true. Of course, you have not seen all the films, and it's not in every picture. But we have had malpractice suits; we lost patients; we filled out insurance forms, Medicare; we told people it's easy to *say* don't worry about the hospital bill, but who the hell is going to worry? You know, it's $125 a day, or whatever it is. We've had all that.

And on the other hand I must say that I am essentially soft-hearted, and maybe a little puerile, but I believe in medicine as a profession. I think that most of the doctors are ethical, most of them want to help. My grandson is just going to medical school. I would have gone to medical school after I got out of high school, except I couldn't afford it. So maybe I'm sublimating and maybe I'm a jerk, because I take them a little bit at their word. But why not show what a good doctor *should* be. And if you're going to have a show, this is maybe to inspire somebody more.

I think that all of us are so insecure, all of us are so preoccupied with our own mortality, that if you keep talking about all the failures that doctors may have, and how they don't give a damn except they worry about their tax shelters, and they go and play golf on Wednesday (of course some do) then you merely contribute to that insecurity. There are an awful lot of good, dedicated doctors like Marcus Welby.

So maybe I err on the side of being optimistic, and glorifying, idealizing the medical or legal profession, but so be it. You know, on the other hand, I think that's one of the reasons why the shows are long-lived. People do want that assurance, and at ten o'clock at night, before the news and after all the other things, there's a little assurance in the fact that maybe somebody cares.

Two of the awards I most cherish, believe it or not, were the only awards that the American Medical Association I think ever gave to a layman, and I got two of them; one for *Dr. Kildare* and one for *Marcus Welby*. Well, you can understand why, because I helped the image, the positive image, of medicine. But, as I say, I don't particularly apologize for that and it's a matter of degree and a matter of philosophy. I believe that I can also do a tough, hard show like *Medical Story* or George C. Scott's *Hospital*. You saw that picture. You're afraid to cross the threshold of a hospital from that point on.

And, as I say, I'm not stupid. I know that there are abuses, and I know there are, like any profession, the bad apples and all that. I prefer, in the long-lived series, to concentrate on the good people and their business without being stupid, never showing that there are other facets. Maybe in 170 episodes of *Welby* we lost fifteen or twenty cases. Well, what should we do, lose one every week? Nobody's going to really want to watch that time in and time out.

Q. *How do you deal with actors, particularly strong ones? Do they have in-put?*

They are usually intelligent and well-meaning people and you never blame anyone for wanting to contribute in-put. They're going to play that character and they think that they have something to say about it and they do. And, again, I told you one of the requirements the producer has is to be a diplomat. You cannot put yourself into an either/or position because you're not perfect and because you can't win in the final analysis. You certainly cannot with your lead because no matter how important I am to the series, my star is more important since he's got to be in front of the camera. And if he doesn't show up, and he says he won't show up on the stage when David Victor's around, there's no choice from management's point of view. I mean, I may be very valuable and work from a distance, but you have to be smart enough to be able to handle that kind of situation and still not put yourself into a bind to which there is no answer.

Now of course you learn a few tricks again. I hardly ever go down to argue with somebody on the set. He has to come up here. This is my place. I have a beautiful office, right? Nice view—and this isn't quite on top of a mountain with a halo shining on it (I'm not done yet). But I keep them out there, give them a cup of coffee, let them wait for five minutes, and then let them come in and talk to me, like a gentleman. I'm the court of last resort, because, as I say, unfortunately, somebody has to make the final decision. But we can—and should—talk about it. And if somebody's screaming, I learned a long time ago, I drop my voice. Higher, lower. Higher, lower. Until I'm whispering and he wants to hear what I'm saying. And he leans over and I say, "Now, we've reached a certain level of decibles. Now we talk like gentlemen, right?" We discuss all these things.

Usually it can work out because they have a legitimate complaint in their mind sometimes, and I have the job of keeping an overview of the whole proposition. I have to worry about a whole script and the whole series and the whole concept. This is an immediate problem that the actor has and it's very important to him and to me. But I also have a bigger view. I'm the man with the concept and I'm the producer. So therefore we have to sit down and discuss it. You can usually meet halfway somewhere along the line.

Q. *How do you conceive of your audience?*

You cannot fracture your audience. In other words, if you give away a chunk of your audience, you must be doomed to disaster in the ratings system. See, you're trying to really hit the big, general audience. By its very nature you're going to lose some people. I don't think we had too many kids, young, really young people watching *Marcus Welby*. That's why it was a ten P.M. show. So are all of my shows ten o'clock shows, as it happens, because I think you reach a more mature audience. I am not trying to hit only the elderly people, obviously, because then you go right down the drain. I cannot concentrate only on men or women or adolescents or anything else. Somehow the audience finds you.

They told me, for instance, that we were going to have a complete fiasco with *The Man from U.N.C.L.E.*, which was put on on Friday night when they say that all the kids are dating. That's date night. Well, the series generated a cult. People used to date and watch *The*

Man from U.N.C.L.E. in college. So the one thing you learn very quickly is you cannot tell what your audience is going to be. That became a big audience of young people because we had a tongue-in-cheek attitude. "Really don't take it seriously, kids. We're only joking, you know, about all those fancy gadgets, all the stuff that we've done." But I really don't aim at any one kind of audience.

I think audiences will respond to people with whom they can emotionally identify in the early stages of any script. When I say emotionally identify, the emotion can be hatred or love, or curiosity, but they had better get involved emotionally or else you're not going to keep them for an hour or two hours or whatever you're working with. So you do have that much of an instinct of what you think the audience is going to find interesting.

There are a lot of tricks, of course, such as you must get the story started at some kind of high point—unlike a theatrical motion picture, where you have them inside a movie house and they have already paid their four dollars and then you can take a slower development. I also don't agree that their nervous fingers will turn you off and people will sit with stopwatches saying "Boring" or "Slow" and all that. I've fought many a battle with that notion. I think that once they know I'm going to entertain them for an hour, I can take a legitimate amount of time to develop my stories and to develop character interestingly. There is, however, the feeling that you ought to get started quickly and, as you all know, a script is a combination of scenes. You have to have an instinct on how a scene should be written, played, developed, and whatnot. And what you avoid a lot in a show is buildups and goodbyes. In other words, unlike the stage, where a maid will have a duster thing, give you all the information, then in comes the master with a tennis racket and says all that nonsense, you pick up a scene at a high point; you make your point and get the hell out without all of the goodbyes. That keeps the pace of the show going and keeps the excitement going. So you can't even call it a trick. It's a means of storytelling.

Don't forget, people have now become very sophisticated. Where in the old movies you have to allow for the passage of time—that could be a fade-in and a fade-out—in one commercial now, in thirty seconds, viewers see four stories. So they're quite used to it. They'll

shift their mental gears. They'll accept all the changes if you tell them
so. With *The Man from U.N.C.L.E.* we invented the smash cut with
all the crazy colors going from one to the other, just moving right
along without giving the audience too much time to get adjusted to the
new scenes. Those are more or less professional trade secrets that you'll
learn because they're proven and they work.

SOCIAL RESPONSIBILITY AND EFFECTS

[VICTOR] I am, I guess, one of the older people in the business and
I've been a producer for more than twenty years. Twenty years is a
very short period of time in the great scheme of things, as you know,
and I can tell you one thing—on *Kildare* back in '61 and '62, twenty
years ago, I did the first story on mastectomy and, believe it or not,
could not use the word breast in talking about it. That was Broadcast
Standards stuff. I said, what the hell are we doing fellows? I mean,
what are we talking about? This is breast removal.

And since then, of course, we've done all kinds of things, and
we're constantly improving and constantly doing what we consider
more daring material. Of course it has to be done, hopefully, in good
taste. But I've never yet had to turn down a subject because they
wouldn't let me do it.

With varying successes we did the story of homosexual rape, an
unwed father, unwed mothers, abortions, drug addiction, indecent exposure. You say it and I've done it, because if you say it straight
out—I'm doing a show about a family doctor, and if you legitimately
came to him in the course of his practice, and we closed the door, and
this was Robert Young, not some punk kid who's trying to write dirty
words on the toilet walls, we are talking about a problem. We're discussing it legitimately and in scientific terms. Nothing has to be
avoided. We've done stories of epilepsy. We showed a "grand mal"
seizure. You say you can't, well you can. As long as you also explain
that it's a short-circuiting of nerve signals to your brain. You explain
it and it's alright. People don't turn away from disgust. And they'd
better not— Because next time they see somebody writhing on the
sidewalk they may know something more about it. I'm proud of that.
I think I educate as well as entertain.

Q. *It seems that particularly in* Marcus Welby *and in* Owen Marshall *there was almost a specific intent to give real information and directions for how to get more.*

We often had a specific goal. We did the first episode on Tay-Sachs disease, the genetic disease affecting Jewish people. We did sickle-cell anemia; we did autism. Sometimes people ask me why I don't do another medical series right now. Not that they're willing to write me out a check or anything. But I say, why should we do that because every week on the networks they're doing two-hour versions of all the things I've done on *Owen Marshall* and *Marcus Welby*. And that's all right. I mean they do the deaf child, the autistic children, the retarded older people deciding whether to marry. We've done all of those things. I'm not saying we had a patent on them. But those will always be popular because they reach a very common chord in all of us. We're all afraid of cancer. We're all afraid of dying. We'd love to have a father-figure like Marcus Welby at our side. We really served a very good purpose, I believe.

Q. *One of the criticisms, as we are sure you know, of the kind of thing we've been talking about, is that television gives people the wrong impressions about doctors and lawyers and so on. Figures are often cited about how many people think of Welby as a real character.*

There's no defense against stupidity, fellows. I mean if somebody wants to think that there is such a person, or they hear on the air his name is Marcus Welby, and they write to him, what can I do about that? I mean I can go around beating my breast. *Welby* was a conscious effort to do a series about a doctor, leaning a little heavier on idealism and good work. It was about good people and nice people, not an exposé, not realism. We're not doing a documentary; we're not doing a White Paper. Of course there are letters where somebody says maybe we encourage a malpractice suit because we idealize Marcus Welby. They compare their doctor with the fictitious Welby. And I said of course there is no such person as Marcus Welby. Nobody concentrates for an hour on one case. But if your office hours were from ten to eleven on Tuesday night and that's all you did with your life, you'd find time.

For every one of the people who may have gotten hurt or misled or misdirected, what about the people who learned how to do artificial resuscitation, went to a doctor to examine a mole on their leg because we said it could be cancerous? We taught viewers about breast removals, that this does not destroy the person. We did all the other things. Now how do you measure that against the fact that we do misrepresent or make it more ideal than it is? It's a matter of choice. And I still say, please don't say that we never lost patients or it was syrupy to the point that a diabetic can't watch. It was not so. If we started to do the realistic, grainy story about modern-day medicine in the ghetto, obviously it would be a different kind of series.

Q. *Was it possible to do the kind of human focus, the emotional identification story, in some of the adventure shows, or do you see that as entirely different?*

There are certain things that never change. When I was doing *The Man from U.N.C.L.E.* I would say to the writer, ''The fact that you are doing a wild story does not violate dramaturgy.'' In other words, you're only concerned if somebody's chasing somebody when you care whether he's caught or not. That's a prime requirement. I made it a rule when you're talking about a series which is as wild as *The Man from U.N.C.L.E.* and has to do with fates of nations and diverting the Gulf Stream and all the other nonsense that you're talking about, that people can't comprehend that except in fun. Therefore, we always had what I define very clearly to all my writers as ''the innocent.'' You always reduced it to a person. A secretary who goes to get a ham and egg sandwich for her boss happens, presumably, to be involved in something. They think that she has something and all of a sudden you have Julie Sommer being pursued and all that. So you care about that one unit of humanity rather than entirely about the cuckoos who have ice palaces at the North Pole. So you have certain elements which are true, even if it's a wild adventure. And of course *Name of the Game* was not a wild adventure; therefore you dealt with people. That was people under stress. But even in *U.N.C.L.E.* I always tried to show a human being with whom you can identify, with whom you can believe that something terrible can happen.

We made it a point that we always cared about somebody who's being pursued. Otherwise there's no fun in the pursuit. And we made it a point never to feed the lack of belief. For instance, if our two gentlemen, Robert Vaughan and David McCallum, were caught somewhere and were hung up on meathooks and a slicing machine was going to slice them like bologna, they could never make a comment, "Here we go again." Then you know they're going to get the hell out and safely. You must keep the suspense that somehow they can get killed.

Sophisticated people know we've got an order for twenty-four episodes and the characters are going to come back. We knew that Jim Arness was not going to get killed. But if you do the show skillfully, and if you do pay attention to detail and to humanness, then for the moment you can make them believe that there's something at stake. So, to answer your question, yes, even in a wilder show, certain elements of humanity do have to be adhered to.

I am known as the "human condition" producer. I love people. I love to do stories about people. I don't know how good I'd be at out-and-out comedy, although I've written some situation comedy. I don't know whether I'd be particularly good in science fiction and all that. I don't want to be labeled as the avuncular David Victor who's a schmaltz barrel or something. I've done *Name of the Game* and *The Man from U.N.C.L.E.* But given the choice, I think there's nothing more interesting than the human condition. I don't think there's anything more susceptible to variation than people. Therefore, instead of depending on the seven basic plots which we're supposed to have, I never care about plot.

If I take interesting characters and put them into a stress situation, their peculiar interplay as those particular characters is what the plot's all about. And those, of course, are different each time, as are the people who are involved in my stories. Therefore, for purely selfish reasons, I love to do stories that originally stem from the human condition.

Q. *Is the moral climate of Los Angeles and New York different from that of middle America? A network executive recently told us his job was to protect middle America.*

I really don't think that's true anymore. I think that as many shenanigans go on in a country club in Scranton, Pennsylvania, as they do in Brentwood or San Fernando Valley. I mean, I think that so much communication has taken place all over that there are no such things as hinterlands or yokels or rubes. I don't know how people are in your part of the country, but for instance right here in wicked Hollywood I go to sleep at a pretty reasonable time. I've been married to my wife for fifty years, so has Robert Young been married to Betty, so has Arthur Hill been married successfully, and David Hartman is happily married, and Dave O'Connell is. You know, I think that to make a generalization like that is fraught with peril. I can understand there's a very good rationale why we should curb too much of anything, and I'm all for that. But I think that might be too simple an answer.

I think a producer, above all, is a human being in his own right. And all the things that he's lived through, and all the things he's learned in his life must affect his particular philosophy and affect the way he operates.

John Mantley

John Mantley began his career as an actor, and after several roles he determined to enter the field of television directing in New York. In the fifties he had at one time three live productions on the air each week. From New York he moved to Rome where he directed over fifty films for American TV as well as several Italian features. Returning to the United States he wrote two novels, *The 27th Day* and *The Snow Birch*. He turned again to television, writing for *Desilu-Westinghouse Playhouse* and *The Untouchables*. After serving as story consultant for *Gunsmoke,* he became executive producer for that series, a position he held for eleven seasons. He served briefly as executive producer of *The Wild, Wild West* and thereafter in the same capacity for four years for the series *How the West Was Won*. His most recent television activity was as executive producer of *Buck Rogers*. In 1982 he produced the three-hour TV movie *The Wrathful Man*. He has produced one motion picture, *Firecreek*.

Mantley is a native Canadian, who served in the R.C.A.F. during World War II. He is a graduate of Victoria College, University of Toronto, and holds a master's degree from Pasadena Playhouse.

Unlike both Martin and Victor, John Mantley has produced television shows that do not bear the surface marks of contemporary America. Having written poems, novels, screenplays, and television scripts, and after serving as an associate producer, Mantley became the producer of *Gunsmoke* in that program's tenth year. He worked on other westerns as well, including *Wild, Wild West*. After *Gunsmoke* left the air, Mantley teamed with his long-time friend and star, Jim Arness, to create a television mini-series, *How the West Was Won*. Still later, Mantley was called in to re-design and attempt to save an expensive NBC failure, *Buck Rogers in the 25th Century*. Though Mantley's experience and talent could not perform that miracle, his observations on the problems involved in revamping a show in mid-stream are among the most informative that we present. They illustrate what becomes, for us, a major theme of this study. Creativity in television, perhaps in any medium, is not a solitary act. Rather, it is a process of negotiation. Programs are often made—or unmade—quite literally out of struggle.

In the beginning, of course, there must be something for which to fight, an idea, a concept, a "vision," to use David Victor's word. Mantley's comments indicate that, like the creative process itself, the concept or vision is also best seen as a continuing series of adjustments. Vision cannot remain static. Series television, far more than literature or film, exists in relation to the real time of its society. It is not a product for reverie, for recalling, for repeating. Only in rare instances—*Star Trek, Barney Miller, M*A*S*H*—do audiences return to works and re-enter them with pleasure, and even some of these shows seem remote and isolated, their vitality drained by the passage of time and the shifting of context.

To ignore this sense of social and historical milieu is to take an enormous risk. Yet some programs never change. For a few, the sense of the eternal, timeless nature of the world of television seems to work. For many it is the seal of cancellation.

How, then, was *Gunsmoke* able to remain on the air long after other westerns? How did it survive the shifts in social and cultural attitudes? Mantley made adjustments, read the signs, changed the show. This was no simple matter, no stroke of blinding genius. Indeed, it involved trial and error, and could have resulted in disaster. Looking back, Mantley sees the problem clearly. It began in the anti-violence campaign that followed the assassination of President John Kennedy.

I decided that every other producer with an action adventure show on the air was in terrible trouble, but I was not. I was riding the crest of the wave because I had four great actors and all I had to do was write stories around them. It was, as I said, the single biggest mistake that I've made in this business, and I can't conceive, in retrospect, how I ever thought it would work, since the essence of drama is conflict, and I couldn't create conflict between these people! They thought so much alike. They had such a strong sense of honor, such a family communion among them, that it was impossible to create honest conflict between them. So when I found I was in as much trouble (perhaps more) as any of the other producers in town, what I did was revert to the technique I used in writing *The Untouchables,* which was to bring a guest star with a problem into the center of the series situation, have the story revolve around him, and get our people involved with his problem.

By bringing these strangers into his tightly defined and familiar community, Mantley could weave elaborate interactions involving insiders and outsiders, past and present, the familiar and the unexpected, the frontier and established society. To put it in the baldest of pairs so often used to describe the western, he dealt with the conflicts between civilization and savagery. Thematically, of course, these new patterns were used to establish a resonance with the world of the viewer. *Gunsmoke* drew repeatedly on mid-twentieth-century issues, which were then treated in a frontier context. Almost always the outsiders represented or brought with them some sort of question or problem for the community. The questions were usually veiled—sometimes thinly— references to social issues common in the audience's own experience, issues which would be resolved in a manner that brought the awards, from religious, educational, special interest, and civic groups.

Several years after the end of *Gunsmoke,* Mantley produced *How the West Was Won.* The show first aired, with six segments, in the winter of 1977. It was successful enough to be returned for more segments, and in 1977–78 became a semi-regular series. Reruns and new segments carried through into the fall of 1979. Mantley cites this experience to describe a new wave of network interference in the production process, interference at the business/scheduling end of television that has strong implications for the creative process.

In *How the West Was Won* Mantley again explored those contem-

John Mantley

porary topics that concern him, and used the contextual frame of history with the formulaic world of the western as his focusing devices. In following the lives of a single pioneer family he dealt with the problems of establishing order from a personal rather than the institutional perspective that often informed *Gunsmoke*. In the show he treated problems of racial prejudice, religious intolerance, the horrors of war, the threat of injustice. Often specific family members were called upon to act in ways that strained their relations with one another and with the various communities through which they passed or in which they settled. Again, these are problems that Mantley senses as problematic in contemporary life. In treating them he calls attention to the fact that we have not yet, as a nation, dealt with them successfully.

This later series emphasized these topics in yet another way. The style of the show was far removed from that of *Gunsmoke*. While the older show relied on studio sets and an audience's familiarity with a regular group of townspeople, *HTWTW* took on the look of the "realistic" western. Extensive location shooting lent an air of actuality to the stories. The continuing narrative of the mini-series, a form in which good characters could die or change, added to the realism. As a result, the problems faced by the Macahans and their friends and enemies seemed to be more directly rooted in history than in the formula world of the western.

Contributing to this sense of the actual was the skillful use of Jim Arness in the Zeb Macahan role. Here Arness no longer appeared in the polished, responsible, authoritative frame of the bringer of order. Neither Mantley nor Arness wished to recreate that role. Instead they created a character who had left his family years before in a personal search for freedom and individuality. Macahan was a mountain man, a role used numerous times in *Gunsmoke* to signify a threatening and powerful attack on the maintenance of order and civic development. When mountain men roared into Dodge City they were usually intent on drunkenness and temporary delight. They brought violence, and Matt Dillon was required, despite a visible affection for many of these characters, to put the lid on their jar of exuberance. By placing Arness in such a role Mantley worked both with and against the typed character of Dillon, the face, bearing, and meaning so well known to the television audience. It was a true stroke of artistry, for with the settling of the west we see the decline of Zeb Macahan. By the end of the series Macahan's nephew is the embodiment of a younger Matt Dillon, a man ready to accept responsibility and enforce it on others. We lament the passing of the old order as we lament the decline of the character. It is almost as if Zeb Macahan is our own Matt Dillon, having fled deep into the mountains, leaving behind the civilization he helped to create. Even there he is brought down by the onslaught of settlers, cities, and occasional sissies. In using Arness in both these roles Mantley explored the meaning of the west's many facets in the American consciousness.

In 1980 he jumped to the other end of the spectrum of history and assumed the role of executive producer of *Buck Rogers in the 25th Century*. Despite heavy network investment this series had failed miserably in its original design, a thin science-fiction parody that attempted to draw the *Star Wars* audience to television with surface flash and gadgetry. Mantley's reputation as a series fixer won him the difficult task of revamping the entire concept, style, and structure of *Buck Rogers*. His job was to reconceive characters, change format and focus, and, once again, to introduce new, more serious thematic material. He entered the project enthusiastically, not merely for the love of the fray, but because of a long interest in science fiction. He quickly eliminated the show's central plot device—twenty-fifth-century Chicago under constant siege from aliens. No longer would Buck, the twentieth-century man reborn after five centuries of suspended animation, be faced with defending New Chicago against threats from without. Instead, he and a crew of close companions would explore space in search of remnants of Earth's civilization.

The parallels with the western are evident, as they always are in comparisons between the two forms. Even more interesting in this case, however, is the way in which the show's two structures parallel Mantley's earlier work. The first design, the city under siege, though not Mantley's conception, reflected the notion of *Gunsmoke,* a city on the edge of the civilized world, with its own group of colorful characters, beset by threatening outsiders. In the case of *Buck Rogers* there was little else. Plots offered none of the rich character development or sense of community that defined *Gunsmoke*. Instead there was a superficial humor, a flat attempt at satire. The character of Buck Rogers served two primary functions. He was to be the town's hero, the never-say-die protector of order and property, something of a gunfighter who rode into town in a spaceship and stayed to help the pretty women and the too-tame men. On the other hand, it was through his historically specific character that the new world was to be commented on, laughed at, called attention to. As in all science fiction, the removed perspective allows the audience to examine its own rules and systems of order, its customs and habits. But in the first version of this series, that was taken as a childishly light-hearted task.

Mantley's revision, however, immediately introduced a more serious note. The pilot episode introduced a bird-man character who became Buck's side-kick. But Hawk, as he was known, also called upon Buck to examine the values of humans, to criticize certain patterns of thought, to highlight the arbitrary, constructed nature of all cultural and social systems. By including this sort of criticism and thought in the structure of the wandering family, Mantley was able to introduce a new topic each week. The show, then, took on many of the characteristics of *How the West Was Won,* as well as of *Star Trek, Lost in Space,* and *Land of the Giants,* shows from the history of television science fiction.

Not even this clear and well-defined concept could save the show. Its own past, its production values, the speed with which Mantley was required to work his magic, all contributed to a sense of sameness, a sense of thinness about the show. The revamping of older plots, many of them with specific western overtones did little to bring the potential to life. In the end the show was merely another expensive television failure.

Buck Rogers, however, is an example of work that many producers do. For Mantley it was a good job, interesting, well-paying, a challenge. Our central concerns in this book, concerns for the self-conscious nature of certain television producers, should never be taken to indicate that every work, even by the strongest producers, is by definition excellent television. In John Mantley's work, *Buck Rogers* is quite likely, and most deservedly, to be forgotten. What will be remembered is that Mantley has given us superb examples of that television innovation, the adult western.

In using this form Mantley relies on a world removed from contemporary experience to relate us to a set of older values. There is no simple glorification of the ideas of that time, however. We are put "in relation" to it in order to examine the assumption that "things were better then." Indeed, given the tension and violence that come into play in these worlds, the past looks far more difficult and harsh than it may have been in historical reality. But by magnifying that time Mantley involves us with broad abstractions, with generalized questions of conflict and decision-making.

These questions are rooted in the central ideas of the western itself. It is America's primary story of social authority, of the legitimate and illegitimate uses of violence in the process of creating order, making civilization. If, in the mystery, violence is an exploration of social rules, in the western it is an exploration of our reasons for having rules in the first place. The large issue is always a rampant freedom posed against a tight community. Mantley is an astute historian of the American west, aware of its quasi-mythical relation to the western. His use of motifs, then, such as the gunfight does not reflect ignorance of the fact that such events were rare occurances in the historical west. It is, rather, a choice employed for metaphoric and dramatic effect, a familiar shorthand that could be used in the midst of an erratic schedule that played havoc with scripts and their production.

To all this Mantley adds the sense of family among his characters, a kind of "communion" he calls it. Even though we generally end up affirming social rules in Mantley's shows, these rules are mediated by the humane vision of the "families": the *Gunsmoke* cast, the biological families in *How the West Was Won,* the crew of close companions in *Buck Rogers.* The power in these shows is power conferred on individuals by social authority, power to be used only in pursuit of legitimate ends. And it is a power that must be forever tempered. There is less an idealization of social force than a probe of its intentions, its humanistic, almost religious roots.

Mantley speaks specifically of the western as a "simpler" form. It enables him to strip away a layer of actual social problems, represented most often by multiple, conflicting points of view, and to concentrate on the underlying principles. A story on compulsory education, then, does not have to deal with ideas expressed by teachers' associations, by parents' groups, by special-interest organizations or political parties. Instead, it concentrates on the value and need for universal education in any democratic society, on the principle itself. It brings the values of the settled east to the frontier west, and in so doing, raises in the minds of audiences a consciousness of an assumed, taken for granted social component.

Such treatments of complex topics might verge on the simplistic— the right answers are always known and are always arrived at. After all, it is precisely the complexity of contemporary society that makes it difficult to apply those "basic" values in their purest form, makes it difficult to live "by principles." This criticism of television overlooks the dramatic presentation of the issues and the function of fiction itself. It also overlooks the fact that television producers are well aware of the charges, the implications, and for the most part, better aware than their critics of the complexities of their programs. In structure and character, in the manipulation of plot and formula, television comments on the world we live in by presenting elements of it in purposely distorted form. Exaggeration and stylization are part of the way in which we come to think through problems that are still unsolved. In these forms we find the richness of television's voice. In the individual voices of self-conscious producers such as John Mantley, we find the muscle and bone of television's function in American society.

INTERVIEW WITH JOHN MANTLEY

THE PRODUCER'S PERSONAL STYLE

Q. *Do you believe that the focus for creativity and power in television is the producer?*

That's right. Not in motion pictures. Motion pictures have come to belong to the director. Television is a producer's world, not because we make it so, but because of the exigencies of television. A director comes in to me and he is handed the script six working days before he shoots, twelve working days if it's a two-hour show. In many studios in this town, or in many operations, the director is not allowed to change that script. He has to shoot it the way it is. I never expect that. I sit down with the director, and if he's got a problem with the script, I try to resolve the problem. If his suggestions are not as good as what is there, but are not really destructive, most of the time I will give him what he wants, because he's alone down there in the cut and thrust of shooting, and he has to feel secure with his material. If his suggestion is bad, of course, I won't use it.

Q. *Do you do the same with actors and writers?*

There is no time to do anything with actors. I mean, if a man—a good actor and a responsible actor—has a real problem with a scene and feels he can't handle it, then I will talk to him, sure. And I have made changes. But I will not permit an actor to pick at a script on the sound stage. That just upsets everyone and destroys the show.

I also let directors cast their shows. I sit in on the casting and I read with every actor who appears on one of my shows, because I can tell when I read with the actor whether they're going to be good on camera or not. That knowledge is very valuable to me and the director. I have only one rule in casting: I will not let a director use any actor that I feel is wrong for a given part, because I think that puts too great a burden on both actor and director. They have to "sell" me, and they shouldn't have to do that. So if it comes to the point where I say, "I really can't see this actor," I will say, "Okay, let's find someone we agree on." The two or three occasions when I've really been against someone and allowed my instincts to be swayed, it has usually been disastrous, not just from my standpoint, but from the network's, the studio's, and everyone's. I said usually, but not always. Once I had that instinct and was forced to use an actor who was not my first choice, and it turned out superbly! The actor was Lloyd Bridges. I really didn't think Lloyd could create the sort of image that I wanted—and I had a very firm image, because I wrote the script. But when we gave Lloyd the corn-cob pipe and the battered hat with the trout flies in it and the big walrus mustache, he just ate that part up! I thought he was brilliant, and I don't think anyone could have done it as well as he did!

Anyway, as I said, the director comes in, he's given a script, and when he's finished shooting, he goes out to do another show. Even if he's still working for me, he's probably in production on another show, so he really has no time to cut his own film. And he is entitled to a first cut—to look at it, and, by union contract, make changes if he wishes. But all the directors who have been with me for any length of time don't make any cuts. They view their film and make notes, or they just come and talk to me and say, "Gee, I think this and this and this," but they know me so well that they generally leave the final cut to my discretion, and so far none of them has objected to the way I've cut anything.

Q. *Do you supervise the cutting personally?*

Oh, yes. My line producers have often complained that they don't really have enough to do, and some of them have been extremely creative. Leonard Katzman, for example, almost left me. He said, "Jesus, John, you don't need me here. All you need is an expeditor!" It isn't because I don't trust the people that I hire. I do, implicitly, or I wouldn't have hired them. But I find that unless I am deeply involved, I don't understand the problems when I'm called upon for a decision. Leonard Katzman, who is now doing *Dallas,* was my line producer for years. He was very creative. On the other hand, John Stephens, who is also a splendid line producer, is not a writer or director as Leonard is, but his contributions are still invaluable. How extensive my line producer's talents are has not been that important to me in the past, although I have been blessed by having outstanding men at my side. However, the last couple of years, I've not had the luxury, for the first time in my life, of getting into all the aspects of the business in depth. Sometimes I was so busy, I didn't even know where the company was shooting.

That's why this is a producer's medium. There is no way [in TV] the director can control, to any great extent, the material he gets because he's hired sometimes a year in advance and he, in most instances, has to take the script he's given. That was never true, as I've indicated, on *Gunsmoke,* because I always had many scripts in advance (until I got down to the last three or four shows, and then every director understood, whether he liked it or not, he had to do the script given him). But, before these last few shows, I always presented an unhappy director with two or three other scripts and let him choose one he wanted to do. The show was so well organized that I could switch from one script to another in mid-stream without any serious problems.

But that's why this is a producer's medium, and that's why, more than anybody in any other medium, I think, the taste, the energy, and the creative powers of the producer are so important. The fact that a one-hour show must be shot every six days does not allow much time for a democratic society! The truly involved executive producer hires the line producer, the executive story consultant, the director, the composer, and, in concert with the director, the guest cast. He also makes the final cut, okays special credits and, in the first season, creates main and end titles. Incidentally, that list of authorities holds true for all executive producers, but not all of them become that involved in all of those areas. And there are executive producers in this town who just come in at eleven and look at the dailies and scribble a few words on a script and go home. When that happens, nearly all the functions that I perform are then relegated to the line producer. So you can't tell by a man's title what he actually does.

Q. *He is a producer, at whatever level—he's going to be a producer.*

That's right. Norman Lear used an interesting term the other day for the people that we are talking about. He called them ''strong'' producers, and I think that wherever they come in, that's a good designation.

CREATIVE CONTROL

[MANTLEY] The problems of producing dramatic network prime-time shows are far greater now than they were in years gone by, which means that it is more difficult today to make good shows.

Q. *Can you amplify that—and tell us why producing is a more difficult profession now?*

I'll try. You understand that what I say is only what *I* perceive as the reasons for the increase in the number of problems in the producing function and in the escalation of pressures resulting from those problems. I think the biggest problem is that there is almost never time enough in TV today for the producer of a dramatic series to do his best work. In the early days of television, all three networks finalized their schedule on or about Washington's birthday, and the new season began in mid-September. That meant that the producer of a new show had seven months lead time in which to prepare scripts, put together a production company, and to grapple with the thousand and one jobs which are inherent in the creation of a smoothly functioning production unit. Enough time, in other words, for him to do his best possible work.

Today, schedules are rarely finalized before the first week in May, and networks frequently want the series on the air by the end of the first week in September, which gives a producer only half the lead time he once had to prepare his product!

Perhaps I should mention that with the plethora of new-show disasters suffered by all three networks in recent years, there has come into being a sort of bastard "mid-season" rescheduling period. During this period, defunct shows are replaced by hastily cobbled-together new entries, most of which promptly fail more disastrously than the shows they have supplanted. But, for the sake of simplicity, I'll try to confine the problems of lead time to the conventional September premieres.

The reasons for the steady erosion of that lead time can be traced, I think, to two major factors. The first of these is the escalating cost of television production, coupled, ironically, with the steadily increasing profits which have accrued to all three networks—profits so enormous that, today, a single share-point lead by one network over another at the season's end can represent as much as fifty million dollars! When this much money is involved, it is evident why the competition among networks to be first in the ratings has reached traumatic proportions. No network, for example, wishes to be first to announce its schedule, because that gives the two remaining networks the ability to program against that line-up. Thus, with each passing year, the chess game over which network will declare first has resulted in the start date for productions being moved deeper and deeper into the year. With only half the time to prepare that was once available, and with several other devastating new problems, which we will discuss in a moment, it is not difficult to understand why the quality of series television continues to deteriorate.

Secondly, shows which do not succeed immediately in today's television market are rarely kept on long enough for the audiences to find them, or for producers to find the most successful way to produce them. (The number of highly successful shows in recent years which started out with ratings which would cause their immediate cancellation today is legion. You can number among them, for example, *Gunsmoke, Bonanza, All in the Family, The Waltons,* etc.) The major factor in this is, once again, cost and the frantic scramble for ratings.

Q. *Can you give us some specifics about the escalation of costs?*

That's easy. Where a one-hour action-adventure show could be brought in for less than $200,000 per episode eight or ten years ago, it can cost $600,000 or $700,000 today. So when a network is losing a time slot badly, not only must it swallow the high production costs of the failing series, it must face the additional blow of plummeting revenues commensurate with low ratings. It is not, then, unusual to see a show with apparent potential yanked after less than half a dozen episodes because its ratings are marginal. (Think how close we all came to losing *Hill Street Blues*!)

I'm sort of lost, now, but I think that I'm at the third point, which is interference in the creative process. This is not, perhaps, the most crucial, but it is certainly the most consistently irritating aspect of producing television for today's market.

To understand the genesis of this interference, it is necessary to go back some years to the days when there was no network interference with the creative process at all, or at least none to my knowledge. I'm going back, now, to the early sixties, when the advertising agencies controlled the shows. They did so because the entire cost of a dramatic series in those days could be borne by a single sponsor. (*Gunsmoke,* for example, was sponsored by a cigarette company, and *Bonanza* by an automobile manufacturer.) To my knowledge, the only people who read my scripts were the sponsor's advertising agencies. They read the scripts and they came to the rough cut, to make sure you didn't "ford" a river if you were sponsored by Chevrolet—honest! As a result, on *Gunsmoke* we always "forded" rivers—on *Bonanza* they only crossed them!

Thus, for the most part, the advertising agencies were only periph- erally concerned with the show's content. They rarely took exception to anything, except those points which might adversely affect product identification.

However, as the years slipped by, two things happened to bring the networks into the creative process. First was the shattering scandal of the *$64,000 Question,* which enabled the networks to insist that producers must be more carefully supervised! And two, the cost of producing an episode, as I pointed out earlier, escalated to the point where no single company could afford to bankroll an entire year's product of a series. Sponsorship became spot-buying, and the leverage of any single sponsor was far, far less than it had ever been. By the same token, the network "in-put" was far greater, until, in today's world, the networks are, more and more frequently, insisting on cast approval, director approval, writer approval, and, sometimes, even editorial and composer approval.

In bygone days, the network liaison personnel were men who dropped by every week or two to see if there was anything they could do to help. They have been replaced by zealous, young film-school graduates who are "helping" producers by showing them how to re-write scripts, re-cut their dailies, and telling them who they should hire as actors, directors, composers, et al.

Additionally, in order for the network to become involved in the creative processes to the extent that they have, it has been necessary for them to increase their staffs to such an extent that each network now has separate departments for dramatic series, comedy series, mini-series, specials, variety shows, etc., and each of these departments is staffed with several executives, the majority of whom have only the authority to say "no," not to say "yes." Thus, producers who once dealt directly with two or three senior executives (all empowered to say "yes"!) are now obliged to deal with relative neophytes, who must pass problems up the ladders of power until they eventually get to someone with the authority to act on them. And for all of these problems, the initial contact is the network liaison man.

When I began *Gunsmoke* seventeen years ago, for example, the liaison man from CBS would show up in my office every week or so and say, "Gee, is there anything I can help with? Anything you need?" He never told me who should play my guest leads. He never suggested that my scripts needed more action or more sex. He never looked at my dailies and said, "Do you really want to keep this director?"

But all of that has gone by the board. The network liaison men, with few exceptions, are now looked upon almost as enemies, and all the old-time producers I know, men who once felt that they worked in concert with the networks, now feel, almost to a man, that their relationships are adversarial.

Q. *You've told us when you think the creative intrusion began and what prompted it. Can you give us some specific examples?*

Sure! I'd like to give you some of the incredible ones—full of unintentional humor, such as Ed Friendly's two-volume battle with the network about the recurring *Laugh-In* line, "Look that up in your Funk and Wagnall!", but it's too good a story for anyone but Ed to tell. However, we've all had our share.

In my case, it resulted in my resignation as a *Gunsmoke* exec. producer. I guess it was around the seventh or eighth year after I came on the show, and for the first time, the network really came up with an ultimatum I couldn't sit still for. At the time, I was getting ready to shoot two unique *Gunsmoke* episodes, and to understand the seriousness of the problem, you should know something about the shows. One of them was written for Amanda Blake and another was written for Milburn Stone. They were both extraordinarily fine shows. Amanda thought her episode was the best show she'd ever had, and Milburn was very excited about his. Jim thought they were both great. The first episode was a show in which Jim was shot in the back in the opening scene and Doc labored all night long to save his life. Always before, when this had happened, we had had Kitty there, acting as a nurse and assisting Doc—helping and so forth. She wasn't doing that this time. She was standing in the back of the room, looking ashen and shaken and not participating at all. Finally, after what appeared to have been an all-night operation, Doc straightened up, took a deep breath, and said: "Well, he's going to make it!" Kitty never said a word. She just turned and went out. It was night, dark. She made straight for the Long Branch, got a water glass, poured it full of bourbon and belted it back, and poured another one, at which point Doc came in and said, "What's the matter with you? I told you it was going to be alright!" She tossed back the second glass of liquor, looked at Doc, and said, "Great! What can you tell me about next time?!! Eleven times up in that room I've watched you dig bullets out of that man's body, never knowing whether he was going to live or die, and I've had all I can take! I love him, but I can't live with it any more." The next morning there was a "For Sale" sign on the Long Branch, and Kitty was gone. And the whole story was, would Jim go after her and bring her back, or wouldn't he? It was a damn good story, and, finally, of course, he did go after her. She did come back and agreed to live with the problem, recognizing it was his problem as well as hers. She thought it was a hell of a show. We all did.

The Milburn Stone show was built around the fact that, in the opening scene of the show, Doc was the sole witness to a killing outside the Long Branch. He'd come out for a breath of air on the upstairs landing. Seeing the killing, he shouted for Dillon, who ran up and shot the man. The man was brought up to Doc's office and Doc began to operate on him in an attempt to save his life, knowing, as he did so, that he was the only witness against this man who would obviously be hanged for murder. In the middle of the operation, a young man runs into the office and says his wife is having a breech birth, and he wants Doc to come at once! Doc says, "I can't come. I've got this man on the table." The kid said, "But the man's a murderer! Your testimony is going to hang him! If you don't come with me, my wife is going to die!!" And Doc says, "I can't leave, son. I have a Hippocratic oath. I cannot leave a patient on the table to die." Well, the young mother's baby died. And the story was the boy's need to learn the priorities in a man's life. Milburn loved the script. We all loved it. The network called and refused me permission to do these two scripts on the basis that they were "the wrong broadcasting image for Doc and Kitty." I got very angry. I said, "Look, I've done seven or eight years" (or whatever it was at that time) "of the show, and I think I know what a good *Gunsmoke* is. The people who are going to portray these roles have been here long before any of you executives were in the positions you are in now and long before I arrived here. They should certainly know better than you or I what the audience will accept and what they won't. And they like both these shows."

The network wouldn't recant, so I said, "Okay, I resign!" Well, there was a big meeting with the brass, and they wanted to know why I was being temperamental because (according to them!) I'd never been temperamental before. I said, "I'm not being temperamental. I'm only protecting my value to you." And they talked about how good the network had been to me, and, all of a sudden, I said, "Come on, gentlemen. That's absolute nonsense. This isn't a philanthropic business. The bottom line is, am I right or wrong? In my opinion, you have to live with my failures as well as my successes, and I'm not always going to be successful, but we both know that if I make more wrong guesses than right, the ratings are going to go down and you're going to fire me. Those are the simple economics of this business. So far, I've been right more than I've been wrong." I should tell you that, at that time, *Gunsmoke* was the number one show or the number two show in the nation.

And I went on to say, "But it goes far, far deeper than that. If you refuse to let me do a show because you don't like the plot, then you emasculate me, and I am of no further worth to you,—because the way any creator creates is that he gets an idea for a show and he calls in a professional writer he thinks is right for this kind of episode, and he says, "Listen, here's an idea. Do you like it?" If the writer says, "Lord, yes!" then you tell him to go write it. Or a writer may come to me with an idea, and I listen and I say, "Yeah, that'll make a good *Gunsmoke*; go write it." And so then I said to them, "But, if I permit you to do this to me, from now on, I'm useless to you, because every time I think an idea's good, I have to stop and think: Wait a minute, wait a minute—what will that corporate mind over there think of this script? And once I have to begin to think with that mind, that corporate mind, I mean—then I can't function anymore. So gentlemen, I've had a grand time, I've learned a lot, I've enjoyed it; you paid me a lot of money, so let's part friends—and get somebody else to do this show."

Well, the upshot of that, of course, was that Jim Arness got involved. He was very angry, "I'm not going to work anymore on this show unless John does the show and these episodes are done the way they are written—and that's all there is to it." And, of course, we did the shows. And they were both enormously successful.

To the best of my memory, that was the first time that the network attempted to intrude in my particular creative process, and with Jim's help, I was able to stop it.

There was another time, later on, when CBS put a lady on my show as network liaison. She was pretty and quite charming, in the social sense, but she was determined to prove how dedicated she was.

She had done some film editing in New York, and all of a sudden she was into everything: editing, scripts, casting—she even changed the titles of the shows. We had a lovely title, for example, about an actual place in New Mexico where, in this period, white women and Indians were brought and sold into slavery. It was called, "The Valley of Tears." It actually existed. That was a lovely title, "The Valley of Tears," and it came out, with this lady's "help," as "Women for Sale." I took it as long as I could, and I finally called the network, and I said, "You either take this lady off of my show, or you make her the producer, because I can't take this anymore! I can't get anything done, because I'm constantly fighting with this lady about what she's trying to do with this show." It became a truly monumental battle, but eventually they did remove her, and in her place gave me a marvellous man, who's now a senior executive at the network. Intelligent, knowledgeable, courteous, and tactful. He loved the show. And, since it was doing very well, he hardly ever interfered. As a matter of fact, he was so complimentary about how smoothly the show operated and the ratings that I found myself actively soliciting suggestions from him. Now *that's* a liaison executive! He never, for example, called me after looking at dailies, and said, "Listen, John, what the hell happened to the coverage on the waterhole scene. It looked to *us* like the director was out to lunch." I can't tell you how that makes a producer's hackles rise! First of all, the royal "us" and "we" falls so easily from the lips of the network liaison people! It's the first word they learn, like a baby's goo-goo! And the producers don't have the remotest idea whether that "us" or "we" represents anybody but the liaison man himself. When somebody calls me and says something like that, my first instinct is to shout, "What the hell is the matter with you?! Why are you calling with such an insane question? I've shot hundreds of shows—if I can't accurately assess coverage, why the hell do you think the network hired me to produce this show? When I see a scene, I know whether there is enough coverage or not. If there isn't, I'll reshoot it, or if not, I'll have a damn good reason for accepting the coverage that is there." What puzzles me and every other experienced producer in this business is why anybody at any level of the network feels that such calls are necessary. When they come, I immediately say to myself, "*Gunsmoke* was the number one show in this nation before the man who made this call (it's inevitably true) came to work for the network. It's still number one, and how in blazes does this idiot think it got there?! And has stayed there through all the years of his puberty! Enormously talented people like John Meston and Norman McDonald and Charles Marquis Warren, and fine actors like Jim and Milburn and Dennis and Amanda and Ken Curtis brought it to life, and kept it vital and entertaining through all of these years, and all of a sudden some Johnny-come-lately is finding all kinds of flaws, and arrogantly pointing out how it ought to be done!'' I tell you, it's damned aggravating!

Anyway, those are two of my specific instances, and I'm sorry I got so hot just thinking back on them. But you're going to find, if you talk to other producers, that each one of us gets to the boiling point at one time or another.

The problem is not just with the arrogance or the tactlessness of the liaison people, but frequently its the numbers of people with whom you have to deal. Every producer has to deal, all the time, with the script concerns of the writer, the story editor, the director, and sometimes the actor. So by the time he reaches first the studio solons, who feel that they must contribute, then the network people getting into everything, his patience wears a little thin. And his sensibilities are further frayed by the time he has to spend dealing with all of these people. Very often, the people at the studio are in total disagreement with the people at the network, and it often happens that the director disagrees with both. But even if everyone who wanted to contribute was truly knowledgeable, their input would still be destructive. Everything that is offered may be sensible, reasonable, and in its own way perhaps creative. But if all of these suggestions are incorporated, the script will have lost one very important thing—a single point of view, and a certain sharp, clean edge of intention will be dead. It will begin to feel like every other show you look at. In my estimation the finest book ever written in this business was *Name above the Title* by Frank Capra, who said, sure we all make mistakes, but my pictures reflected my taste, my instincts, my belief of what the people of America would like, and for the most part they worked very well.

Then the time came when the studios began to tell me who I could cast, what they wanted in the scripts, how they wanted the scripts changed, who the writers should be. I left the business.

I think today's television could take a lesson from what Capra said. In what was called the "Golden Age" of television, we had a whole procession of splendid shows: *Playhouse 90, Show of Shows, Studio One, Kraft Television Theater, The Defenders, Desilu/Westinghouse Theater,* and dozens of others. The reason that television was so interesting in those days, in my estimation, was that every one of those shows had the unique mark of its creator—his taste, his thrust, his energy was in the show, and the excitement that that energy generated communicated itself to the television audience. You rarely feel that energy anymore, because with all the testing and the postcards, and the computer printouts that are used by the networks to rate shows, the shows end up being done by test scores and committee, and the end result is that everything looks the same. This syndrome is compounded by the fact that shows are frequently butchered for the sake of the network schedule. Fine shows are bumped from pillar to post around the schedule until the audience no longer knows where to look for them. *Centennial,* for example, which could have had a magnificent reception, was aired so infrequently and at such odd times, that it never found the audience it deserved.

In my own case, I made a twenty-hour motion picture called *How the West Was Won,* which was divided into ten two-hour segments. I think they were the ten best westerns I ever made. America never saw one single show the way it was conceived, written, directed, and produced! Not one!! We started out with two three-hour shows, then went to eleven one-hour shows, and ended with another three-hour show. I presume, if you've written a book on television, you know that the structure of a one-hour show is totally different from that of a two-hour show—the act breaks, the timing—everything's different. It cost hundreds of thousands of dollars to make those odd-length episodes, because the network had time to fill and nothing else to fill it with. There wasn't a damn thing that I could do about it! The network has the right to program material in any fashion it wants to. And I could have refused to restructure the series, but the network would simply have brought someone else in to do it. And the "someone else" would not have done it as well as I could, because I, at least, knew where transitions could be made, what scenes could be cut, and all the rest of it. So I was obliged to destroy my own best work. The one-hour version shows were the worst I have ever made! There were three, sometimes four stories, running side by side and/or interlocked, in forty-eight minutes (which is the amount of actual dramatic time you have in a one-hour TV show), and this was totally confusing to the audience. I got hundreds of letters that said, "Thank you, we loved the production, we loved the action, but we can't follow the show!" They didn't know what the hell was happening. . . .

The three-hour shows got such splendid ratings that we ended up being the twelfth show nationally on the air. But it's indicative of how subservient to programming needs the networks have become, that they are prepared to savage any show to the expediency of the schedule.

In the previous year, the three two-hour shows we did were in five different structural positions before we finally went to air! When I had those shows cut and was dubbing the first one, the network called and said, "No, we can't use two-hour shows—we must have six one-hour shows." So I stopped everything. I spent ten days figuring out, on paper, how to make six one-hour shows out of the three two-hours. At the end of the tenth day, I handed the blueprint to my editors and they began to do the actual re-structuring. Five days later, the network called again. This time, the caller said: "Forget the six one-hours. The schedule's been revised and we want you to go back to three two-hour shows." So we stopped the revisions we'd already made and went back to the original two-hour version. I had one of the shows in answer print and a second one ready for answer print when they called again: "Sorry as hell, but there's been another revision. We want to go back to the one-hour version. At least it should be easier this time—you've already got the sequences on paper!"

Now, at any time during all this, I could have quit—one of my editors did! But Jim Arness is my friend. We've been together for fifteen years. All the kids who worked for me were lovely people, and their jobs were on the line. No matter how frustrated you get, you just can't walk. Finally, unbelievably, we went into a fifth position, which was (thank God) our original position, and we aired three two-hour shows. Those three two-hour shows were the second-highest-rated mini-series in the history of television. *Roots* was first, and we were second. We had a 50+ share.

Q. *When you had to go from one position to the other, and sat down and redid them in ten days, did you do that yourself?*

I'm the only one who could. First of all, I knew every foot of film that had been shot, and I had been responsible for writing a good portion of it. My executive story consultant, Cal Clements, who is a splendid writer, had only seen the dailies—he hadn't worked with the editors, putting the episodes together, and so was at a severe disadvantage. Jack Fagan, who was in charge of post-production, had worked with the editors and is a brilliant editor in his own right—but he's not a writer. When you're starting to change the entire structure of a show, and you realize that you've got to cut a dramatic scene because it can't work where it is in the new format—because it's got to be in next week's episode—only someone who has seen every foot of dailies and who has been with the script since its inception has the tools to do the job. I sure as hell didn't *want* to do it! But I realized that if I walked then, not only did the product suffer, but the performances of Jim and everybody in the show would also suffer. And I just didn't figure that I could do that. But I tell you, I wanted to walk away and wash my hands of what I feared was going to be a total disaster.

But when you talk about where creative control rests, it begins with me deciding what kinds of shows I want to do and persuading the network to let me do what I want (because I've got some clout now) on shows that they really don't want me to do, like "China Girl." Until this year, I've been trapped in the middle of the post-production season, so to speak—into changing things, and there was no way for me to prevent that. Now there is, because I have the agreement up front, and because this show—in spite of what they did to it—was very successful this year. They really don't want me to walk, or Jim to walk. If the show is a disaster, well, those are the risks you take in this business.

SOCIAL RESPONSIBILITY AND EFFECTS

Q. *Could you define for us that particular "keen vision" that you wanted to get in your shows? What is your view of the world as it transposes into television?*

Well, I've been told by people who have looked at a lot of my work that I have a penchant for doing things that have something to say about the world. I almost left *Gunsmoke* after the fifth year, because I couldn't do that—make shows with some meaning to them. After five years, I was tired of *Gunsmoke,* because it was what was called a "traditional" western. There was always the mandatory shoot-out at the end, and it was always "We're gonna cut 'em off at the pass'' or "I'm gonna kill you because you killed my brother.'' And every script was the same, with a few variations.

But . . . that was the year that the anti-violence campaign came in, and no one knew what to do with *Gunsmoke*. I thought I knew what to do—and, thinking that, made the worst mistake of my professional life.

I decided that every other producer with an action-adventure show on the air was in terrible trouble, but *I* was not! I was riding the crest of the wave, because I had four great actors, and all I had to do was write stories around them. It was, as I said, the single biggest mistake that I've made in this business, and I can't conceive, in retrospect, how I ever thought it would work, since the essence of drama is conflict, and I couldn't create conflict between these people! They thought so much alike. They had such a strong sense of honor, such a family communion among them, that it was impossible to create honest conflict between them. So when I found I was in as much trouble (perhaps more) as any of the other producers in town, what I did was revert to the technique I used in writing *The Untouchables,* which was to bring a guest star with a problem into the center of the series situation, have the story revolve around him, and get our people involved in his problem.

It is interesting that in the five or six years preceeding this new attack, *Gunsmoke* had won only three awards. Milburn had won one as an actor . . . and the show won both an editing and a sound award. In the five years that followed, we won a whole potfull of major accolades. We did a show called "The Fires of Ignorance," which was a show about the need for compulsory education. It received a special citation from the N.E.A. We did "This Golden Land," which won the mass media "Brotherhood" award from the National Conference of Christians and Jews. We won six consecutive Fame Awards, three Western Heritage Awards, and it just went on and on—an award from the President's Council on Mental Retardation for a show called "The Deadly Innocent," and another—the Black Image award (Cicely Tyson's first major accolade)—for a show called "The Scavengers." The crazy thing is that I never sat down and said, "I want to do something important," ever. But, obviously, problems intrigue me. . . . So, in answer to your question, I guess that I do have a predilection for doing shows which have some substance.

I know one other area that I care a lot about, because writers keep telling me they hear it in their sleep—"Where are the people?" I don't care where the gold is buried. I want to know why the man buried it and what happened to him when he dug it up. I think the essence of all drama is involving an audience with the hates, the loves, the fears of your protagonist. And if you can do that, then I think any show can be successful. And when people say to me, "Do you think the western is finished, or is coming back?" I say, "I don't know the answer to that question." But I do think we can't do traditional western anymore—they just won't work. That's what was wrong this year with *How the West Was Won*. I did a traditional western, because I had no choice—no time to do anything fresh and original. (Remember, I started all this by talking about "lead time.") People are too sophisticated today to accept the old-fashioned western, but I think that if there's a hell of a good western, with very good stories and interesting actors, that show will succeed. I think any show can succeed, whether it's set in the past, the present or the future. Drama is drama, and the frame in which you put it is unimportant if the characters are real and the audience learns to care about them and is involved with their stories.

Q. *Does the western give you a special handle when you want to do that—because it's a basic American form?*

I don't think it's because it's a basic American form, but it is simplistic and I think I can give you a very good example of that. That show that got us an accolade from the National Education Association was called "The Fires of Ignorance." As I told you, it was about the necessity of compulsory education for children. Now, if you did that show today, you would have to deal with the National Education Association, with the Parent-Teachers Association, with federal funding to schools, with state funding, with all of the multi-various problems that surround schooling today.

But see how simple it was to make the point, hard and clearly, in a western. You start out with a fox trying to burrow his way into a henhouse; you cut to a barn; there is a little boy (he's about ten or eleven years old); he's got a lamp hanging over him, there is a shotgun across his lap, and he's reading *The Iliad*. The fox gets under the henhouse, and the hens are screaming, but the boy is back in the Trojan Wars; he doesn't hear. But his father, upstairs in the bedroom, hears. He comes racing downstairs, drives out the fox, then walks into the barn with two bloodied chickens in his hand, and the boy looks up in horror. . . . The father takes the book and tears it apart, and says, "You're finished with school. You can read and write, and that's all any farmer needs." It turns out the boy is a brilliant student—the best his marvellous teacher's ever had. The teacher comes to plead with the father to let the boy go back to school. There are no laws saying the boy has to go to school in this state. The father says, "No, I'm a farmer. My father was a farmer. He's going to be a farmer. He can read and he can write, and that's all he needs!" The boy does his best for ten days, can't stand it, and runs away and goes to school. The father comes to school, tries to drag him out of the classroom. The teacher interferes and the father knocks him down. The teacher sues the father for assault and battery. But we know that's not what the show's about. The trial is about the right of the child to an education. Now we wrote a beautiful speech, which was brilliantly done, in which the attorney says to the jury: Thomas Jefferson was a farmer. George Washington was a farmer, and he lists all of the good men of this country who were farmers. But they had something more, he insists; without the knowledge and the learning that these men possessed, they could not have led our country to where it is today. Here, in this room, there may be another George Washington, another Thomas Jefferson . . . and so on.

Q. [In 1980, John Mantley assumed the producer's position on a failing show, *"Buck Rogers in the 25th Century."* That move shed new light on the producer's function.] *Are there special difficulties in taking over a project like this that has been on-going, that has some definition to it?*

Oh my, yes. A lot of them. I've had some experience before with shows in difficulty, and this whole thing came about—my being here, that is—through an extraordinary set of circumstances. You know that *Buck* was cancelled and was almost off the charts last year. Well, many years ago, when I was at CBS with *Gunsmoke,* I was sent over to try and rescue another show whose ratings were slipping, called *The Wild, Wild West.* I left before a year was out, after I got the show back on track. I think part of the reason I'm here is because of that. I had, also, gone into *Gunsmoke* with Phillip Leacock when it was slipping in the ratings. Phillip left after a year or two to produce the very prestigious *Cimarron Strip*. So I sort of inherited *Gunsmoke* from him and did it from then on by myself. But neither *Gunsmoke* nor *The Wild, Wild West* was in the condition of this show when I came aboard. Both were in the middle and sliding, but *Buck* was close to being the lowest-rated prime-time show on TV last year.

I had publicly announced that I would never do any series television again. I mean, it's just become impossible now—for the reasons I've been discussing up to now—but I was told by Fred Silverman, when we met together, that if I did the show, I would only have to report to Paul King, an old friend, and there wouldn't be any interference. I was also told, by Don Sikes, who, as I'm sure you know, is the president of Universal TV—that the studio wouldn't bother me. . . .

The problem was that they'd really taken a bath on this show. I was told they'd dropped 3.5 million last year *over* budget. The only way to recover part of the money is if the show can be kept on for a year or two. Then merchandising and syndication cut the losses. So a lot rides on the show. That's really the reason I'm here, I guess—that and the fact that in eleven years of *Gunsmoke*, I was never a penny over budget. I never have been, on any show that I control. . . . That was true of *The Wild, Wild West* and *How the West Was Won*, as well as *Gunsmoke*.

When I took over *The Wild, Wild West*, for example, they were eleven days from the end of principal photography to "air," and they were several hundred thousand dollars over budget. They also had no scripts of any kind. I came in on a Thursday afternoon and we had to shoot a new show on Monday morning. Except there was no script for Monday—there was no writer anywhere in the world working on a script! There were no outlines out, nothing! I took over about two o'clock on a Thursday afternoon and I called Cal Clements—we've been together off and on for years. . . . And he came down and we blocked out a story. He went home and put a script on my desk at 8:00 the next morning. In the meantime, I called the art director, explained the sets and told him to start building. The director and I cast the show in twenty minutes from people we knew. We shot on schedule Monday morning. It wasn't a bad show, it wasn't great—but it was acceptable.

So the people who wanted me to do *Buck* knew I had had some experience—that I had sci-fi experience (my first novel, *The 27th Day,* was a Sci-Fi Book of the Month and made into a movie by Columbia from my screenplay), that I had controlled budgets, or had been able to in the past, that I had experience in rescuing two shows, that maybe I could do it with this show. And, as I told you, one of the reasons I came is because a lot of people whom I like very much—who have been very helpful in my career—wanted me to come. I felt that, at the very least, I owed them my best efforts to make *Buck* work. And just so I won't sound too altruistic, they also offered me a helluva lot of money! In answer to the other part of the question—are there problems? Oh, my yes, there are problems. The show didn't work the way it was. So I now have to try and figure out how it can be made to work. But I've got other problems besides just making a good show. I'm told that virtually the only solid audience this show has left— according to the demographic experts at the network—is children through young teenagers. *Buck* has (again, according to the demo-graphic experts) long since lost most of the science fiction addicts, because it isn't true science fiction, and it has almost no general-type audience at all. So my job is to hold the kids and to try to draw back at least some of the science fiction audience that *Star Trek* had, for example. And, at the same time, to try to suck in, with good stories, a reasonable portion of the general audience. Now, whether I can do that or not, no one, including me, has any idea. But I have changed the show, radically, and I have changed some of the characters, and I have conceived a new approach . . .

I'm trying to get away from the comic strip to a certain extent and do a little more adult science fiction. Let me explain the new concept of the show. First of all, I think the producers were trapped last year, at least to some extent, by being based in Chicago. They were fighting an inter-galactic war almost every other week. . . . I felt that was a restrictive atmosphere, in Chicago, and so I decided to eliminate the menace from space, which I've done in the first show. So the Earth is now free of that menace. And it seemed to me that in the five hundred years since the holocaust, many, perhaps tens of thousands of the peo-ple, would have left Earth, for various reasons—because the capability to go to the stars presumably existed. And, just as the Pilgrims left England in search of freedom from religious persecution, and the Thai boat people are leaving their homes for fear of their lives, people left

Earth. Within the five hundred years, Earth has been too busy defending itself against the menace from space and in rebuilding itself to find out what happened to those lost tribes of Earthlings. So now that Earth is at peace, finally, we developed the Searcher. It's not a military vessel, it's not "Battlestar Galactica," it's not the "Enterprise"—it's the "Calypso," if you like. It's a vessel with a couple of fighters on it and defense capabilities. But it's not a war ship. It's much smaller, and it's got a much smaller crew, and they're going out to look for the lost tribes from Earth. Now that puts us in space, where I can run into derelict ships, find different planets, encounter strange cultures— but it also does something else. It eliminates, for me, the necessity of creating every week a new race of lizards or tortoises or some other form of intelligent life. I will, from time to time, meet with those strange creatures. There are some in several of the shows we've already conceived. But, from time to time, I will meet colonies of Earth people. These colonies have different mores, different sexual practices, different religions, different governments, and so forth—and we'll try to make a story about those things. These people are Earthlings and, therefore, they don't have to have pointy ears or huge brain cases, or what have you. So that's the concept of the show now. We're in space, and we'll be in space most of the time. We may occasionally return to New Chicago. We have the Star Gate, where we can get back. But our concentration is going to be out there in the galaxy. . . .

Q. *Do you keep working on two levels throughout, as you develop? Is that part of the plan to keep the younger audience and develop the others?*

Yes. I didn't really need the extended aerial fight between Buck and Hawk, but the kids will love it. They'll love the Hawk's talons coming down, and if the character Hawk "takes off"—then that puts money in the studio's pocket too, for all the merchandising. And if Creighton (a robot character) takes off, there'll be Creightons all over the nation. Nobody knows whether any of these things will succeed, but if they do—then I will have done my job as well as I can, and there'll be money to be made from merchandising. There'll also be money from syndication, if I can keep it going for two years—we both know by now that if a show doesn't run for more than a year, there's not enough product to be a "viable"' syndication vehicle.

Q. *Given the amount of money involved in the show, do you sense a kind of freedom, or a kind of pressure to make the show go—besides your own instincts to do that?*

Oh, there's enormous pressure. I mean, I've been asked to do something that everybody thinks is impossible. I'm not at all sure I can even come close. All I'm going to do is do what I did with *Gunsmoke* and *The Wild, Wild West*—go back to basics. Try to do stories that are interesting, real stories. It's a marvellous form, as was the western, in which to do so. In some respects I think the western and the future are easier areas in which to do shows than the present, which is enormously complicated. You can make the future as simple as you want. The west probably wasn't simple, but we have made it so in drama. You know, if you had courage and persistence and guts, legend said, you succeeded in the Old West. There are a lot of similar advantages to science fiction. Not just as a television medium, but as a writer's medium. . . .

Q. *Science fiction has always, of course, been a form of social criticism for many people—to tell us how we live and what our values are. Do you plan to do that kind of thing? Do you see those possibilities, especially given the interest of children?*

It's a hard question to answer. I said before, I think, that people keep saying that my shows have had a lot of social content, and I guess in retrospect they have. . . . And I guess, subconsciously, there must be something in me that makes me reach for that. But I don't consciously sit down and say, "I'm going to find an issue and I'm going to write a story about it." I never do that. But things happen. . . .

Q. *When you say that you want to make the best show that you know how, what does that mean to you in terms of character and emotion and plot?*

Well, you've really said it for me. When I say the best show I know how, I mean a show that people will look at and will enjoy, and, without knowing it, will learn and expand, I guess. I can't put it any differently than that.

. . . The shows that I like the best—and I have never had a show, I think, that I really liked that the audience didn't like—have all been shows which said something about the human condition. . . . About the fascinating, eternal, interesting, complicated relationships that we get ourselves into.

Q. *It is often said that you cannot do that in television—that, by definition, it is not an art form.*

That is not true. It's damned hard to do, but I've been very lucky. . . . I wanted to quit *Gunsmoke,* but, when the violence restrictions came in, nobody knew what to do with the show and they got out of the way because they didn't think I was going to be able to save it . . . and nobody wants to be associated with a failure! In one sense, that is good, because I love it if they don't "help." But, you see, when those violence restrictions came in, I was suddenly able to have the freedom to make shows of my own. Can you imagine any network permitting me to make a show about a Jewish patriarch in a western, not just about the patriarch, himself, but about his dedication to the Torah?! I mean, it was impossible before those restrictions came in. Or to make a show called "The Fires of Ignorance," about the need for compulsory child education. All of these things I was able to do because nobody knew what to tell me to do with the show. So, it isn't easy. It is tough. They're accepting my new concepts for *Buck.* They say they like them and everybody, so far, has appeared to like the first script. I say "appeared" to like, because I don't really know whether they're saying it's good because they don't know what else to say, or because they don't want to be involved. In the long run, however, it doesn't really matter what anyone thinks, including me. The public will deliver the answer.

Q. *But when you have the sense of freedom, television is just like any other raw material?*

You bet your life it is. . . . There are a lot of really good things on television. There's a lot of trash, too. If you look for them, there are a lot of fine things on public television. There are also some excellent things on network television. Ed Asner does some really fine shows. *M*A*S*H* does some lovely stuff . . . and *Barney Miller* does really lovely things. I mean to say, they do very important things on that show, and you don't know, unless you're a producer, how cleverly they do what they're doing, and how difficult it is. But you're learning so much about human interaction on *Barney*—about all kinds of things: about prostitution, about homosexuality, about man's inhumanity to man, about tenderness, about compassion; it's all there in that show. It's really a beautiful show, and I never miss that if I can help it. I think it is just splendidly done. Important things are being delivered in a package that's fun to look at.

Q. *Cable television, with re-broadcasting rather than syndication, brings a question about the future of the producer, because it raises serious problems for everyone. Nobody will pay the money they've been paying, so you can't make the money that way. Does that leave you with questions about the whole future of the producer as the creative force in television?*

I think they're going to need producers, and it appears from the disasters on the tube now that they need experienced producers more than ever. There isn't any substitute for experience. I mean, I don't care how dumb you are, if you make six hundred television shows, you've got to learn something—if only by osmosis. You learn where the money goes. You learn—nobody ever learns all of this, but you know some of the answers—how to grab an audience's emotions . . . because, in my opinion, if you don't you lose. That's really what I'm trying to do with *Buck*. I think they made the same mistake with *Galactica* and *Buck Rogers*. In both instances, they've tried to make pyrotechnics and hardware substitute for really good stories. And I don't think you can do that.

Richard Levinson
and William Link

Link and Levinson began their writing collaboration while in high school in their native Philadelphia. After serving in the army they went to New York to continue their writing efforts in the arena of television. Their first scripts were produced for Canadian Broadcasting Corporation. They then sold a script to Desilu, *Chain of Command*, and with that success, they moved to California in 1959. They wrote for *Johnny Ringo, Sugarfoot, 77 Sunset Strip, Wanted Dead or Alive, Black Saddle,* and *Slattery's People.* They went to work under contract for Four Star Television and after two years decided to return to New York to write a play. The result was *Prescription: Murder,* which opened in San Francisco and toured the country for half a year. Commuting back to Los Angeles they wrote for *The Rogues, The Fugitive, Dr. Kildare, The Man From U.N.C.L.E.,* and *The Alfred Hitchcock Show.* After some years they returned permanently to Los Angeles, early reworking their play into a TV movie for Universal starring Peter Falk as Columbo. Following that venture the two men signed a contract as producers for Universal. For the studio they produced several movies for TV, *My Sweet Charlie, That Certain Summer, The Execution of Private Slovik, The Gun,* and *The Storyteller.* They also created and produced several series including *Columbo, Ellery Queen,* and *Tenafly.* They have written scripts for several theatre films, among them *Rollercoaster* and *The Hindenberg.*

Since leaving Universal in 1978 Link and Levinson have produced four movies for television, *Murder by Natural Causes, Crisis at Cen-*

tral High, Rehearsal for Murder, and *Take Your Best Shot.* They have now returned to Universal in a consulting role. In 1983 they wrote the script for the Broadway musical, *Merlin.*

Both men are graduates of the University of Pennsylvania.

William Link and Richard Levinson form one of television's most successful partnerships. As writers, as studio producers, and in their own production company they have established an easy working style that finds them speaking, and one supposes, thinking, as a single creative force. Their collaboration is no recent matter. It extends to their junior high school days when they created their own mysteries on wire recordings, modeled after the popular radio mysteries of the day. In television the long relationship has paid off in creative power, for they are among the masters of the sophisticated crime-detection drama. *Columbo,* a series which they created and for which they served as executive producers, is perhaps the best example of the high style and polish of their work in this area. But they have also participated in the creation, development, or production of series like *Mannix, McCloud, Tenafly,* and *Ellery Queen.* Some of these series have been among television's most successful, embodying all the elements of familiar formulas but polished to the hilt, varied in significant ways, creatively transformed into superb television.

Simultaneously, Link and Levinson are noted for a succession of highly acclaimed movie-length television dramas dealing with complex and often controversial social issues. *My Sweet Charlie,* their first film, aired in January of 1970. It dealt with race relations in a time of tense social circumstances, and it did so with style and gentleness. *That Certain Summer* (1972) portrayed male homosexuality in an understandable, sensitive manner, exploring a range of relationships without condemnation or easy acceptance of difficulties. *The Execution of Private Slovik* (1974) studied the case of the only soldier executed for desertion in World War II, a case notable for its complex web of human emotion and bureaucratic insensitivity.

In some ways, which we explore later, these two types of television production are almost antithetical. Certainly Link and Levinson maintain a strict distinction. ". . . we think of Graham Greene's handy semantic device of dividing his works into 'entertainments' and 'serious novels.' We do this, we hope with some sense of irony, since it's a rather pretentious concept. But it does serve to differentiate one's *intentions."* In spite of this basic, underlying conceptual difference, the producers point to a similarity crucial to our understanding of their use of television. Both types of production, they insist, are "well made." As they endeavor to define this term we come best to comprehend their particular view of the creative producer's role and general function.

At the start of their career Levinson and Link, as writers, created for many types of television. Indeed, on one occasion these specialists of puzzling mysteries even wrote a western for Canadian TV. Like many, if not most, series writers, however, they saw that they had little opportunity to shape the end product. Their authority, their very authorship, was always superseded by those with more extensive control. Particular designations of who exercised such control hardly mattered so long as it was taken and used. In some rare cases, like that of Paddy Chayevsky, a writer could control the work. In other cases a star, a Barbra Streisand for example, could maintain creative control.

> The point is auteur again. Most films don't have an author. They're simply happenstance and collaborative enterprises. Most television shows don't have an author. The author emerges as whoever has control and exercises it.

Recognizing this, Link and Levinson determined to become writer-producers and were thus able to make far more precise choices affecting the design and final development of their written work. They are, as a result, exceptionally involved in every level of detail. As they put it:

> There are many producers who don't choose to exercise the control. They have line producers, executive producers, and all they do is handle stores. But we—and the more we've been doing television the more we like it—out of a compulsion for better work, make every decision.

In order to work at this level of detail the two men have had to adjust their career to suit their goals. In 1977 they formed their own

William Link and Richard Levinson

companies and concentrated on made-for-television movies because they were convinced that no one can work to full creative potential in series television. Their only connection with the series form at present is as consultants at Universal Studios. By concentrating their efforts on the "one-shot," the serious telefilm, they are able to define for themselves and for many creative producers one of the theses of this book.

> We protect ourselves by producing. Now we go a little further and say you can even "paint," you can use the various areas of production as a part of the writing art: set design, your choice of other people, your choice of music.

It is this perspective, the view that the very limitations of collaboration can be used as creative possibilities, that sets the self-conscious producers apart. With such an idea in mind we can reinterpret and better understand the traditional notion of the "well-made" dramatic production and move to clearer insight into the work of Link and Levinson.

It is unlikely that they are able, finally, to attend to every detail of their work. Still, it is their ideal, the goal that structures their work patterns and underlies many choices. In the case of their most recent film, *Take Your Best Shot* (1982), we observed them as they participated in every aspect of sound dubbing, scoring, and final cutting, even to the extent of debating at some length with the director the subject of bird sounds in an outdoor scene.

The partnership itself facilitates their attention to detail. One is often attending to "business" while the other oversees more artistic matters, and the interchange and mutual assumption of duties is constant. As an example they point to their concern with the soundtracks of their television works. With *Columbo* for instance, one of them was on the dubbing stage for every episode, supervising an area of the show often disregarded by producers with different aims or styles. Similar concerns are expressed with choices of set design, wardrobe and lighting. This same expanded and shared role of producer is evident in their "social dramas" such as *Crisis at Central High*.

This precise attention would be futile, of course, without purpose, without a clear and coherent sense of how each of these elements contributed to the whole, to the "well-made" product. In the "entertainments" this principle is rooted in tradition, in a strong sense of the continuities of popular culture itself. Quick to acknowledge the influences of classic mystery writers they are dismayed at young critics who, in their ignorance of these traditions, might even classify *Columbo* as a "whodunit." Keeping all these formal distinctions at the forefront, Link and Levinson give scrupulous attention to matters of plot and action. Weapons are placed within reach and reason of users, noted carefully for the audience long before their actual use. Poisons and their effects are seen to with care. Even the most elaborately planned murders are outlined with fully rational explanations. Hours are spent, they tell us, in deciding on such minutiae as how to move a character upstairs so that a part of the puzzle will fit most precisely.

At the juncture of tradition and technique, of course, is meaning. It should hardly surprise us to hear that they require changes in set decoration.

> You say to the art director, "The man we've written wouldn't have these paintings. He would not have that dreadful *objet d'art* sitting there. It's much too cluttered for a guy of his sensibilities. So clean out the set. Replace the paintings with a different kind, more contemporary graphics. And so on." The man's environment is an extension of him. We created that person as a character. We're also interested in how it's extended.

Similarly, we should more easily understand why Link and Levinson see it as part of their role as producers to engage in the following exchange regarding the lighting of *Columbo*.

> With *Columbo* when we talked with the cameraman about lighting, we said, "Artificial." The first cameraman, who had worked with Orson Welles, was lighting great bars of shadow across Peter [Falk's] face, and we said, "It's too moody. It's too down."
> And he said, "Well, the little fellow has a bad eye."
> And we said, "He doesn't mind."
> He said, "You want to light this like a musical."
> We said, "Yes."
> He said, "But it's a cop show."
> We said, "No. It's not."

Complete accomplishment of such precisely fashioned television art depends, as these examples indicate, on others as well as the executive writer-producers. Link and Levinson select personnel as carefully as they plan scenes. They know that there are differences among directors, designers, editors, or actors. Again, the choices are made on a conceptual basis: a director whose sense of style suits their particular intention, an editor who can produce a final cut without constant directorial supervision, an actor whose presence and persona carry a prior meaning that can contribute to the story. Even when such choices have been made Link and Levinson go a step further, working closely with production personnel in ways not often attended to. Not only, for example, do they provide auditioning actors with scripts ahead of time, they also see that technical personnel such as sound mixers have access to scripts before photography begins.

The conventional wisdom regarding television has it that such choices are, in spite of their contributions, useless in the long run. In this view the network, as final arbiter of what is used or cut, programmed or shelved, makes creativity of this sort redundant and, indeed, wasteful. Link and Levinson refuse to accept such a view. Television, they point out, is an industry of "the track record." Their success—a success brought about by their care and attention—wins them "clout" with the networks and enables them to gain still more creative freedom and control. With this behind them they can fight for what they want, and, most often, win. As they describe their use of this creative power, and add to it other descriptions about how producers can learn to use "loopholes" in the production system to gain more creative control, they speak for many of the self-conscious producers. They make it quite clear that commercial constraint need not reduce artistry. In their "entertainments" all these concerns tend toward a delightfully playful sense of excellence. Using the twentieth-century's most popular medium, Link and Levinson continue a tradition of diversion and pleasure begun with Poe's first stories. (Not surprisingly, they have on two occasions won the Edgar Allen Poe Award for mystery-writing.)

In the serious social dramas, however, there is another tendency, another use for this precision. When asked to define the style of these works Levinson and Link quickly reply that they are grounded in "understatement." The topics dealt with in the social dramas are exceptionally serious ones and the producers have no intention of being exploitive. The realism and probability that went into the making of a well-constructed mystery remain central in this genre as well. They

have consciously avoided, for instance, a style they define as more
"rhetorical," exemplified for them by works such as Chayevsky's
Hospital and *Network,* or in some of Norman Lear's more specifically
polemical work. Admitting, and in some ways admiring, the enormous
energy and effect of such works, they maintain a base with actions
and characters more realistic and familiar. Acknowledging that outrageous humor, thrilling effects, bizarre characterization or other single
aspects can "carry" an otherwise flawed, less-than-well-made film,
they still opt for precision and control, for a fine balance in which all
elements fit. As they say at one point:

> In the films where we have serious intentions, we tend to un-
> derstate. This comes from a feeling that if you're going to deal
> with subjects such as homosexuality, or race relations, or gun
> control, you should show some aesthetic restraint and not wal-
> low in these materials like a kid who's permitted to write dirty
> words on a wall. Our approach is that if you're going to use
> these controversial subjects—play against them. Don't be so
> excited by your freedom that you go for the obvious.

The somewhat rigid distinction between the "entertainments" and
the serious works implied in such a comment and expanded upon in
other observations is not merely a matter of taste, choice, or commercial expediency. For Levinson and Link it grows out of a deep concern
for how television operates in society. They describe themselves often
as products of the fifties, pointing to their immersion in popular culture and their continuing interest in entertainment as part of the un-
critical attitude of that decade. The innocence of that time ended for
them, as for many others, with the assassination of President Kennedy. And after the deaths of Martin Luther King, Jr. and Robert
Kennedy in 1968, because they were forced to admit the possibility of
television's contribution to an aura of violence, to a sense of impa-
tience with complexity and frustration, they began to create something
other than the formulaic, excitement-filled television programs with
which they had achieved first success.

It is as if they attempted to divide the elements of television that
we have seen so often combined in the work of other producers, creating a kind of internal dialogue within their own body of work. Ironically, in their overview of television, they feel that their social con-

cerns will never be able to balance the world of more conventional programming. They express serious personal doubts that single programs, no matter how accurate, how complex, how superb in presentation, can change social attitudes. Television's effects, in their view, emerge from ongoing, long-term, submerged attitudes.

In our own view the distinctions between the two types of work are not so rigid nor is the gap between their effects so wide as Link and Levinson would have it. Their two styles are actually complementary expressions based in the same vision. Taken in the context of television's larger dialogue, the dialogue we have been outlining, their contributions of both sorts add to the overall resonance, the "discussion" of varying social views.

Their "entertainments" in spite of their "baroque," highly stylized, playful elegance are hardly insignificant diversions. In spite of Levinson and Link's disclaimer, for example, that the class differences structuring *Columbo* are incidental and are included merely to provide conflict and juxtaposition, many other techniques could easily have been developed for the same ends. The plots of that series do in fact continually ring changes on its basic pattern, on the theme of social distinctions. When the nagging "prole" finally brings down the sneering, condescending snobs who flaunt the rules of social order, we can always score one for the working class.

A more subtle comment emerges when *Columbo, McCloud, Ellery Queen,* and other near-comic detective shows are compared to the more straightforward, straight-laced cop shows. Quinn Martin makes no apologies for his use of popular entertainment forms to present "idealized," bigger-than-life, heroic police officers, nor for the ideology that stands behind such decisions. Even in their grimest, most rigorous representations he uses them and the popular formulas in which they are presented as patterns and goals, indicative of the attitudes that *should* support social structure, even if, in his view, they do not always do so.

Obviously no such idealization is possible in Link and Levinson crime and detection series when standard police procedures become the basis for humor, when maverick law enforcement officers continually undercut their authoritative superiors, or when brilliant private detectives outwit their dull official counterparts. While some sort of more critical, more caustic view of authority could result from such presentations, there is clearly no subversive intention involved. Indeed, just the opposite is intended. The far more specific, more precise goal of Levinson and Link is to *avoid* serious content in such shows by insulating crime and detection within thick layers of popular fantasy. It is as if they are saying that none of this touches reality; these are the fluff, the dreams that remove us from actual worry about such matters. Every attempt is made to assure the audience that popular entertainment does *not* represent or comment directly on the realities of harsh, serious social issues.

If we recall their ambivalence regarding television's effects, addressed directly in their 1977 movie for TV, *The Storyteller,* we can better understand both the formal distinction of style and the philosophical concern with content. For Link and Levinson the content of the typical "realistic" TV detective show is precisely what is problematic about television. The reliance on authoritarian uses of violence, presented repeatedly through years of television experience, is potentially more capable of changing audience behavior and expectation than those programs presenting individual problems and well-defined, complex situations. They choose, then, in their "entertainments" to avoid violence or other forms of social controversy, or to couch them in patently *un*realistic fictions. They do so not to mislead or divert the audience from serious social problems, but because they believe that no combination of social problems and popular fantasies can be truthful to the issues. The audience will, in their view, be so thoroughly seduced by the familiar formula that it will never penetrate to the level of serious content. It will devalue the real issues by easily accepting their inclusion in these unreal worlds, and this is precisely what leads to social problems in the first place. An audience that can accept this toying with problematic areas of social life will hardly, in their view, deal with them appropriately. In the larger television text, then, their "entertainments" are packed with meaning and social significance. They stand as a pointed alternative to attempts at realism and idealization.

This view of television relates Levinson and Link to some of television's severest critics. If this were all of their statement, its perspective would be profoundly conservative. But they are no more willing to accept this narrower attitude as the total picture than they are to assume easy answers to other social questions. Even when they are unsure about ultimate effects on the audience, they respond to the more conservative approach to television with their other productions. Unwilling to stand by waiting for evidence that they have changed lives or attitudes, they continue to create. And the things that they create are hard-hitting, precise, naturalistic, social-problem plays.

In these "serious" works, questions of authority, power, socially established rules, prejudice, or violence, topics that are taken for granted in popular entertainment, become the subject matter for their complex and moving works. If they are to be properly understood these tough topics must become the center of dramatic focus, highlighted and removed from the periphery of formulaic television. Small moral tags, submerged "lessons," overtly idealized authority figures cannot do the job. In the dense escapism of ordinary television they are easily lost or overlooked. At their worst, they mislead. Serious television about serious issues must provoke the audience into questions, into potential criticism. To make this sort of statement the producers must strike for the real experience of humanity. Just as they avoid the formulaic fantasy, then, when dealing with important topics, so they avoid the "rhetorical" style of Chayevsky. That particular style, certainly in television, is as diversionary as fantasy, drawing audience attention from the realization that the problems presented in social drama are problems touching real lives.

In these social dramas, as in those lived experiences, there can be no simple, formulaic, idealized solutions. Even in the interest of presenting their own personal views—humane, tolerant, classically liberal social views—Link and Levinson remain true to the ambiguity and multiple perspectives of social issues. In their dramas good people get hurt. Well-intentioned people make terrible mistakes. Human beings find themselves unwittingly caught in horribly frustrating circumstances. Brave people act, even in the face of potential failure. Committed citizens discover the burdens of legal tangles. Neither a small dose of seriousness in the midst of entertainment nor strident, skewed polemic is adequate to accomplish Link and Levinson's goals for television. For them it is the carefully crafted, naturalistic, dramatic presentation that best approaches the realities of social life as most of us live it.

Like a microcosm of television itself, then, Levinson and Link productions offer audiences a range of styles and meanings with which to argue, choose, explore, and experience the realities of American life. They offer a personal internal dialogue which, in their own view, engages us with serious works and diverts us with "entertainments." In our view the distinction is not so complete, precisely because we find a healthy and fully warranted seriousness in those entertaining pieces. But whether the separation is valid or not Link and Levinson move us another step toward an understanding of the medium itself. In all their works they demonstrate that it is a medium as capable of complexity, variety, and excellence as any other. Indeed, they make it clear that the very meaning of the concept of the creative producer is that there are television works exhibiting an awareness of difference and distinction, a knowledge of television's larger social and aesthetic meanings, and a willingness to create the unique yet familiar work that touches a mass audience in meaningful ways.

INTERVIEW WITH RICHARD LEVINSON AND WILLIAM LINK

THE PRODUCER'S PERSONAL STYLE

[LEVINSON AND LINK] The influences on us as young people—and we've known each other for a long time—were a combination of junk and high art swallowed whole: from Salinger to Jules Verne to *Lights Out* and *Escape*.

We loved movies when we were kids. We used to follow Hitchcock. Years before the television series went on the air, we used to say, "Oh, that's Alfred Hitchcock." The culture co-opted our private interests. For example, we were making wire recordings of our own radio shows, even music, in a time when little music was out: mostly Miklos Rozsa scores, back in the forties.

Our mysteries are clear because of our whole background. Some of the reading we did when we were young was in the field of the golden age of the mystery story. And what that teaches is structure, a sense of structure and a sense of internal logic. So we had a predilection to stress that. We used to read maybe five mysteries a week: John Dixon Carr, Ellery Queen. Now whether or not the people are puppets, manipulated by these authors, the structural sense in these books was excellent, very cleverly plotted. We've read hundreds of mysteries. It really seeps into your work.

Everything we wanted to do when we were kids presupposed an audience. Our initial ambition was to direct and we thought of writing as a way to direct. We love the directors of the forties and the fifties.

A man like Norman Lear, who has had a great impact on the thinking of television, has a sense of tradition. He comes out of a certain thirties attitude, perhaps from a lower-middle-class environment. His attitudes were forged in that time.

We come out of the fifties which was much more skeptical. We were much less ideologues in the fifties. The writers in the fifties were Salinger and Sartre and these were the skeptics. Holden Caulfield thought everybody was a phony. We weren't forged with any great social consciousness.

Maybe some of the social shows we've done are trying to compensate—because in our day, though we went to an integrated school, the one girl who was a social worker and played the guitar in settlement houses, was an object of derision. She was, oddly enough, a girl from the sixties stuck in the fifties, where she was mocked. "There were no blacks in the fifties"—it's a famous line. And, to paraphrase, there were no poor in the fifties. We went to a musical-comedy high school where we put on shows and where our concerns were dating. Our personal concerns were putting on our shows, getting a car, driving around, going to the local malt shop, necking, and those are the values. And should we steal our father's bottle of Scotch and have a drink?

Occasionally, you'd turn on the television set and see McCarthy getting demolished, but that didn't really impinge on us. It was a period of great triviality, but it was the last moment of innocence in the history of this country; the last moment of all the traditional, romantic, sweet, movie-forged attitudes. And of course, our lives were lived in books.

Sometimes we get the feeling that it's hard to find a common denominator in our work, and searching for one is something usually best left to critics. Films such as *The Execution of Private Slovik* and *My Sweet Charlie,* and *That Certain Summer*—and even a series such as *Columbo,* in a way—all seem to deal with outsiders, those who go against the grain. But then up pops a *Murder by Natural Causes* or a *Rehearsal for Murder,* which do not come to grips in any way with social issues, nor are the characters at odds with society.

This is probably because we like to vary the work and the process of filmmaking itself. It's a grim experience, day after day, to be involved with a project such as *Slovik.* In the most basic sense, though there may be a feeling of accomplishment, no one has any fun on the set. Everyone is glum. We're all weighed down with a self-imposed burden of responsibility, and we tend to take ourselves too seriously. But when we do one of the mysteries, the set is a happy place to be. There are no responsibilities to real people or real events, and so we can enjoy ourselves in the old-fashioned hey-we're-making-a-movie sense.

Sometimes, when we go back and forth between a *Crisis at Central High* and a *Rehearsal for Murder,* we think of Graham Greene's handy semantic device of dividing his works into "entertainments" and "serious novels." We do this, we hope with some sense of irony, since it's a rather pretentious concept. But it does serve to differentiate one's *intentions.* And it's important for us to make the "entertainments" for two reasons. One is that we have a particular affection for the traditional mystery story, the thriller, the whodunnit, the puzzle piece. And the other is that it's useful to refresh ourselves creatively so that we don't become mired in the solemn and the discursive and the overly earnest. Social drama tends to get a little heavy-handed if you're not careful, and a change of pace can help to keep you from boring yourself and your audience by hitting only one note.

Our style is, in a sense, "literary." Not being directors, we're probably more interested in words than images, and we write a great deal of dialogue, often to the despair of some of our directors. If pressed, we'll admit to writing "well-made" films, and the phrase "well-made," at least in the theatre, is currently out of vogue. Structure is important to us. Interestingly, many of the works we read by young writers have marvelous dialogue and characterizations, but there is no sense of form. Of course, form has many faces—in our view an apparently formless writer such as Sam Shepard does have a structure and an internal logic in his work, even though he may evolve it unconsciously. But plot and structure seem to be problems for new writers. Whatever else it may do, by the way, the mystery genre does teach one how to plot and bring various story strands together to make sense.

We've tried to be looser in some of our films (*Take Your Best Shot,* for example), but our pictures never seem to turn out as ragged as we may have wished. Films such as *Mean Streets* and *Taxi Driver* spill out over the edges—they may be sloppy, but there's juice there, and energy, and we have great admiration for this kind of work. Fortunately or unfortunately, it's not our style. Our influences were more formal and traditional.

In the films where we have serious intentions, we tend to understate. This comes from a feeling that if you're going to deal with subjects such as homosexuality, or race relations, or gun control, you should show some aesthetic restraint and not wallow in these materials like a kid who's permitted to write dirty words on a wall. Our approach is that if you're going to use these controversial subjects—play against them. Don't be so excited by your freedom that you go for the obvious. The danger, of course, is that sometimes you get so muted that you boil out the drama. In *The Storyteller* we were so concerned with being fair and with balance that we lost energy and dramatic impact.

If you ask about our film-making style as opposed to our writing style, we'd say that we ask, from our directors and actors, for a sense of naturalism. We don't like make-up and ask the actors not to wear it whenever possible. We tend to cast unknowns rather than "names" or familiar faces. When we did *The Gun* we didn't want a single person in the picture the audience would recognize. Later, some of the actors became famous, but at the time most of them had not been on television to the point of familiarity.

We tend to prefer practical locations to sets. Actual sites present problems, particularly with sound, but they give great reality. We hate looping, and we'd rather have less-than-top-quality sound than the kind of antiseptic artificiality that comes with looping lines. We like natural light, and shadow—anything but the kind of flat lighting that prevails on most TV series. And we tend to use less and less musical underscoring. It's so often a crutch to juice up a weak picture. *The Gun* had no score whatsoever. *Slovik* had a few records of the period. And, though we like good composition and fluid camera work, we ask our directors not to have the camera intrude and call attention to itself.

Having said all of that, we totally reverse ourselves when we're doing a mystery. Then, in pre-production, we sit down with the director and say, "Dance. Have fun. Play games with your camera. Take a look at *Citizen Kane,* or Hitchcock, and be as flamboyant as you like. This isn't *The Bicycle Thief* or *Umberto D,* where the camera sits there and the intention is to create the pain and intensity of the human condition. This is artifice, and style, and flair, and, if we're lucky, well-crafted entertainment."

We'll spend days on how to get a woman upstairs. I mean, occasionally we get angry with ourselves over why we are spending all this time to make it seamless, to make a move, a manipulative move, be very smooth. And the audience isn't going to know it.

Your own sense of pride and craft is involved—because writers are always saying that the audience won't ask why a central character in a given script arrives at a certain place at a certain time. And you do have a problem in that if you explain why you've plugged up a plot hole, you may be boring the audience, putting the audience to sleep with exposition. So you have to strike a balance.

When we dub a picture and spend a lot of time carefully mixing sound and everything, someone would say, "Why are you doing that? It comes out of a ten-inch speaker."

Partially you're doing it for your own ego. And maybe, fixing all these elements improves the picture by 15, 20 percent. And it's a sense of your own compulsion. We don't know that one can always say that it's wonderful of the individual to to this. Sometimes the individual is just compulsive about it. But those compulsions lead to better work in our view.

Q. *In relation to this compulsion idea, do you apply the term auteur to a producer?*

One of the things Universal Studios prides itself on is being a general service studio. Universal's position is, "We can produce a show without you. Our casting department can cast it. Our editorial department can edit the film. Our production department can board and budget it."

Some of the old-line producers resent the advent of the hyphenate [the writer-producer]. They say, "We need you people as writers so we make you producers. You don't really know anything about the mechanics and technical side of production. We can do that. Now you, of course, stop writing and want to hire story editors which costs us more money, and all you want to do is produce because that's the power."

And a lot of the old guard resent that terribly. They have a concept—many people in this business have a concept—of below the line personnel. They do not realize that some editors are more creative than others. Some make-up people are more creative. Some art directors are more creative. Some of them care. So the in-put from a producer to these below the line people is resented by the production departments of the studios.

We like the people with the egos: the editors that have an ego, the art directors, the composers. Because you have to grapple with them more. You're still trying to impose your vision on them. But you get more in-put because they care more. They care about their work.

We provide the sound mixers with scripts, too. These are very technical people. At a place like Universal movies run through them; they might do two or three television shows a week. They couldn't care less. But they're stunned when we say, "Hey, before we get into the room we'd like you to read the script, so you know what's going on and you're not going to be confused, and so on." And surprisingly, they love it, because no one really cares that much about their part of the operation.

And there's another thing—the dubbing of a picture. When you're doing a television series you have to have your producer, your line producer, or some associate dub the film. Dubbing is very important but it takes up from nine in the morning until six at night. You're trapped on the dubbing stage and you can't conduct business. One of the problems in a series is you don't dub your own pictures. When we were doing *Columbo,* Bill would dub one and then I would dub one.

There was always one of us in the office, which is the advantage of a partnership.

But on all of our television movies, we do *everything*. We go to wardrobe and look at the wardrobe.

The auteur of any collaborative art form is the person who has creative control and chooses to exercise it. Be it the writer, like Paddy Chayevsky, or in film the director, or the actor—Barbra Streisand, for example.

There are many producers who don't choose to exercise the control. They have line producers, executive producers, and all they do is handle stories. But we—and the more we've been doing television the more we like it—out of a compulsion for better work, make every decision.

Frequently this includes directorial decisions. You say to a director, "This is the kind of directing style." On *Natural Causes* we said to the director, "This is Hitchcock. We're confined in a house, therefore fluid camera, as much camera movement as you can give us. Ceiling shots. The old-fashioned, schmaltzy, baroque, Orson Welles approach." You sit down and give that director in-put. And you give him in-put every day after you see the dailies. You go back on the set. You discuss performances. One actor may seem to be overacting. You say to the director, "Can you hold him down?" This is not to say that the director hasn't decided these things for himself. But it's an endless daily dialogue.

We produce for two reasons. One is to protect the material. And the second is that we've discovered that producing is an extension of writing. The day before they're going to shoot it you walk on a set designed for a character you've written. You say to the art director, "The man we've written would not have these paintings. He would not have that dreadful *objet d'art* sitting there. It's much too cluttered for a guy of his sensibilities. So clean out the set. Replace the paintings with a different kind, more contemporary graphics. And so on." The man's environment is an extension of him. We created that person as a character. We're also interested in how it's extended.

This is not to say that if you have an art director who is extremely talented, or particularly an editor who is extremely talented, you don't look at what he's done. For example, on our film *Murder by Natural Causes* Frank Morris, who did *Slovik* and *The Gun* for us, was the editor. He makes the first cut. The director in this case didn't go to dailies. He was too tired. So most of the choices were Frank's, with some in-put from the director on the telephone. Now what we did was see Frank's first cut and adjust that cut.

With *Columbo,* when we talked with the cameraman about lighting, we said, "Artificial." The first camerman, who had worked with Orson Welles, was lighting great bars of shadow across Peter [Falk]'s face, and we said, "It's too moody. It's too down."

And he said, "Well, the little fellow has a bad eye."

We said, "He doesn't mind."

He said, "You want to light it like a musical?"

We said, "Yes."

He said, "But it's a cop show."

We said, "No. It's not."

And by giving him a box—two boxes—of Havana cigars and a lunch, he was "coerced." He brought the key up. He did the lighting the way we wanted it.

We protect ourselves by producing. Now we go a little further and say you can even "paint," you can use the various areas of production as a part of the writing art: set design, your choice of other poeple, your choice of music.

We thought *Columbo* would be successful. We never knew it would be the kind of success it was. We thought *My Sweet Charlie* would be a ratings failure and a critical success. It was, in fact, both. With *The Gun* we had no idea about its reception. *The Storyteller* we assumed would be highly criticized, and we assumed it would have low numbers. We were right about the numbers; we were wrong about the criticism. We got some of the best notices we've ever received. We know when we've got something good, but not about how "popular" it will be. You can't always guess. We can't measure "popular."

Q. *How do you try to measure? Obviously you want both.*

No. We don't want both. Perhaps we shouldn't say this for attribution, but we want something good. That's it. That is our main criterion in the work we do. If you gave us a choice between a bad and very popular show or a good show and unpopular, we would choose the good and unpopular show. That's *The Storyteller*.

In the best possible world you want one of those wonderful things like *My Fair Lady* or *Death of a Salesman*, which is, on all levels, a success.

A mass audience responded to *Roots*. In our view *Roots* was, aesthetically, highly flawed. And *Holocaust* was aesthetically highly flawed. Now the interesting aspect of *Holocaust* is that we didn't think it was a good show. We didn't think it was well done. However, its social ramifications transcend the narrow view of aesthetics: the very fact that the statute of limitations in Germany was extended, possibly because of *Holocaust*, the very fact that people were reminded!

Q. *So "good" for you, in many ways, leans on the social side? You do concern yourself with social impact?*

In that sense "good" for us does lean toward social significance, yet we secretly feel that television has very little effect—the effect we intend, let's put it that way. It certainly has an effect over time. We're still confused about that.

CREATIVE CONTROL

[LEVINSON AND LINK] At the Writers' Guild of America there are endless discussions about "We want creative control." And the answer to that is, the only way to get creative control is to hyphenate, to become a writer-producer. Many writers don't want to spend their mornings yelling on the telephone. They don't want to get their hearts under that kind of pressure. And, of course, they always point out that the final option is the network's. For ten years in film for television we had as close to creative autonomy as you could get. However, the studio could supersede us, and did on occasion. And the network is the final arbiter. Fortunately for us, after you've had some successes they tend to leave you alone.

Here again, you're dealing with people. You're not dealing with monolithic black towers. There are a lot of nice people and there are some bad people. Usually you scratch their back and they scratch yours. But we do lose. For instance, we did not want the title of *Murder by Natural Causes* changed from *our* choice, *Natural Causes*. We were simply overruled. Now we could have possibly said, "We'll never work for CBS again." We might have been able to get our title back again. But you don't want to use up your capital that way. And of course this wasn't *Slovik*. If they had tried to superimpose their title on one of our serious pictures—No Way!

When the producer knows where the network draws the line and will not cross it, that's what Chayevsky calls pre-censorship. First of all you have to distinguish, as always, between a series and a one-shot. For example, *Columbo* was finished, the first six shows were finished before it went on the air, which creates one environment. Other shows go on the air and you begin getting reactions to them. Then the network has a lot of power—*if you are failing*.

The one-shot is finished before it's exposed and therefore you have more room to negotiate. Because if you're failing in a series, which is getting low ratings, you are very vulnerable and there's very little you can do because you haven't got a talking point. In *Columbo* we took a very strong position against the network that wanted the lead character, as in traditional, to make an entrance very early in the show. We convinced them. We're talking about the head of the network. We convinced him we were right by pretending a confidence that we didn't necessarily feel.

Also, the summer before a series goes on the air, everybody, networks included—it's the nature of the medium—tends to be very busy. So there are loopholes through which one can slip. And we have used them on occasion.

An example: We want a certain actor to play the lead in *Columbo*. We call our liaison to the network and say, "We would like so-and-so." They say, "We don't want him; he doesn't mean anything. We would rather get Laurence Olivier. Or, I'm sorry, we'd rather get Paul Newman." And sometimes they make suggestions that are ludicrous. We say, "We can't get Paul Newman." And they say, "Well, you can try."

So we play a game that they are half aware we are playing, which is this. We pursue Paul Newman. We pursue others. Meanwhile, we call the actor we want and tell him what we are doing, and say please stand by. The night before the show is to film we call our liaison at the network and whine and complain and say we have tried so-and-so, and so-and-so, and so-and-so. In good faith we may have tried some of them. Others may not have been tried. Now the liaison may know he's being tricked or he may not know and he says, "Alright, alright, you gotta shoot tomorrow, go with who you want." Bingo!

Now what they've done is display their power, but finally give you what you want. Muscle flexing. So it may, in a sense, be a psychological ploy to show you who the boss is, but the fact of the matter is, you've wasted energy, but you've gotten what you want. Other times they can be persuaded by reason. But they can be more malleable if you are powerful. You will win and you will lose, but you will always lose if you never take a stand.

If you're a producer who creates an image, you have another bid in that on a one-shot that you care very much about they realize you can come up and feed that network a good idea for a series. They'll sometimes be more lenient and be off your backs much more because they figure a little way down the road you're going to feed them a television series that might become quite popular. That's another bit of leverage.

Yes, you can win battles. One lesson we've learned is that we tend to do things better when we have a certainty about us. When we are genuinely confused about a creative choice it gets difficult because as soon as there is a vacuum, someone will fill it and that someone is usually the network. They will make your decisions for you if you vacillate. If you are strong and reasonable and have a history with these people of responsible conduct, you can get your way frequently, though not always.

Television is an industry of the track record. That's so important. The tendency is to say, "Well, if Dick and Bill really want Marty Sheen for *Slovik*, even though we want Jeff Bridges, they're the creative people, let them have what they want. We're doing this for prestige reasons: we don't expect high numbers on this. They've been productive for us in other areas. We don't want them angry. They tend to blow up and get temperamental. Indulge them."

One line we've got to hand you. Somebody said the other day, "Television is a business of people, not ideas." You going in with an idea and us going in with an idea, the *same* idea, if they won't buy it from you, they will buy it from us—for human reasons.

Almost anything that we want to do would be accepted by one of the three networks. I mean we have literally carte blanche. You can't do anything pornographic. The industry has limitations. What we have found is that in theatricals we just don't have control that we do when we write and produce our television dramas. Virginia Carter, vice president of Embassy Pictures, is correct when she observes that "Everyone wants greater control." There's no reason why the producer should have it. There's no reason why the director should have it. Whoever can get it will get if they want it.

It's what William Goldman, in his book *The Season,* called "the muscle." Every production has a muscle. We believe that the purpose of all this stuff, of everybody, is to tell a story. And we believe in the primacy of the writer. We believe everyone else is an interpretive artist. We've had many arguments and an actor will say, "What about when I'm improvising? Is that interpreting?" And we say, "No, that's writing. You are then the writer."

We believe in the primacy of the writer and we know that somebody has to have an organizing vision. The economic nature of television, happily for us, makes that somebody the producers. Now the ideal hyphenate is the writer-producer-director. We simply can't direct.

SOCIAL RESPONSIBILITY AND EFFECTS

[LEVINSON AND LINK] When we began writing for television, we did the westerns and the private-eye shows and made no moral distinctions. This is part of the times and the period. Then, with the spate of assassinations, we said, "Wait a minute. We have no idea whether television contributes to this general tone or not, but we don't want to do it."

Now there are many writers who take the position that fairy tales are violent, Shakespeare is violent, and that it's not violence, it's action. They see it as a reflection of society that is violent. We, on the other hand, determined in 1969 to move away from violent shows. *Columbo* is a non-violent show. It starts with a bloodless murder and then it's a cat and mouse game. The Columbo character does not carry a gun. There are no chases. It's rather a static show. It was a conscious decision on our part.

Now as for *Mannix,* when we created *Mannix* it was before we developed that kind of social conscience. We had nothing to do with the series. And the people who made it—we think made it well—don't agree with us.

There are arguments among writers and among producers about violence. Many people feel that it has no effect, that it's exciting, that the audience perceives that it's make-believe, that it's legitimate conflict. *Mannix* is a violent show. *Starsky and Hutch* is a violent show. Many, many popular shows are very violent. We just don't want to do that. And there are many who disagree with us. But, we would add, it's harder to do a non-violent show than a violent one.

See, it would seem if we would do a movie for television like *My Sweet Charlie,* which is thematically about "the races can live in harmony," that that has a liberal beneficial effect. But it probably doesn't "take" as far as the mass audience goes. Whereas violence, we think, has a negative effect. You solve problems through the use of violence. You get that on every night and kids watch it from three years old and up. That would seem to have some type of negative mass effect, although no one can prove that. It's just a suspicion we have, and other people as well.

Of course, if you believe George Gerbner, Dean of the Annenberg School of Communication at the University of Pennsylvania, and others, there's a reinforcement of racist, and elitist, and anti-feminist, and anti-age, a reinforcement of totally establishment values as opposed to more radical and theoretically humane attitudes. Television eschews those and deals primarily with establishment values. And if television does reinforce establishment values in any given country it may be damaging to the fringe areas of humanity.

In Ben Stein's book *The View from Sunset Boulevard,* he discusses *Columbo* going against the very rich people, but that was not intentional on our part. That was for purposes of drama and juxtaposition and contrast. But what's a black kid take out of that? What does a Chicano kid take?

The Stein book has some interesting half-truths in it and we would say that he's more right than some people seem to think. But there are too many exceptions. And if there is a conspiracy, it's simply the fact that when a lot of people make a lot of money, certain political attitudes come along with the vested interest. Either the guilt about "I had too much, therefore I'm concerned about my fellow man,'' or the conservative sense, ''I got it and I want to hang onto it.''

As we sometimes say, there aren't any shows putting down welfare on television. There is a liberal cast. We might say that there is a liberal cast because it is the right attitude that anyone enlightened would have. One could make that statement.

One of the problems in television is that everyone says it's junk. But there are some shows, like the *Mary Tyler Moore Show* and the Norman Lear shows, which are very well done public entertainment. If you're going to do entertainment, you might as well do it very well. We think that people can rightly object to the badly done popular entertainment.

The movies for television, the so-called ''socially oriented'' dramas, those are one at a time. You have more money; you have more time to make them. You somehow care about them. And those are the things we're proudest of.

In the fifties, the ''Golden Age,'' there was the anthological period when people like Paddy Chayevsky and Reginald Rose and Rod Serling were writing little closet dramas, little slices of life, kitchen-table dramas, and they were quite good. And then the wasteland took over for many years, and you had your westerns and your private eyes.

And in the past ten years there have been two significant trends in television. One is Norman Lear opening to intelligent and reasonably adult situation comedy. And the other is the movies for television dealing with subjects, taboo subjects, that reach forty million people. The question you must ask yourself is whether or not you *reach* thirty or forty million people with a piece of work you do. Do you really change them? We don't know.

The best play about American marriage may be *Who's Afraid of Virginia Wolff?* and we feel that people don't come out of that theatre with ''Oh, my God, I've gotten a great insight into my marriage; now I will change.'' We do a show saying homosexuals have a right to conduct themselves the way they choose. We don't know that people are suddenly going to say, ''My God, we've seen this show and let's change. We're going to be kinder to homosexuals.'' Or *My Sweet Charlie* and ''We're going to be kind to blacks.'' We doubt very much whether, as much as many people in the business think, they have this mighty influence. We think all of it together, night after night, year after year, may have a little bit of effect.

There was a movie on TV two or three years ago, called *A Case of Rape*. It was quite famous. It was non-exploitative. And there was social legislation in Sacramento which changed the rape laws in the state of California which made it much more slanted toward the woman victim. That was a definite case in point where one television program enacted social change.

So we go back and forth. That's not the answer to your question. The answer is really that you have to have some awareness that you may have an influence. You have to have some respect for what you are doing and some respect for your audience. And then the majority of problems are creative. One doesn't sit down and say, "What are the social implications" unless you are treading on a very fine line. And a few of the shows we've done are like that. How is it to show homosexuality to forty million people? Is this going to be upsetting to them? Taste comes into it. Your responsibility really is to write as well as you can, produce as well as you can, cast as well as you can. You've a creative responsibility.

Earl Hamner

Earl Hamner held his first job in broadcasting with a Cincinnati radio station, WLW, where he was a part of the writing staff. From there he moved to New York as a staff writer for NBC radio. His first assignment in television came with *Today* followed by writing for *Matinee Theatre* and *Theatre Guild of the Air*. Following the writing of two novels, one of which was *Spencer's Mountain,* later a theatre film, Hamner moved to California where he wrote for dozens of major series. Then in 1971 he adapted his novel *The Homecoming* for CBS-TV and that in turn led to the series *The Waltons*. He followed that success with *Apple's Way*. In 1981 he began production of *Falcon Crest* for CBS. Hamner has been associated with Lorimar since the beginning of *The Waltons*. Hamner has also been responsible for several movies for television including *Heidi* and *Charlotte's Web*.

Hamner was born in the Blue Ridge town of Schuyler, Virginia. He attended the University of Richmond and Northwestern University.

Earl Hamner's production of *The Waltons* presents one of the purest examples of the central theme of this book. He was writer, producer, executive producer, and narrator. He created *The Homecoming,* the pilot for the series. And near the show's end he produced a documentary study of the program, an affectionate tribute in which his "fictional family" was introduced to the "real" family members on whom their characters were based. His involvement was detailed and extensive, a daily immersion in questions of story, casting, design, and overarching concept. The show was not, however, a new direction for Hamner, some brilliant stroke of insight into what was missing from television. It was rather an extension of a career focused on the personal and the regional, on special experiences that would have great potential for mass appeal.

When he created *The Waltons,* Hamner was a successful television writer who had worked on several shows. In addition, he had written a strong novel, *Spencer's Mountain,* which had been made into a movie of the same title. Always, his strongest work had been selected from personal experience, which is common among all sorts of writers, but takes on special significance for Hamner. A committed regionalist, he places himself in the line of southern story-tellers stretching from local colorists to the latest novelists. The role of the writer, as his character John Boy makes clear, is central to cultural and social coherence. It is as the mature, experienced, remembering John Boy that Hamner speaks his framing narration for each episode of *The Waltons.* Throughout his interviews the primacy of the writer emerges as a constant theme. While most self-conscious producers have their roots in writing, Hamner is surer than many of them that he is still, primarily, a writer who happens to produce.

While he has taken to producing well in some ways because it gives him a measure of control beyond that associated with the script, he clearly dislikes other aspects of the position.

I do enjoy being on the production side, approving costumes, approving location or suggesting costumes, props, etc., seeing us come in on time and on budget, discovering new talent and taking the chances on young, untried people. . . .

I think basically business and art are at war with each other. Sometimes we would have a richer scene with more extras, but probably because I have a percentage of the show I say, "Let's go with twenty rather than forty." As producer I don't think a great deal about the business aspect of it when I'm trying to come up with an idea. I am aware that that TV is a business and that in order for it to be successful the concept or the idea has to be one that will appeal to a large enough audience to allow it to stay on the air in the first place. But I try not to get bogged down by considerations like: Will a sponsor like this particular idea? or, Is this offensive to an audience?

What Hamner does enjoy is the opportunity to tell stories that appeal to a mass audience because of, rather than in spite of, the special, identifiable qualities of those stories. This special sense puzzled the typical Hollywood television production community. As Hamner put it, ''none of the other executives at Lorimar Productions ever understood what made *The Waltons* work.'' Hamner realized from the beginning, however, that his show operated simultaneously out of a long tradition and in opposition to conventional television programming.

> From *Leave It to Beaver* as one of the earliest shows down to a modern show like *Family,* there has been a trend away from cardboard cutout figures toward people with more reality, more dimension, more meaning to our lives. For reasons I've never been able to figure out, in today's society, the family does seem to be in danger. And I hope that television can remedy that or be an antidote to the disintegration of the family because the family has always been the unit through which society has survived. I would hope that through television shows, like *Family,* like *The Waltons,* we can show that families are valuable, can be a uniting influence, can provide stability and some solid base in a society that seems to be trembling on the brink of disaster most of the time.

This particular vision of what his show meant formed the center of a complex interaction of history and memory, society and individual, fiction and reality. From its inception *The Waltons* was taken to task for its idealizations. Hamner's responses notwithstanding, the picture of America's Great Depression that emerges from the series is a partial one. Economic strain is evident, but is more apt to be masked by a creative response than by depictions of ruined and wasted lives. One need not question or doubt Hamner's account of his own family's experience to realize that the show has no intention of analyzing or criticizing specific political and economic choices that pushed the nation to the brink of *that* disaster. It is not, in that sense, historical. Its thrust is toward memory. It transcends Hamner's personal memories pre-

Earl Hamner

cisely because the Depression is part of America's cultural memory, and part of the genius of his conception is in tapping into that larger memory in ways that seem personal to a mass audience. There, in that great collective remembering, the meaning of the Depression is quite likely akin to Hamner's smaller personal one. Here was a test well-met, an ordeal survived. As part of national memory it is recounted primarily in terms of personal experience, passed on from the generations which experienced it to all who will listen.

Translated into fiction, this burden of memory fell upon the Walton family as viewed from the vantage point of the adult John Boy. It was presented as personal narrative within the larger national story, and it focused on emotion, on individuals, and on small groups who felt the force of large social events in personal ways.

This does not mean that social commentary and criticism were eliminated. Rather, as in so much of television, it is displaced to the personal and domestic arenas which then serve as the appropriate perspective from which to judge the meaning, power, and effectiveness of the social order. If it is not good for the members of the family, it is not good for the society.

In a series such as *Gunsmoke,* for example, we might say that outsiders enter the Dodge City community as a threat. They must either fit into the social structure, obeying its rules and contributing to its stability, or they must leave. If they refuse either choice, they must be punished, banished, incarcerated, killed, or they must be taught. Many learn, and many are punished. To be sure, here too the social order is rendered more compassionate by the family structure of the central characters. But this family remains a representation of order and authority.

In *The Waltons* the outsiders come into the bosom of a compassionate biological family seeking refuge. The "outside" world has beaten and battered them into angry, hurt, damaged human beings. The Great Depression stands a symbol of a failing social order, a system that harms individuals. This is not, of course, a sustained critique of an America failed. Insistent on making it through the Depression on their own, the Waltons are the truest patriots, ultimate believers in free enterprise, supporters of "the system." Their criticism enters whenever the system loses sight of its ideals, when it ceases to protect either the individual or the general welfare. Hamner's meanings revolve around the search for these values. Seeing a contemporary world in crisis, he offers stories about people who bought into a social system and made it work because of their deep-seated, humanistic, and religious concerns for the communal good.

If these characters are framed in Hamner's pleasant personal memories and the rosy mists of cultural nostalgia, the realistic structure of the show demonstrates the importance of the values in another way. Through Richard Thomas's career development, Ellen Corby's stroke, Will Geer's death, and the visible growth of the actors playing the fictional Walton children, the show accommodated change. It dealt with real growth, injury, and death within its fictional framework, and audiences witnessed the inclusion of these events in the storylines. As the historical time-frame moved the stories out of the Depression era and into World War II, the show's emphasis shifted to the lives of the young adult Waltons. The world of the program became more prosperous, an occurrence that reduced the tension between Walton's Mountain and the "outside" world. Some episodes took us to new locales, following the Walton boy-men into war. A new actor appeared to play the long absent John Boy late in the series. New children were born to the characters we had known as children themselves.

With it all the sense of cultural texture, no matter how idealized it may have been, diminished. This new world looked much like our own, and, at the same time, our memories of the war and its immediate aftermath have little of the power of the Depression. The people and their problems were remote, shadowy. The series took on a thinness in the final years, and when early episodes of *The Waltons* now reappear as the show is syndicated throughout the country, these reruns are reminders of a different time and place, reminders almost as powerful as our own family memories. We have known these people, visited with them before, and now they are gone. Watching the show in rerun is much like looking into a family photograph album.

In 1973, while *The Waltons* was at its height, Hamner ventured into a fictional version of contemporary American life in *Apple's Way*. George Apple was the central character, and his "way" was the way of the Waltons, plunked down in late twentieth-century America. The show didn't work. It was far too sugary, too simple. Surrounded by tough cop shows that spoke of a different, harsher America, and by the new socially conscious comedy shows, *Apple's Way* appeared as a pale anachronism cloaked in new fashions. It died a quick and merciful death, and as Hamner says, "taught us some things."

In 1981 Hamner brought another new show to the air as executive producer of *Falcon Crest*. Placed in the 10:00 PM (EST) slot following *Dallas,* which is also produced by Lorimar Productions, the show was an immediate ratings success. Its resemblance to *Dallas* was obvious, for although it was set in northern California and was not so geared to the steamy sex and dingy power-grubbing of the Texas show, it did bring its share of "adult" themes to the stories. Critics and audiences, then, were both quick to point to a lack of Hamner's former homey tone.

The original conception, however, was considerably different, and sounds, in the telling, something like a tougher, wiser *Apple's Way.* The show was intended to focus on a contemporary family's search for meaning, their flight from a pressured, hectic, high-anxiety urban life to the rural setting of the father's boyhood home. All this was planned, in Hamner's overview, as an "eight o'clock" show. That is, it would be suitable for children, pitched to families in that time slot when children often control program selection. The focus was changed, in decisions influenced by Lorimar and by CBS. Obviously, the enormous success of *Dallas* and, to a lesser extent, that of *Knots Landing,* had much to do with the choice to make the program a "ten o'clock" show.

The *Falcon Crest* that came to television still focuses on families, on extended networks of them, in fact. At the level of plot we deal with murder and extortion, eager and relatively frequent sexual activity, financial chicanery, and internal family stress. But the differences from the earlier design and certainly from *The Waltons* run deeper than this. Here generation plots against generation in efforts to build or thwart dynasty. The wisdom of age still functions, but now the wisdom is tainted by secret knowledge of past scandals and is directed toward the manipulation of power. The exuberance of youth is marred by ambition and misdirected desire.

Still, in all of this, Hamner's concerns run like a counterpoint to contemporary problems and styles. The struggle is carried on in the interest of preserving family ties, dignity, and a sense of tradition. Our sympathies lie with those characters who wish to preserve, in the midst of this modern swirl, some sense of community, mutual respect, support, and creative individualism. Even the "bad" characters exhibit a form of ambiguity, driven as they are to place *their* branch of the family in ascendency. All of them, in some ways, are more interesting than the Walton clan, perhaps because their problems are played out in the familiar surroundings of our own lives, but also perhaps because we are as intrigued by family secrets, family gossip, as by family beauty and harmony.

In a way, then, *Falcon Crest* can be seen as the story of what could happen to any unlucky Walton who might have grown up and followed the national hunt for the sun in a move to California. Living now with the nagging, hopeful sense that something of the older ways and older days might become useful again, they hold onto the memory. These are new times. *Falcon Crest* may be the "ten o'clock" version of *The Waltons* as *Dallas* may be the "ten o'clock" *Gunsmoke*. Perhaps we live in a "ten o'clock" world. It may be fitting then, that the creator of one of television's most famous and familiar families has now brought his characters and his vision into the later hour, the hour in which many viewers must live their own lives. Maybe the world of *Falcon Crest* is closer to the world Hamner sees "on the brink of disaster," but if it is, we can be sure that he will never present us with a world that goes over the edge. Hamner is a believer. No matter how bad it gets in this show or any other, there will still be reason for the parents to pull their young close and say, "It's all right. Stick together. We'll make it."

INTERVIEW WITH EARL HAMNER

THE PRODUCER'S PERSONAL STYLE

[HAMNER] It was never my idea to become a producer. I think Lorimar bestowed the title upon me as an honorary thing because *The Waltons* had done well and because my contribution had been very meaningful.

And, I thought, "producer, that's fine." But then the first time I was called upon to make a big decision I thought, "Gee, I wish I were back in my office being a writer." But I have learned, although it doesn't come naturally, to make decisions involving people's jobs and consequently their lives. Now I can say, "Yes, let's hire that person" or "let's let go of that person" or "let's do this so we can cut down on the budget. We can combine these two characters and save money." I have learned to produce. But it was not something that I had aspired to. I was quite happy to be a writer. I do enjoy being on the production side, approving location or suggesting costumes, props, etc., seeing us come in on time and on budget, discovering new talent and taking the chance on young, untried people. Today we are required by the Directors' Guild of America to hire a certain number of minority directors such as women, blacks, and Chicanos. On *The Waltons* we were doing this long before it was demanded by the D.G.A.

In the case of *The Waltons* I think simply because I was sort of resident authority on that part of the country, everyone deferred to my judgment. So even though I didn't have the title of producer, I still was able to function in that capacity. Lee Rich, president of Lorimar Productions, is consulted and kept abreast of major decisions. The nice thing about Lee is that he has a marvelous business sense and the ability to get along in the hard edge of business. He also has a marvelous creative sense that doesn't hamper you. A lot of people would look at just the business side of it and forget the creative side. Lee, fortunately, has good judgment in both areas. He is on first-name basis with every network executive. Some of them I don't even know. But, I think to Lee, who sells these shows and works with these people on really hard issues, it's to his advantage to know them. I go to meetings and I don't know half the people there.

Naturally, if I find we are going way over budget, then I get in and examine the script, see if we can, without hurting the show, trim scenes, if we can simplify scenes, or if we can find an alternate way of filming a scene. I would say that takes up only 10 percent of my time, as opposed to 90 percent of creative contribution. We have a meeting with the director after he has read the script. We do it to make sure the director sees the script pretty much as we do. Sometimes a director will ask for some changes in places where we can heighten the drama and sometimes we make minor adjustments in the script. After that there is a reading of the entire script with, if not the whole cast, at least the actor who is featured in that particular episode. We listen to the script being read by the actors and frequently make changes.

To me it all begins with the script. I know, at least in my case, I am in on the conception of the idea, the discussion of it, and then follow it all the way through in all aspects of the production of the particular script. But in the beginning it is a script, and the producer and the story editor and the writer have to get it off the ground. I think, particularly if you are the producer-creator, you are able to infuse some of the original energy into each subsequent episode. Also you are able to impart a kind of production attitude or style which you can keep uniform as a producer. Maybe it's just in the selection of personnel you are going to work with, or story material, or costumes, or sets, or furnishings that you are able to determine a look, a style, a statement that you are going to make.

In *The Waltons* the very tragedies that we had, like Will Geer's death and Ellen Corby's illness, which we have integrated into the show, have given the appearance of life. When Richard Thomas left, after having worked valiantly for five years, it was at a time in the family's evolution when a young man should move on. We dealt with young John Boy's leaving in that way. Each of those losses we have dealt with in, I think, a credible way. For instance, Michael Learned appeared in the eighth season in nine shows. At the end of that time Olivia Walton would never really leave the family unless there were a need to, some need that involved the family. So we devised a way where John Boy, who was working on *Stars and Stripes,* was shot down over Belgium in 1943. He recovered and was sent to a hospital near Washington, D.C. So in the eighth show Olivia went to be near him in the hospital. Once again to accommodate a contractual agreement, we solved a problem in a creative, believable, and acceptable way. We have a great sense of obligation and responsibility to the audience because the audience believes so in these people and they've come to know them and to care so deeply about them that I think it's as much a sense of responsibility to the audience as any other thing that made us give something extra in the way of thought and production to these episodes.

Q. *What about your current work as producer on* Falcon Crest, *how does it compare with* The Waltons?

When we started *Falcon Crest* it was designed to be an eight o'clock show, more in the tradition of *The Waltons*. The emphasis was going to be on family life. The whole thrust was going to be to try to repair a troubled family by moving to the Napa Valley. But CBS felt that with some modifications it could become a ten o'clock show. We made those modifications and one of them was to shift the emphasis away— not totally away—from the attempt to build a strong family. We moved to conflict with neighbors, conflict with other family members, the kind of thing you do at ten o'clock. I was not totally pleased that we had to make those changes because I felt more at home with the eight o'clock time period and with persons whose goal was to strengthen the family unit. Consequently, when we moved into the ten o'clock time period it was not an area that I felt as at home in. I still have the same degree of control as I did with *The Waltons* but I don't think I have the same amount of confidence in myself at that time period. I notice sometimes I have a tendency to go overboard and will find myself suggesting the most outrageous plot developments. I am really unfamiliar with the kind of storytelling, serialized drama, like *Dynasty* and *Flamingo Road* and *Dallas,* although I have consistently said that *Falcon Crest* is not like any one of those. It's Gothic drama, it's human conflicts. The other series do not have the same dimension that my characters do on *Falcon Crest*.

I must say I get more input on *Falcon Crest* than I did on *The Waltons* both from Lorimar executives and from the network. I don't think any of them ever understood what made *The Waltons* work, they sort of left me alone, but I think that they feel more secure in drama like *Falcon Crest*. They have more to say and it's really a script by committee. You negotiate lines of dialogue, you don't write them.

You constantly get input from the networks simply because they are in the business of trying to get ratings. Their considerations are not artistic, but mechanical, mechanical ways to grab the audience. I'm not opposed to that because I want to grab the audience too, but I want to do it in an arresting, dramatically accurate way, a way that's indigenous to the material.

I think basically business and art are at war with each other in television. Sometimes we would have a richer scene with more extras, but probably because I have a percentage of the show I say, "Let's go with twenty extras rather than forty." As producer I don't think a great deal about the business aspect of it when I'm trying to come up with an idea. I am aware that TV is a business and that in order for it to be successful the concept has to be one that will appeal to a large enough audience to allow it to stay on the air in the first place. But I try not to get bogged down by considerations like: Will a sponsor like this particular idea? or Is this offensive to an audience? I think in many ways my taste is the taste of the mass audience. And I don't say that in a derogatory way because I think of the audiences as being very intelligent and receptive to the best that we can do. I don't think we always live up to the best that we can do, but at least that's my goal, and I think it's a goal of most television producers. Certainly you want something on the air that you're proud of, something that your family won't be embarrassed by. And also, since we spend so many hours on these jobs, it has to be something that you enjoy.

CREATIVE CONTROL

[HAMNER] On *The Waltons* we wanted to do an episode which involved Mary Ellen's first period. The script was written by Joanna Lee, one of our finest writers. It was very sensitively done and there was nothing clinical. As a matter of fact, when the network advised us that they would prefer that we not do it, then president of CBS, Robert Wood, said that if he had a daughter he would like her to read the script to help explain to her what was happening to her body and mind at that particular time. But his reasoning was that people would turn to *The Waltons* for one particular subject matter and that menstruation was possibly something the audience would go to a Norman Lear show for. We did compromise, but not without a struggle. It was a discussion. In the end CBS, in the person of Bob Wood, did not prohibit us showing the episode. He did not say, "You can't do it." He said, "We would prefer you did not, and we leave it to your own judgment." That is the closest to any kind of censorship we have ever encountered. A couple of times CBS has suggested that we take out a damn or hell. We do if we feel that it does not harm the show, but on the whole we have probably encountered fewer censorship problems with the network than any other show that I know of. Because basically we are nice people and we deal with nice subjects and *The Waltons* simply doesn't attract controversy.

We *have* had violence on the show. John Boy was once shot protecting ancestral land. John and John Boy were in a barroom fight on one occasion. We have even seen John Walton come home staggering after having stopped in a road house, but essentially we don't encounter censorship. One thing going for us is the fact that the network is not nervous about the show. They know that we have taste and that we will exercise that taste, so they trust us.

I think it should be worrisome to all of us whenever censorship could emerge that would stifle free speech. There was something of this kind touched on in the battle over the family hour, but there it represented censorship in that the networks and the FCC got together and decided what kind of programming we were to have in early evening. I think the only true censorship should rest with the audience itself. They have remarkable power if they knew that power existed. If they knew what a letter could accomplish then the audience could rule the airwaves. But the power is in the hands of the advertisers and there are citizens' groups forming now who realize how to express themselves. The air belongs to the people and it should be up to the people what they see on it. I would worry if we were to program by government decree. I think that we should program to all different groups. No matter what subject we treat, we do hear from some people, but their voices would be more strongly felt if they were to approach the advertiser, not us.

I remember one occasion—Olivia Walton says, "Damn this depression." But that came as a culmination of an hour in which the depression had put her through hell, and so it was terrifically justifiable and understandable that she would need to use that word. I suppose we self-censor ourselves. We know that the audience comes to us expecting a certain kind of entertainment, so that certain stories we simply wouldn't try to do, or we're not attracted to. Which is not to say that we don't do tough stories. It's simply that we think we know what the audience comes to us for and we enjoy having that trust with the audience. So that in effect we censor ourselves in the selection of material or in the treatment of certain situations. Once the concept is clear I don't think we've ever had any dictates from the network.

We keep in close contact with the network, and they know what we are doing. We have one person who is our liaison person with the network who clears ideas and sees rough cuts so that changes could still be made. And there has been input from the network. You know, I haven't had much problem in that area, thanks mainly to our liaison person with CBS. She has been totally involved in the show, cares terribly about the show, and has a feeling for the pulse of the show. So that if we had interference, if CBS would call, sometimes it would have to do with the way a scene had been cut—I'm trying to think of a specific example, because if it had to do with a story plot, or a turn in the script, usually it was good. Mainly because we don't deal in controversial material I haven't had that much interference from the network.

There's a project that I'm working on right at the moment and it's a half-hour fantasy anthology, like *Twilight Zone* and *One Step Beyond,* that genre of entertainment. I am so schooled in "family entertainment" that given a totally clean, open space I immediately inject a family kind of story into it. In this particular case it had to do with a family of mannequins who become animated at the strike of a clock. Immediately following, an intruder breaks in, breaks up the family group, kills the father, even though when he kills him he's simply a mannequin. The wife mannequin decides that she will seek revenge and knows that if she can bring the intruder, the robber, back to the store, there will be enough mannequins there that they can punish him. She goes out and flirts with this young man, entices him back to the store, and then you see a lot of mannequins closing in on him.

At the very end, the mother mannequin is back in her place, the little girl mannequin in back in her place, and sitting in the father's seat is a mannequin. But he is the robber. The store decorator comes in and says, "Well, we got it all back together, but I don't like the looks of that father. Don't we have another head up in the storage room?" She picks up the head of the father who was killed and exchanges heads so that the family group is back together again.

But see what happened is that I have gotten brainwashed. I've brainwashed myself in that the family must remain together. And here I'm talking about network interference, but network interference in a good way. When I took my story over they said "OK story, but it's not really about people.'' And I said, ''But look what artistry I've brought you. I have made these mannequins alive.'' They said, ''They're still dummies.'' So I said, ''OK, let me rewrite it.'' And I rewrote it. But it was in doing the rewrite that I was able to sort of liberate myself from this set that I had in my head that says families must stay together even if it means changing heads.

I rewrote the story so that it's the decorator herself who is terrorized by these three young gang members. It's also much more timely. She has fired one of them because he was clowning around. They then proceed—they're really there to rob the store—but they find her working late and they make a clown out of her. They make her face up and they find a clown suit and they make her get into it. But in the meantime they have vandalized the window. We can see the mannequins gathering, and it gets really creepy. And in the very end, instead of the happy ending that I am so prone to supply, you see the mannequins again gather. Then we switch to the next morning and an assistant comes by and says to Mildred, the display lady, ''Where do you want these clowns?'' And she's pushing the three clowns on the dolly. They are the young gang members and she says, ''Put them down in the bargain basement, in that circus display.'' And her assistant starts pushing the dolly away with the three mannequin clowns on it and you see the distressed eyes and you hear their voices saying, ''Help me, save me, help me!'' So it really became a much creepier story and a much better story than the one that *my* discipline imposed on me.

SOCIAL RESPONSIBILITY AND EFFECTS

[HAMNER] I think what motivates me is that I am basically a storyteller. I enjoy telling stories—and that's sort of a lost art—especially in television, where a story should have a beginning and a middle and an end. We seem to have recaptured that way of telling a story in a medium where it is now commonly practiced.

As soon as *The Waltons* came to the attention of critics they pointed out to me that there were moral values in the material that I was dealing with. These values I think came out of the fact that the family that we modeled *The Waltons* after is my own family and the things that we underline or that we attempt to show are simply values that were taught to me as a child by my family in Virginia. I think what motivates me as a writer is the fact that I am first of all a storyteller, and whether it's film or television, or radio or a book I set out first of all to tell a story. When we began *The Waltons* as a series all I was trying to do at that time was tell stories about my family and what our life was like. The moral values and judgments were not a calculated thing on my part. It was not what I set out to do primarily. And as a matter of fact, it came to me with something of a bit of surprise when the critics first discovered the show and said that we were affirming basic pioneer virtues. They were simply inherent in the characters of the people I was talking about.

We never set out in an episode to say, "Now we are going to affirm the value of motherhood or mom's apple pie." Yet I think almost without exception, at the end of each story, we have said something, something I hope is of value to the audience. So, the underlining or pointing of the moral is a byproduct of essentially an attempt to entertain. Yet this particular series seems to have inherent in it the ability to be a forum for making an affirmative statement about mankind. I think it comes primarily from the soundness of my own family background.

Our show is unique in many ways. It is unique because it is based on life and has a life of its own. It lends itself to such tragedies as losing an actor through death or having an actor's work diminished by illness, as happened in the case of Ellen Corby. We've always been guided by a sense of responsibility to the audience and of being honest with the audience. From *Leave It to Beaver* as one of the earliest shows down to a modern show like *Family,* there has been a trend away from cardboard cutout figures toward people with more reality, more dimension, more meaning to our lives. For reasons I've never been able to figure out, in today's society, the family does seem to be in danger. And I hope that television can remedy that or be an antidote to the disintegration of the family because the family has always been the unit through which society has survived. I would hope that through television shows, like *Family,* like *The Waltons,* we can show that families are valuable, can be a uniting influence, can provide stability and some solid base in a society that seems to be trembling on the brink of disaster most of the time.

I've always had a prejudice against stereotypes, and this family, for instance, is not a stereotyped family. In the first place, it's based on my own family, and growing up during the depression in Nelson County, Virginia. So that family isn't an invented television family. It wasn't dreamed up by someone who had to make a deadline the following morning. I draw material from my own family: from the character of my mother and father; from the characters of my brothers and sisters and myself and the people who lived around us. They tended to be God-fearing, country people from Nelson County. Their values were the historic values that the country is founded on: thrift and independence and self-reliance, going to church and trying to make something of yourself. Anyway, my point on stereotypes is that this was not a stereotyped family. So I had built-in values that we could affirm.

Whenever possible I try to go away from images of people that could be harmful to them. The character Olivia Walton is sometimes thought of by people as being sort of perfect. So I try not to give images that make it difficult for a woman who is at home with seven children and not enough money and tired feet to live up to. I try to present Olivia as a dimensional woman, who has courage but also whose feet do get tired and who experiences despair as well as great elation. And so, hopefully, we are helping the image of women by showing in Olivia a fully dimensional, believable character who is not always right but who is not always wrong.

We try to do that with any stereotype. So often on television you see black people depicted as people who simply shout at each other. I find that terribly offensive. I think there is room on the air to show any minority family life realistically, so that we get away from images of minorities as being less human than, say, a WASP family. There's a great deal of work to be done. I have tried to get a black family life series going but there is a prejudice at the networks against treating minorities seriously. You can only treat it comedically. But I haven't given up.

There is another show that I'm taking to the networks that is called *Beach Patrol* and it's about three young people who live at the beach. Their base is the fact that all three of them share a house together.

One of them is a lifeguard. The second is a young black woman who is a rookie cop. She comes from a very liberal Eastern college and is quite a liberated young woman who came to California and fell in love with it and stayed. The third is a driver of a jeep that patrols the beach as part of the Parks and Recreation system. The story that I want to do, and it will be interesting to see what the network reacts to, is about a couple of elderly people who live on the beach in a recreational vehicle. They aren't able to make ends meet and they turn to a life of crime. They rob stores, they shoplift, they will even, maybe, do one bank job simply in order to keep living. And these young people become involved with them. And in the end, I think, they will be influential in possibly finding the couple some kind of work. I think it could be comedic, but, at the same time, I think it can say something about old people. There are loads of elderly people in this particular area I'm thinking of, which is in Venice. And there are a lot of young people as well. An old woman was killed over there not long ago by someone on a bicycle. It's a teeming, fascinating area, but I think that if the audience sees my name, and I think I've come to typify in their minds some kind of decent and thoughtful and meaningful work, I think that they'll stay tuned and see what that old man is up to now. But as you can see, it's still a story that has to do with people in believable situations, and with an affirmative point of view.

I've heard from a lot of school teachers saying that they are able to interest children in the depression era or that they can have a livelier discussion if they pick something like a television show that the kids might have seen the night before as the beginning of a discussion; and that occasionally they will give the children an assignment to watch *The Waltons* that week. I like to think *The Waltons* has affirmed things that have made people feel good about themselves or helped them in their lives somehow. It may have helped overcome adversity in the Ellen Corby case where she had her stroke dramatically there on the air. The knowledge that she has struggled to attain even the limited speech that she has, that personal example of the actress in this case, must be encouraging to some people who've had a stroke or have some disability to overcome.

In time it will be tougher and tougher to get acceptance for what I do best. The trend is more and more toward a comic approach to life. We were in the kind of T & A period and now it's gone toward the torrid and steamy. You can get away with a one-dimensional character as long as you have them suggesting that they are getting in and out of the bed, or they are taking off their clothes. It's the leering kind of suggestive television. I hope people get tired of it because I feel like what I do, and not to say that it's wonderful, but I think it's what people really would like, is also necessary.

I remember a letter once from a girl who said she was thirteen, and estranged from her family. She had become a street person and was on dope. And she saw one episode of *The Waltons* and it brought back the kind of family she had come from and she got back in touch with her family and, at that writing, was straightening her life out. I hope that happens a lot.

We had a show in 1978 about alcoholism. It was directed by Ralph Waite who is a recovering alcoholic who does a great deal of work with groups like AA. He has a great deal of conscience about kinds of things that bedevil us in today's society. We've done shows about Indians, trying to show some of the atrocities that we committed on the Indian people, again trying to present people who are usually stereotyped and often not presented in a human way as human beings. I'm beginning to sound like a Baptist preacher, but I think that what you see on any television show reflects the morals and the conscience of the people on those shows who have influence. I have an affirmative, upright, cheerful view of humanity, and I think that that's reflected in the show.

Norman Lear

After serving in the Air Force in World War II Norman Lear returned home to enter business and moved to Los Angeles after an unsuccessful venture producing novelties in New York. While involved as a salesman Lear collaborated with Ed Simmons in writing comedy, soon selling work to local comedians. After selling one routine to Danny Thomas, Lear and Simmons were signed by David Susskind to write for *The Ford Star Review*. This led to the writing of all the Jerry Lewis and Dean Martin shows for the *Colgate Comedy Hour*. Lear soon began writing on his own and in 1959 teamed with Bud Yorkin to form Tandem Productions. The company produced several theatre films, *Come Blow Your Horn, Never Too Late, Divorce American Style*. Alone, Lear wrote the script for *The Night They Raided Minsky's*, was executive producer of *Start the Revolution Without Me*, and directed *Cold Turkey*. Moving back to television Lear and Yorkin produced *All in the Family* in 1971 for CBS. There followed *Sanford and Son* (1972), *Maude* (1972), *Good Times* (1974), and, under a new TAT label, *The Jeffersons* (1975), *Hot l Baltimore* (1975), and *One Day at a Time* (1975). Syndicated series by Lear included *Mary Hartman, Mary Hartman* (1976), *Forever Fernwood* (1977), *All That Glitters* (1977), *America 2Night* (1978), and *The Baxters* (1979). Leaving active TV production in 1978, Lear continued with occasional series such as *Palmerstown, USA* (1980). In 1982 Lear founded People for the American Way and in the same year he acquired Embassy Films.

Lear is a native of Connecticut and attended Emerson College, Boston.

We went over to CBS one day and the guys in the programming department said, ''We want you to look at something and give us your honest reaction to it.'' It was before we went on the air with the *Mary* show and we were feeling pretty good about it, cocky about it. We felt it was going to be *the* show. Then we sat down and watched *All in The Family* and we came out with very mixed feelings. We were very impressed that something was going to be that competitive with us. To be honest, we thought it was going to steal a lot of wind from our sails. At the same time we were exhilerated to think that the network was going to have the guts to put that on, and it was Bob Wood who had the vision to take the face of his network and make it different.

These remarks by Allan Burns, made ten years after the debut of the *Mary Tyler Moore Show* on CBS in the fall of 1970, contribute to the reconstruction of the industry environment at that time. At the close of the sixties the term ''social melodrama'' was not applicable to series television comedy. From 1948 through 1969 the thrust of ''sit-coms'' was certainly not in the direction of social or political comment. That is not to assert that the family half-hour comedies were without substance. Many scripts of shows such as *Mama, Leave It to Beaver* and *The Andy Griffith Show* dealt with significant personal decisions and demonstrated a genuine concern for the personhood of the child, for instance. A close analysis of such programming can rescue it from the easy dismissal as ''mindless.'' Nevertheless, the 1970–1971 season inaugurated an unquestioned new dimension in network comedy.

Norman Lear and Bud Yorkin had been inspired by a British series, *Til Death Do Us Part,* to develop the theme of that show for the American audience.* After initial interest, ABC rejected their idea for a series and the two were in possession of a free-standing pilot. They approached Robert Wood, president of CBS, with their show. It was a fortuitous moment since Wood was anxious to excise the bucolic humor of *The Beverly Hillbillies* from the schedule and thereby change

---

*From the beginning Lear was far more visible than Yorkin, and though a joint venture, *All in the Family,* as well as succeeding series, became quickly identified with Lear both in the industry and in the public mind.

Norman Lear

his network's image. Reflecting on his decision to accept *All in the Family,* Wood was quite candid in a 1978 interview.

> When Norman Lear came to me with *All in the Family,* which had been turned down by ABC, it was a free-standing pilot. It was very provocative if you consider what television was like in 1971. It was kind of like breaking peanut brittle with a ballpeen hammer. But for a lot of reasons I thought it might take some of the wrinkles out of the aging face of television and put television on some kind of new course. I knew it was a gamble and I took a run at it.
>
> I had no idea at all what the fallout would be to *All in the Family.* I sent teletypes to all our affiliates and told them to bolster up their switchboards. I put on extra operators in New York City. I was expecting an avalanche of public opinion. I think we got eleven calls in New York City!
>
> *All in the Family* really changed the face of television. In the ensuing four or five years we saw *Maude* and *The Jeffersons,* and other programs not derivative of *All in the Family,* but byproducts of it. There were other effects not so obvious. I always felt that the sketches on the *Carol Burnett Show* were a little more chic, the comedy on an ABC show a little smarter, a little sharper, because of *All in the Family.* It got television up on its toes and things became sharper and better. Comedy, I thought, had a much better edge to it. All of television benefitted for a period of five years and I think it did advance the entertainment level of television considerably.

All in the Family was something of a television time bomb. It injected ethnic humor and social comment into series television comedy. Within three months of its premiere in January of 1971, the show had addressed the issues of homosexuality, miscarriage, race, female equality, and cohabitation. Within a year plots centered upon blockbusting, menopause, false arrest, and impotency. And the contrast is startling, for just six years before, on the ABC series *Ben Casey,* a particular episode starring Jack Klugman had struggled for an hour to deal with male impotency without being allowed to employ the term. Euphemisms alone accounted for ten minutes of dialogue.

The wit and classical liberal politics of Lear, combined with a fundamentally optimistic view of human nature, spawned an American "tradition" in television quite distinct from the infatuation viewers in the late fifties exhibited for *I Love Lucy*. From the earliest episodes of *All in the Family* there was little doubt as to the producer's influence, but Lear was loathe to admit that he was conveying values in his work in those first years. Commenting on his series in 1979 he reflected on his initial reticence.

In the early years when I was asked, "What are you trying to say?" I would respond, "I'm not trying to say anything. What I'm doing is entertaining; we're doing a comedy show. Isn't it funny?" But gradually I began to realize that I was not being honest with myself. Of course our primary obligation in theatre is to entertain and I've never lost sight of that. If we couldn't make a story entertaining we would not do the story. But I didn't feel the obligation was to make an audience laugh only. An audience is entertained when it's involved, involved to the point of tears or laughter. So I began openly to say, "I don't feel any obligation *just* to make an audience laugh; I feel an obligation to treat an audience to the best we could provide in dramatic entertainment—laugh or cry."

When I was asked whether I had a *right* to say the things that were said in the shows, in the early days I would avoid admitting that we did more than entertain. Then I began to realize that I was 50 years old, a grown man, with responsibilities and attitudes, and why wouldn't I have thoughts and why wouldn't my work express them? And of course it did! Then it became a question of openly saying, "Yes, as a full grown human being with children and concerns and attitudes, who reads a couple of newspapers a day and pays a lot of attention to what is happening to the younger generations, there is much to talk about, much that interests me." I determined that I need not be apologetic for saying, "Yes."

And neither was Lear apologetic about being an active and respected citizen of the television industry. As a leader he brought vigor to the Producers' Caucus and was largely responsible for their lawsuit against the Family Viewing Time concept. His strength of personality often galvanized producers in the community and, as many attest in this volume, he is a touchstone of comparison on numerous questions related to television production.

The early literature on *All in the Family* makes it clear that from the beginning critics were quick to observe political and social comment in Lear's productions. And the viewing public knew. Yet agree or disagree with Norman Lear, millions watched and made *All in the Family,* and the shows that followed, unqualified successes. Lear respected his audience and sought to elicit from viewers opinions, responses, disagreements. The Smothers Brothers had addressed similar issues some years before on CBS, but even the most ardent admirers of their comic style would have to admit that it was a series of liberal statements intercut with quality entertainment. Lear demanded something different; he asked the viewer to debate the issues, confront the problems, disagree.

Lear's commitment to his concerns and attitudes, and his dedication to social justice, distinguish the productions that bear his name. The wedding of serious issues and comedy, in satire, was not new for television, of course. Even before the brilliant pioneering of the Smothers Brothers, using a sermonic style, *That Was the Week That Was* attended to serious events with high humor. Lear moved beyond these predecessors by developing production muscle in relation to the networks and creating family comedy without the necessity of stand-up comic routines by established performers. Series like *Mama* and *Father Knows Best* and *Leave It to Beaver* had employed light comedy to focus upon human relations, an important ingredient of the Lear comedies as well. But the earlier efforts saw family as a protective shield, warding off external forces. Home was happy, secure, serene. If tempests arose, they would ultimately be calmed there as well, and nothing ever suggested that the security could fail. In addressing problems that lay beyond hearth and home Lear introduced dimensions of fear and doubt into the heart of the family unit, altering the entire concept of the situation comedy.

Since the fifties there has been a sizeable discussion on the national level concerning television program content. The targets have traditionally been sex and violence, but as that debate continued through the seventies, the focus of attack centered more and more on the performance of producers like Lear who were expanding areas of dramatic and comedic concern. The forces that attack television content in the eighties are substantially concerned about the successors of Norman Lear rather than of Aaron Spelling. In making television comedy a forum for the exploration of ideas about the social order, Lear has placed on the public agenda attitudes about some very serious questions. In the process he has created a new American television form. And while such innovation is to be expected in a young medium such as television, and will occur repeatedly in the future, Lear stands nevertheless as a trail-blazing pioneer in contemporary American popular culture.

Much of his success in this role clearly derives from his personal force. He refused to alter his style in the face of network pressure. His mixing of anger, decible-level, earthy language, compassion, and pressing external forces resulted in the creation of a unique group of television families for the seventies. Aware that those components coupled with comic relief provided the key to the appeal of *All in the Family* and its successors, Lear was immovable against efforts to tamper with his style.

The hero in the Lear comedies was inevitably flawed, often bigoted, but human, open to being liked in spite of his faults. Lear is fond of saying that Archie is his father, that the anger and noise of the Bunker family reminded him of his own environment as a child in Connecticut. Such single-minded commitment to his production, such a personal identification, meant that his series sparkled with his touch as writer-producer.

And that producer's touch, always in evidence, came to focus when Lear formed his own company, TAT Communications, in 1974. Shortly thereafter he moved his operation from CBS headquarters to Metromedia on Sunset Boulevard. Since Lear continued his association with Tandem, which he formed with Bud Yorkin in 1959, the company that had produced *All in the Family,* the combined activity at Metromedia was commonly labeled Tandem/TAT. There he expanded the control we have identified as central to the writer-producer. Yet one looks in vain for the term "control" in the Lear interview. This is so because, as one top TAT executive explained,

> Norman has an enormous talent for extracting the best from his associates. He works very hard at the task and the result is total

involvement by all participants and the generation of consensus.

No one doubted that Norman Lear was in control, but his style was to expend tremendous energy to create an environment in which control was not an issue. His encouragement of debate and disagreement was not, for him, merely a ploy to make his staff feel involved. It was his producing style.

Lear was a partner, thinking and doing, a totally involved writer-producer, addressing every aspect of production on a daily basis. The reference in the interviews to the loss of John Amos on *Good Times* reinforces the fact that Lear's scope of concern for his series was total. By 1976 he was so completely absorbed in day-to-day deliberations, he seemed to the visiting observer to be the center of a moving storm at Metromedia.

> With as much as we're doing here, my concern is making a good *Good Times* tonight. It's a sensitive show and I want it to be right. [The episode concerned the death of James Evans.] *Maude* on Tuesday night—we're doing a fairly sensitive, *very* funny show. [The episode concerned funeral parlor activities.] And I will see a run-through of it tomorrow night. So it'll be my concern tomorrow. And next Monday we will read the first *All in the Family* and I will be involved in how that is coming off. So during each day and at the conclusion of most days, I am either reaching a reading of a new script, a run-through of a show that is in progress, or a taping of a show. All of this I am involved in and concerned with and that leaves me absolutely no time to ponder the momentous problems related to television impact.

In fact such a disclaimer is not entirely accurate, for during those years Lear "pondered" as a natural ingredient of his personality. He lived the various series night and day, including weekends. But he lived them in the context of the viewing public. A case in point was a Sunday evening at Lear's home in the summer of 1975 when he and Virginia Carter, vice president of TAT, argued the implications of a turn in the storyline of *Maude*. Should Maude desist in her effort to be elected to public office because her husband, Walter, an alcoholic, was threatened by her potential victory that would require moving to Albany? The debate centered on Maude as a spokesperson for women, a model. Would she serve the cause of women's rights if she capitulated to Walter's needs? In the discussion at one point Lear, with the public clearly in mind, said, "I think the best thing for women is to develop the four episodes so that men and women alike want her to run." The resolution was to have Maude detach with love from Walter's alcoholism and be herself. (This was the point made by Carter.) Maude ran for the state legislature. She lost the election, but in a close vote. Now whether Carter and Lear were correct in their assumption that Maude's decision would have national impact, the thought that it might did affect delineation of character. For them that evening *Maude* was not merely a drama/comedy, it was a statement.

In our view Norman Lear was partial to Maude as a personality. She seemed to reflect the Lear political sense, whether she was commenting on abortion or "grass." Maude addressed the subject of alcoholism with intensity and feeling; she commented upon religious hypocrisy and medical ethics. Indeed, seldom did Maude and her companions merely go for the laughs. "Occasionally we produce a show and fail to notice, ourselves, that we've said something that could be of special interest to sensitive viewers." The occasions were rare.

The attention to every show, the attempt to include something for interested, sensitive viewers and to oversee every aspect of production from concept to final taping, took its toll. After the 1977–78 television season, a season in which his company received six Emmy awards, Lear left active television production. He expressed the need to expand his horizons, to do new things, including features. The "new things" included two notable television experiments. On the network he offered *Palmerstown, U.S.A.*, a work he did in cooperation with Alex Haley. It was a critically acclaimed drama that touched the heart of race relations. Lear also moved into a realm of pure issue-oriented television with *The Baxters,* an innovative syndicated show that offered a problem in comic/dramatic form in a twenty-minute play. It was to be followed by open, live discussion in each locality. In the problems addressed in this series as well as in the operation of his company, Lear continued to exhibit a genuine concern for the rights of women in deed as well as word. Since the fall of 1980 his energies have been directed toward the building of an organization, *People for the American Way,* that seeks to combat what Lear and his supporters believe is the threat to freedom posed by the evangelical Christian right. Withal Lear today is still identified most regularly as the creator of Archie Bunker.

Our assessment of Lear's reasons for leaving television has much to do with the thesis of this book. In large measure it was exercise of control as writer-producer that finally consumed him to the point that he sought diversion. He oversaw scripts, new productions, a host of details in casting and the actual tapings. In addition, as the years passed he became something of a counselor for cast members and creative talent who sought relief from presumed mistreatment by others. He was, in fact, an artistic traffic-director, a role that has driven many executive producers to seek quieter spaces. By 1977 this responsibility was, we believe, taking its toll, and yet Lear wisely recognized that, for him, it was total production involvement or none at all. In 1978 he opted for the latter.

In Lear's place Alan Horn, an able executive, became chief operating officer of Tandem/TAT. Few critics would be prepared to affirm that the shows born in the new era were of the same quality as had been the earlier efforts. NBC might well find cause, in its third-place role, to sing the praises of *Diff'rent Strokes,* but it is hard to imagine that series, as it existed in 1981, as a product of the gifted Lear. Even a show such as *Hello Larry,* which reflected the Lear concern for issues, exuded moral lessons devoid of the crackling wit of earlier days. The deft mixing of moral concern and humor in appropriate doses that made *All in the Family* a landmark, that made the satirical *Mary Hartman, Mary Hartman* a syndication classic, are lacking in the company's presentations in comedy in the eighties.

Norman Lear is a moralist, a social critic, and an able business executive. He combined those qualities with a gift in writing comedy in such a way as to "change the face of television." His penchant for getting on the air in November issues he encountered in September was a marvellous, fresh understanding of the potential for television comedy. His fundamental optimism and his commitment to the family and to traditional American virtues of freedom and justice generated an effective counterpoint to network pressures. And while Lear did not provide viewers with serenity, he, along with MTM, produced 25 percent of Nielsen's top fifteen from 1971 through 1978.

INTERVIEW WITH NORMAN LEAR

THE PRODUCER'S PERSONAL STYLE

[LEAR] In theatrical films there are "creative" producers, but most of them are business people, who put together deals, bring in strong creative people, and hope for the best. Quite the contrary is the case in television. The producer is usually the center of the creative process. It is he or she who sees the project through all of its stages from inception to broadcast. From working with the writers in the development of the treatment, to writing the teleplay, to casting, to rehearsal, to rewrite, to taping, to editing, to promoting the show, to the airing. There are only a few of us who came up from the writing ranks, and so we're in the trenches in a way that non-writing producers can never be.

Garry Marshall and John Mantley are examples of other producers who also began as writers. So in addition to whatever strength we might have as producers and thinking adults, if something is wrong with an episode, we can sit down and fix it ourselves, or sit with the cast and talk through the problem, or get the cast on a set and improvise until we licked the problem on our feet. That is a writer's and a director's technique, not a producer's.

The genuine writer-producer takes the producing reins and produces as well as writes. I was totally involved in *All in the Family* and *Maude* and *Good Times* and *The Jeffersons* and *One Day at a Time* and *Mary Hartman, Mary Hartman*. Now when I say involved, I mean involved from the moment there was a paragraph of the story through the development of that story to the first draft, and the conversations/conferences on the second draft. There was always a tape recorder nearby, and when we sat down around the table to talk about a story or a script, I immediately turned that tape recorder on. Three or four minutes later somebody was typing in another room because the recorder was connected to a transcribing machine. When the writers got to their offices, they already had the first thirty minutes of the conversation. The rest would be sent down later. This was a constant on all of the shows I'm talking about.

In 1976, Mondays meant reading *All in the Family* and a run-through for *Maude, One Day at a Time,* and *The Jeffersons.* That meant a camera run-through and two back-to-back tapings for each. Wednesdays, we read *Maude, One Day at a Time,* and *The Jeffersons,* had a rehearsal hall run-through for *All in the Family* and a stage run-through for *Good Times.* On Thursdays, we taped *Good Times* and had a run-through on *All in the Family.* Fridays, we read *Good Times,* had a rehearsal hall run-through on *Maude, One Day at a Time,* and *The Jeffersons,* and taped *All in the Family.* I also did most of the warm-ups for the audience before the tapings.

In the case of *Mary Hartman, Mary Hartman,* I could not be in the run-throughs because the taping went on all day long, five days a week. I did whatever rewriting was necessary in the early mornings. If, during the day, there was trouble with a scene, I would get a telephone call in my office and I would get to my feet, even if I was in the middle of a meeting, go over to the side, and talk into a tape recorder.

Men and women who follow this kind of schedule and are involved with all aspects of a project really produce. When you look at the credits of a typical television series, you often find executive producers, supervising producers, producers, executive story editors, story editors, and probably others I can't think of. Those titles are bestowed as a way of making it more attractive for the writer to stay where he is on the third year of the show. A large number of those people are not really producers. They don't assume all of the casting functions or all of the below the line functions, or other producer functions. They are writers exclusively. A producer, in my opinion, is someone who touches and effects the whole.

I hear myself saying a lot of "I, I, I," and that must be clarified. I was deeply involved in every detail and nuance of every episode of every show—no story proceeded without me and each had my input. But I am essentially a collaborator—and nothing I have been describing took place without collaboration. Describing my personal involvement as I am results in the "I, I, I,"—but the results of each show were a team effort and it's important that that be very clear.

Q. *How do the seventies compare with previous decades in television production?*

Playhouse 90, Philco TV Playhouse, and *Goodyear TV Playhouse* did some marvelous things. But I think the level in the seventies was at least as good. Many of the people who were directing in the early years are still directing now. And a number of the writers are still writing, or have become writer-producers. Some have moved to theatrical films. Television offers the excitement of having an idea on the fifth of September and seeing it dramatized and delivered to forty million people on the fourteenth of November. Film directors are constantly telling me "I was so in love with this when I conceived it, and now it's two years later and the film is doing well but it really doesn't have the impact it might have had if two years had not passed." The exciting thing in television is to pick up a headline on one day and have a story about it three months later on the air for a vast audience, much larger than ever imagined in the fifties. And, of course, technologically there is no comparison with the early days of television.

Q. *What were the creative ramifications and alternatives you had to consider when John Amos asked to leave* Good Times?

The determination to release John Amos was first of all occasioned by the fact that he was a very unhappy actor in the role of James Evans. He didn't like what he was doing in *Good Times* and I have to assume he didn't like it for his own good and valid reasons. They were not good and valid to the other members of the company— the other black actors in the cast—or those of us on the production team. The fact is, one unhappy actor infuses a company with bad feelings and makes it difficult to perform. And that difficulty was translated on the screen into shows that simply lacked the esprit for which the Evans family was known. The loving family feeling that the audience had come to expect—not on a conscious level, perhaps—was missing and they knew it.

We elected for that reason to go back to find that esprit and warmth again and we released John Amos. Now, we could have simply hired another actor to take his place. It wasn't, from our point of view, the honest way to go about it theatrically. We were telling a real story and didn't wish to drop one actor out and drop another actor in. So we decided that we would solve the problem by dealing with a real life situation: the sudden death of a father or a mother (in this case a father) and what happens to that family.

We knew we would be dealing with what it means to each of those siblings and the wife. We knew it would be a fatherless home which certainly was a phenomenon in either white or black homes. Single women raising children make up a large percentage of the total number of households in this country. We knew that we would have entirely new areas to explore in terms of the family. J.J., the oldest son, would have to assume the strong male role, with circumstances forcing him to reach toward manhood. We felt that would be very good for the character, very good for the young people watching the show, and was a very valuable area for dramatic exploration.

We were not unaware of the fact that John Amos, as James Evans, constituted a very strong, male, black image that was of great social value. We knew that not only from our mail, but also were very aware of it ourselves. And because of that, because life would take Florida Evans into other areas of relationships with men, we knew that we would be exploring the fatherless home for a while, and then begin to bring another male—adult male, father image—into the show. And that meant she would ultimately remarry. So we would be supplanting the role of James Evans with another strong, black, male image which was so important to the show. But we would get to it in a real life way—through the absence of the father, leading to the development of the older son, and then noting the difficulties of getting along without an adult male in the house, followed by the joy of finding a new relationship and seeing it mature.

CREATIVE CONTROL

[LEAR] The networks usually seek to avoid whatever they feel might be controversial. Their total effort seems to be to appeal to the greatest amount of people and to offend no one. You can't deal as honestly with life-problems, with human frailty, if you put on that kind of restriction. Writers, theatricians, should be under no obligation to please everyone. Good drama is often provoking; it stimulates people to think and feel and react. So if they react negatively, that does not necessarily mean the production didn't earn their respect. It *touched* them, made them *feel* something; something strong enough to write about. Too bad advertisers and networks don't understand that.

There is no doubt that if you have done something successfully for a network, the executives listen to you in a different way. You *do* get in the door. Not so true for many a newcomer. But the notion that just because you "have a track record" they will *buy* your idea is completely fallacious. They had better believe your idea is commercial, that it will translate into high ratings—and quickly—or you, too, might just as well be an unknown commodity. They will not buy.

When I went to CBS in 1970 with *All in the Family,* I had just finished a motion picture for United Artists (*The Night They Raided Minsky's*)—and the studio was after me to write and direct three additional films. When CBS told me they were interested in airing *All in the Family,* they also said they wanted me to make changes. I wasn't all that brave; I had something else I also wanted to do. I wanted to do *All in the Family,* but if I couldn't do it the way I wanted to do it, then I would accept the United Artists proposition. I was going to be okay, so it wasn't, I hasten to say, as brave as it always sounds. I have no idea how I would have responded to suggestions, or insistence on changes, if I had had nothing else to go to. So I won every major battle on that first one, because they just wanted to have the show. Once the show was on the air, despite the fact it was very controversial and the ratings were low, two things were going on in the heads of the network executives: one, it was stirring up a lot of controversy, but *good* controversy and they didn't want to lose it; and two, they didn't want a lot of arguments, a lot of public arguments, about what they were not allowing me to do.

Fights with the network continued and the show started to do well in the sixteenth week. Now, with the first smell of success, they would watch a little more carefully how they treated me and argued with me. After the initial episode, the biggest confrontation was over the story about Mike's impotency. Mike was studying very hard for some exams, worried to death about them, and couldn't make his wife happy. Mike and Gloria were in great pain and turmoil. CBS didn't want that show done at all. It was the first time, as I recall, that I said, "If you know what America wants and what America will fall apart over; if you know with such certainty that there will be a knee-jerk reaction here and that it won't fly there; if you really feel you know all that, then *you* produce the show.'' At the last moment they allowed us to make the show and allowed it on the air. Nothing happened, the network didn't fall apart. States did not secede from the Union. America even liked it. The network and I received a lot of letters from individuals and organizations thanking us for the new maturity on CBS. The network did hear from a few affiliates asking, "What is this madman doing in California?" But they also heard from mental health groups and from clergy and other family counseling services with responses like "Those things you were touching on in that show are extremely helpful."

Q. *After you left active involvement in the everyday production of your shows, the sequel to* Maude *created problems with the network. Will you describe your role in the final resolution?*

As you know, *Mr. Dugan* was a series developed after Beatrice Arthur's decision to retire from the role of Maude. It was set in Washington, D.C., and followed the career of a black congressman. I got into the debate over the series at the very end of the process. I saw one act at home and immediately called our producers and exclaimed, "We can't let this go on the air." It was Saturday afternoon and the first episode was scheduled for airing in approximately a week. However farcical it was, we were presenting the first black elected official, he had to be believable as a man people would vote for. I talked with CBS about eight times over that weekend and it reached the point where I told them, "We're not going to put it on the air." They would say, "Well, yes, we are going to put it on the air."

I then called to see if we had delivered the tape. If the network had the tape, they could put it on the air. But we had the tape and I said, "You're not going to put it on because we aren't going to give it to you." Then they said, by way of being reasonable, you haven't even shown it to black people. I said that I had a black foster-daughter and that I would call her and invite about ten of her friends to see it. They came over on Sunday and they were appalled. So I called CBS and told them I had had my little test. They didn't even remember that they had asked. I wound up calling Gene Jankowski, president of CBS, at his home in New York. It was the night our 200th Anniversary episode of *All in the Family* was to air. I was very open. I said, "Gene, *Mr. Dugan* simply *can't* go on the air." He said, "It's wonderful. People will love it. You're wrong.''I told him that I'd gone to several friends who were black who had strongly opposed it being on the air. He said, "You haven't even shown it to one black congressman." I said, "If you will meet me, I'll arrange a meeting for the day after tomorrow with the Congressional Black Caucus in Washington." He said, "Oh, I've got a big day Tuesday, but somebody from CBS will be there." I got on a midnight flight, went to Washington and showed the episode to the Caucus. No one from CBS was there. One man got up and walked out after ten minutes. It was insufferable. Needless to say, the show did not go on the air.

Q. *In your experience, what are the most serious threats that could lead to censorship?*

First, perhaps we should talk about the debate over the so-called Family Hour. The networks wished, by drawing a smokescreen called the "family hour," to drape themselves in the goodness of the term and convince the nation that those of us who write and produce were really in favor of violence on television. Now I think there is virtually no disagreement anywhere that television has been excessively violent, gratuitously violent, and that that is bad. The confusion is in the area of who's to blame. [That suit by television producers against the NAB and the networks was won by the producers in federal court in 1977. The networks were restrained from jointly establishing such an hour or hours.]

It is true that we who produce and write are responsible for physically producing violence, but the men and women in this community who make their living writing and directing television have only three theatres to sell their wares. So when you go to any of the three theatres (CBS, ABC, NBC), you often find yourself writing what it is that they are interested in buying. And if they are interested in buying a cop show or a private eye show, and within that context they are interested in as much action as they can get, then that's what you, as a craftsman, as a person with something to sell and a family to support, must do because that's what the buyer wants. It's so patently obvious that the people who order and exhibit and pay for the violence—and the independent stations that buy them in re-runs—are really the people who are the source for the existence of this much violence. To look elsewhere is to draw red herrings.

Some of the pressure groups that attack television for sex and violence are a puzzlement. I question their motives. I'd like to know what the PTA has been doing about the fact that reading and writing skills have been falling for a number of years. What is the PTA doing about that? Where are they on the question of the quality of teachers? I think they are an organization that needed a public relations shot in the arm, and a good way to get it was to criticize television, swipe at it, make some headlines, and increase membership. The PTA has published a book telling you what shows are too violent or too sexy. That is so ridiculous. There's no real sex on television. There's smarm and double entendre and all kinds of things television cannot be proud of— but there are also some honest presentations of problems in human sexuality—and these groups tend to run them all together.

I question the sincerity of the PTA and the AMA. In light of the fact that hospital care in this country grows in cost a million dollars a day and we lead the world in unnecessary operations, I find it difficult to believe that the American Medical Association is sincere about its interest in violence on television. There is, by the way, violence beyond our imagination occurring behind closed doors in surgery everywhere.

Now I'm *not* about to make a case for sex and violence on television. We have much to correct, but we must also consider very carefully what sources are criticizing. And Sears Roebuck suddenly coming out against sex! And what have they been sponsoring all these years? Won't somebody do a little research into where Sears's spot advertisement dollars are placed?

Basically television, like other industry in America, lives by the law of supply and demand. If the demand didn't exist at the network and among affiliated stations for television violence, the supply would never have been there. As I said, people in this town work, basically, for networks. If they don't ask for it, they don't get it. When the networks bestir themselves ostensibly to deal with protection of the family, it is phony. The whole "family hour" thing was a phony from its inception and we defeated it. And now we have the spectre of the Supreme Court troubling, and even getting involved in declaring that, in the afternoon and early evening hours, children will be prevented from hearing seven dirty words: the seven dirty words that they use all day long on the playground, on any playground in America. And that comes at a time when every bit of research tells us that three year olds are watching television at midnight. Most parents are raising children to go to sleep when they fall over. Certainly at ten o'clock, seven and eight year olds have television sets available to them. That's the way people are raising children today.

But to return to the Supreme Court decision, look at what can happen when some words are used in an honest way. I'm reminded of Ed Flanders, a magnificent actor, who did a ninety-minute portrayal of Harry Truman. At one point, the essence of what Truman said about MacArthur was, "I don't give a shit, I don't want that son-of-a-bitch around." The Supreme Court ruling, if carried forward, would prevent an audience of young people from seeing a marvelous portrayal of a President of the United States using human, ordinary, daily language, language used by 99 percent of Americans. It humanized him. Everybody's entitled to their opinion, but the point is Truman said it, and the portrayal ought to be able to be shown at any hour of the day or night. And the Supreme Court has seen to it that that can be stopped in any community. It's unfortunate.

SOCIAL RESPONSIBILITY AND EFFECTS

[LEAR] It is too easy to be self-serving, talking about one's work. But I think I and the wonderful group of people with whom I collaborate are basically in love with humanity. I think we all step off of the same philosophical base, feeling people are fundamentally good. It would follow from that, I hope, that in everything we do, we are reflecting that love of humanity. This is so regardless of the fact that we are dealing with the problems and the difficulties of living on this planet and interrelating with each other and the environment. People are good, people are courageous, people are indefatigable, people are capable of greatness. And where they do not realize their individual greatness, I think the fault lies more with all the leadership we see around us, be it in the church, politics, or industry.

Of course, our first obligation is to entertain, and I believe the shows meet that goal since they *are* succeeding. But clearly there are many other responsibilities. For instance, I have been, on occasion, a sharp critic of the television industry. Now it seems to me an obligation of good citizenship is to criticize. It has been said all kinds of ways by all kinds of patriots through the years—the basic right of freedom is to tell people what they may not wish to hear. As a good citizen of television, as a toiler in the vineyard, it would seem to me to be my responsibility to criticize the television industry where I think it is wrong.

As far as the content of the series I have produced, in the early years when I was asked, "What are you trying to say?" I would respond, "I'm not trying to say anything. What I'm doing is entertaining; we're doing a comedy show. Isn't it funny?" But gradually I began to realize that I was not being honest with myself. Of course our primary obligation in theatre is to entertain and I try never to lose sight of that. If we couldn't make a story entertaining, we would not do the story. But I didn't feel the obligation was to make an audience laugh only. An audience is entertained when it's involved, involved to the point of tears or laughter. So I began openly to say, "I don't feel an obligation just to make an audience laugh; I feel an obligation to treat an audience to the best we could provide in dramatic entertainment—laugh or cry."

When I was asked whether I had a *right* to say the things that were said in the shows, in the early days I would avoid admitting that we did more than entertain. Then I began to realize that I was fifty years old, a grown man, with responsibilities and attitudes, and why wouldn't I, as a mature writer, have thoughts and the desire to express them in our work? So we did. Then it became a question of openly saying, "Yes, as full-grown human beings, with children and concerns and attitudes, who read a couple of newspapers a day and pay a lot of attention to what is happening to the younger generations, we will write and produce those stories that interest and involve us—and those were usually *about* something." I determined that I need not be apologetic for saying "Yes." At the time, we were a company of some seventy-five to a hundred writers and producers and directors and actors, and we all had a lot on our minds. We all had children, we all had marriages, we all had concerns as citizens of the world and of this country. Our humor expressed some of those concerns.

I feel a keen sense of responsibility in other areas to start thinking in terms of the long-range future and away from the short-term bottom line thinking that seems to motivate everything today. Our country is choking on short-term thinking—we seem to be sacrificing all of our tomorrows for that profit statement, that short-term gain, that momentary gratification which we call success. Success has much more to do with succeeding at the level of doing one's best—and we are forgetting that.

As far as what the shows have or might have done, by way of influencing a large audience, I find myself in disagreement with a lot of the research I read. I don't think we effected much change attitudinally. I don't think the shows have added up to that much at all. Sometimes we're accused of—through Archie—enforcing bigotry, and sometimes given credit for having diffused a lot of prejudice and bigotry. I don't think either is true. I'm proud to say, on the other hand, that I've never received a letter from a bigot or from somebody who agrees with Archie—and there have been thousands—that didn't somewhere say, "Well, why do you always make Archie such a horse's ass at the end of the show?" It doesn't escape the notice of any of those "right-on Archie" people that the point of view of the show is that the man is foolish—his bigoted attitudes harmful. But it is equally true that these people are not changed. There are people who write, "I see a lot of my uncle in Archie, I see a lot of my neighbor in Archie." I've never seen letters saying, "I see a lot of myself in Archie."

I don't believe at all that it reinforces *anything* bad in society. But, again, I don't see that it has changed anything for the good, either. *I* would be a horse's ass if I thought that one little situation comedy would accomplish something that the entire Judeo-Christian ethic hasn't managed in two thousand years. But there have been some specific results, results that were measurable. This usually occurred when we did a show on such a subject as clear and specific as health.

We've come, through the years, to be *very* much in touch with all of the organizations around the country that deal with health: the National Institute of Mental Health, HEW, individual associations concerned with cancer, lung, heart. So when we did a show on hypertension in black males on *Good Times,* we'd follow through on what the show's impact may have been the first time out, and by the time it appeared again in re-runs there was a network of interested groups and organizations standing by to see the show all across the nation. Thus they were able to measure how many black males were calling for help or information on hypertension after the second running.

Counting how many black males checked their blood pressure after seeing the show is an impact that can be measured, but when you address attitudes, I disagree with those who see appreciable change. I think *All in the Family* is a celebration of family life or I wouldn't have done it. But I don't see attitudinally how we have affected anything in that area.

Q. *Do you think the persons in the networks concern themselves with matters of quality of life and values?*

As individuals, yes. But as corporate executives who are trapped in a system that calls for winning in the short-term at any expense, no. No more than the chemical companies that pollute lakes and streams, or the makers of children's breakfast cereals that ought to be labelled "candy." We put too much emphasis on winning today and, because of its high profile, we see that most clearly in television. Indeed, we may be raising generations of kids who feel they have failed themselves and their parents if they are not number one or in the top ten. The ratings create a terrific problem for us. We don't read week by week which cars sound best, which barber is shaving more faces, but we do read what show is attracting more viewers. Television is berserk with that, the crawling around like crazed insects scrambling to climb this tree to be number one. In such a system there is no room for innovation or for creativity. There couldn't be, not when the view is how do we get to be ahead of the other two networks from 8:00 to 8:30, rather than how do we do a terrific show.

Q. *With your strong social conscience and your admitted pleasure at using the medium to express your concerns, why did you determine to leave active production/writing in television?*

The real reasons are very personal. Often the press wants to hear that I'm dissatisfied with television and that I don't like the state of affairs at the networks. But my reasons were, as I say, personal and positive. I just felt like stretching in a different direction. I'm sitting with you this morning, as a matter of fact, in a state of anxiety about exactly what I'm going to do. I'm thinking about a couple of motion pictures. I have some ideas for public affairs programming for television. I am awash with ideas, and am looking to a variety of *different* ways to express them.

Q. Mary Hartman, Mary Hartman *was very different from your network comedies in the seventies. What were you trying to do?*

What we were trying to do with *Mary Hartman, Mary Hartman* was to make the best hunk of theatre we knew how five times a week; as dynamic and exciting and surprising and as funny and as sad as was possible. Our interest was in people and what they go through. There are some marvelously talented people who are interested in what people lived through in the past. There are others who are interested in what people may be living through in the future. We were interested in what people were living through at the moment. And I don't know how you do that except to deal with the problems that people face. So I would be surprised if anybody could point to a problem on *Mary Hartman, Mary Hartman* and say, "C'mon, nobody's going through that." *Mary Hartman, Mary Hartman* simply reflected what we who were involved in the show saw and felt around us.

It created its share of controversy. For instance, we were dealing with an old man who said, "They give us all we need to keep us alive longer—just so they can treat us poorly. So I'm alive, but what do I have to do? I stand, I sit, sometimes I lean." And he was the Fernwood Flasher. But the flashing was a call for help. It was looking for attention. It was wanting somebody to pay attention. And I just loved learning, as we did, that organizations of elderly people saw more than the flashing; they also saw what was intended. And they approved passionately.

We all truly enjoyed the experience. Not only because of the work, but also because we were dealing with stations directly instead of through networks, and it was good to have a marketplace a little more free.

The half-hour comedies that we did were strictly one-act plays, and the reason that they had any content at all was because that's the way we cared to write. I've always believed that the things that make me laugh will make you laugh. I have to believe that or I don't have any guidelines. And the things that make you cry will involve or make me cry. For me then laughter isn't as important if it's not involved with other emotions.

James L. Brooks,
Allan Burns,
and Grant Tinker

James L. Brooks began his career as a writer for CBS News in New York in 1964. Moving to Los Angeles in 1966, he worked as writer-producer of documentaries for Wolper Productions. In 1968 he joined the series *Room 222* as executive story editor, having created the show. In 1970 Brooks joined Allan Burns to create *The Mary Tyler Moore Show*. He was a producer of that series for its entire run. Other series with which he has been associated as creator and producer have been *Rhoda* (1974), *Paul Sand in Friends and Lovers* (1974), *Taxi* (1978), and *The Associates* (1979). In addition he was co-creator and co-executive producer of the dramatic series *Lou Grant*. In the arena of film Brooks produced and wrote two movies for television and the feature film *Starting Over* in 1979.

Brooks is a native of New York, born in Brooklyn in 1940. He is an alumnus of NYU.

Allan Burns began his television career in the sixties as co-creator of *The Munsters* and *The Smothers Brothers Show*. During that decade he wrote numerous episodes for *He & She, Get Smart,* and *Love American Style*. He wrote for and produced several episodes of *Room 222*. In 1970 he co-created and co-produced *The Mary Tyler Moore Show*. As a producer for MTM he also co-created and co-produced *Rhoda* and *Paul Sand in Friends and Lovers*. In the field of drama he joined again with James Brooks to create and produce *Lou Grant*. He remains associated with MTM. His screen credits include the writing of *Butch and Sundance: The Early Years, A Little Romance,* and *I Won't Dance.*

Burns was born in Baltimore and is an alumnus of the University of Oregon.

Grant Tinker began a career in broadcasting in 1949 when he joined NBC as a part of the radio program department. In 1974 he moved to the McCann-Erickson Advertising Agency in their television department. Four years later he became a member of the firm Benton and Bowles Advertising. He was appointed vice president for programming on the West Coast by NBC in 1961, and in 1966 he moved back to New York as vice president in charge of programming. He left the network in 1968 to join Universal Enterprises and a year later became associated with Twentieth Century-Fox. In 1970 he organized and became president of MTM Enterprises where he served for a decade as chief executive. In 1981 he was appointed chairman of the board and chief executive officer of NBC-TV with offices both in New York and Los Angeles.

Tinker is a native of Connecticut and an alumnus of Dartmouth College.

The Norman Lear shows are often said to mark the beginning of a new era in television comedy, perhaps even a new "golden age." Yet the evidence for that judgment is seldom based on the Lear series alone. The first of the new wave of seventies comedies was actually *The Mary Tyler Moore Show,* which appeared some months before the blockbuster arrival of *All in the Family.* The *Mary* show made a far more subdued entry into the world of television programming, a fact that tells a great deal about fundamental distinctions between the two shows. For our purposes here, it also highlights distinctions in the body of work of various producers, in differing styles of industrial organizations, and, ultimately, within television's internal dialogue.

Underlying all these differences is the company style of MTM productions. That group is curiously different from other successful production companies that have emerged in commercial television since the early sixties. Unlike the Lear or Garry Marshall operation, MTM was not the vision of a writer/creator about to turn producer. Rather, it resulted from a highly competent executive employing the considerable comedic skill of Mary Tyler Moore in combination with the writing-producing talent in the team of James Brooks and Allan Burns.

Grant Tinker, executive producer of MTM, began his career in television in New York advertising work and moved to NBC as vice president for programming in 1961. In 1967 Tinker moved to Los Angeles as an executive with Universal. He later moved to Twentieth Century-Fox where he met Brooks and Burns who were then working on the popular show *Room 222.* In early 1970 Tinker began exploring with the two men, separately, the possibility of a new show as a vehicle for his wife, Mary Tyler Moore. Burns and Brooks left Fox and were sent to New York to pitch the new property, which dealt with the efforts of a recently divorced woman to create a new life for herself by moving away from her home. Allan Burns provides a fascinating description of the meeting with CBS executives.

> We went to New York to tell CBS brass what our concept was. They sat there and just stared at us. Then they proceeded to tell us why it was not a good idea. I remember one particular individual sat there saying that their research had shown that there were three or four things that American TV audiences just didn't want. One was divorce, one was people who were Jewish, third was people with mustaches, finally people who lived in New York. Of course, about a hundred percent of the people we were meeting with were at least three of those things. Nevertheless, dumb as we were, we didn't know the meeting had gone all that badly. We left the room and they snagged Arthur Price, Grant's aide-de-camp, and Mike Dann of CBS told Arthur to get rid of those guys. It was two years later that we learned of this. Arthur said nothing but apparently telephoned Grant and Grant said he had no intention of getting rid of "those guys." He said, "They are really who I want and who Mary wants."
>
> Arthur then told us of the CBS misgivings about the show and we had a terrible flight back. We thought, if CBS is too

James L. Brooks   *Allan Burns*

Grant Tinker

old-fashioned to think divorce is a wonderful concept, then we don't need CBS. But then we thought, Grant and Mary were both extremely decent people who had been very supportive and we owed them our giving a try at altering the concept. We gave it a week and we came up with the newsroom concept. We wanted to do something that seemed like it was in the real world. When we called Grant with the new concept I think he was relieved although I also think he was willing to take the risk on the divorce issue.

Of course the new concept had Mary having lived with a guy for a long time prior to coming to Minneapolis. The network was willing to wink at that idea but not willing to go with divorce. It seemed to me a strange standard at the time.

While Tinker was clearly in charge of the new project, Burns and Brooks were given free creative control from the beginning. As Tinker's remarks make quite clear, he considers his talents to be in the area of business and management. He was, as well, through the eyes of critics, a highly perceptive individual with a style and direction of his own, a man who could identify creative people and give them the environment in which they could flourish. Further, a shrewd sense of business led Tinker to sign a unique agreement with CBS, asking only the minimum for production costs, but in the process retaining much broader latitude than other producers. Conversations with Tinker in 1976 revealed that MTM did indeed depend upon its series producers for ideas and show direction. He graciously deferred to Brooks and Burns, acknowledging their creative control of the series they produced, and remained proud of his role in structuring a company in which that creative freedom was intended, and not an accidental result of growth.

In a more recent discussion in 1979, Tinker reflected that same insistence upon creative control by his producers, but there was a strong indication that he was becoming more directly involved in series development. In part this may have been due to a significant drain on the creative talent at MTM as people like Brooks left to become independent writer-producers. Indeed, Burns was one of the few from the earliest days to remain with the company.

As he contemplated the company's history and current position in the industry, Tinker identified an MTM "style" and he was free in his remarks about concerns that the shows his company had created should live up to his standard. Tinker had developed an image, elusive as it may be, of what constitutes an MTM product. The image includes words like "gentle," "simple," "personal," and "compassionate." And overarching all these descriptions is that of character integrity and a "lack of sizzle." In a world that often boasts of selling the "sizzle" rather than the "steak," such a vision is a clear one, strong and potentially dangerous for the program seller. Still these are the qualities that seem to link the *Mary Tyler Moore Show* with the *Bob Newhart Show*, with *The White Shadow*, with *Lou Grant*, and with the more recent offering *Newhart*.

It is not yet clear what impact Tinker's departure to the presidency of NBC may have on the future of MTM. As long as he remained with MTM he was the business head, doing those battles despised by Burns and Brooks, and indeed by many producers. In a way Tinker provided a cocoon in which talented writers could produce, removed and protected to some degree from direct network pressure. Yet the fact that the environment was of the character described by Burns and Brooks is directly attributable to Tinker's quality of mind. Beyond being a businessman and a shrewd judge of creative talent, he possessed his own personal image of MTM that ensured the consistency of the product experienced by the viewer. And within their "cocoon" Brooks and Burns exercised their talents with the same degree of control we have noted for the other writer-producers. Burns remarked,

> In television the producer's authority is total; he has ultimate creative responsibility. . . . As producers the creative overview of the show is ours and we kept it on course. . . . We have in mind exactly who our characters are and what the thrust of the show should be.

There are many ways to mark the distinction of the MTM product, but again, one of the best and most important is by distinguishing it from the shows produced by Norman Lear. Viewers and critics have compared the gentleness of the MTM productions with the shrillness of the Lear shows. Some have suggested other distinctions stemming from a difference in attitudes toward humor. But all these observations are subordinate to comparisons focusing on Lear's concern for con-

tent, on the style and presentation of specific political and social issues.

As we have seen, the Lear shows deal with topical social content
in a most explicit manner. Particular issues become the center of almost every episode and the characters are structured in a previously
identified political configuration. We know them well. Indeed, our enjoyment of these shows is often rooted as much in our anticipation and
prediction of their responses as it is in actual development and unfold-
ing of the plot. And we can be equally amused when a character is
forced to contradict or subvert the bundle of beliefs and stock responses that make up his or her style. Underlying this comic action is
the clearly identified preferred position, the thrust that we are "supposed" to see. Even for those viewers who do not accept that position,
who defend Archie and his values, the message of the chosen point of
view is evident. There is, in other words, a strong attempt in these
shows to persuade, and Lear has never apologized for that aim.

By contrast, of all the producers interviewed, Brooks and Burns
were the most positive in rejecting the use of television to espouse
social change. In a 1976 discussion Brooks stated, "We had pressures
from women's groups on *Mary* that had nothing to do with the way
the majority of the American women felt about our show, nothing
whatsoever. So how dare they?" Burns indicated similar concern over
the issue orientation of *Lou Grant*. And while both men have expressed on numerous occasions their admiration for shows that address
issues, particularly the Lear shows, Burns remarked, "I think that the
difference between our style and Lear's, for instance, is that he probably would have made a big deal of Mary's sex life. He deals with
controversy; we are subtler about it."

Brooks makes a strong case for the fact that the moment he begins
to consider the issues, he feels he hurts the work. While he admits
exceptions—race, population growth, smoking—he does not believe
TV should be employed generally for the making of statements. When
the P.T.A. and the A.M.A. mounted attacks on television violence in
1975 Brooks was caustic about both sides of the debate. "I don't
believe all this nonsense about the family hour. I don't understand. I
think everything tends to be a sham. I think businessmen will always
be businessmen, and we just force them to sound different."

In spite of this firmness regarding television "messages," it is quite

clear that topics and issues of deep human and social concern surface
with some frequency in the MTM shows, certainly in the work of
Burns and Brooks. When pressed on the subject, Brooks is willing to
admit to a style best defined as being "true to character" and seeking
to find the "human factor" in his shows. He makes the point that,
even though he is constantly striving for "good work," "some weeks
I can't do it."

When Brooks and Burns speak of being "true to character" or of
working with the "day to day stuff" they are referring to a concern
that their characters remain consistent. Brooks once noted that he and
Burns reminded themselves of Mary's character in order to ascertain
how she would react in a given situation, even a controversial one.

> We did a show where Mary had to go to jail rather than reveal
> a news source. But if you look at that show it was a very
> human show about somebody caught up in an issue who wasn't
> accustomed to it, somebody who didn't want to get caught up
> in an issue, someone who just felt she couldn't back down.
> . . . So the issue was there, but muted.

And muted may be the most satisfactory definition of the Burns-Brooks
shows for MTM. Issues of social concern appear constantly because
they are often the stuff of dramatic conflict. But issues are used to
define the boundaries of an arena in which to explore character. By
contrast, in the Lear shows, characters are used as symbols with which
to explore issues.

From the very beginning of their work together, Brooks and Burns
developed their style. In *Room 222* the concern was with drugs, drop-
ping out, and racial prejudice. But all these were examined through
the central character of a gentle black history teacher, a man whose
chief concern was with the well-being of his students rather than with
the exposure and alteration of social attitudes. When they were given
the freedom that came with the *Mary Tyler Moore Show*, these two
writer-producers plunged into some of the most important topics of the
American seventies, but they plunged in their own fashion.

Much of their emphasis has been on family relations of various
sorts, and perhaps because of the time when they worked for MTM, a
central concern was with divorce. As we noted, CBS rejected the original plot line for the *Mary* show because it presented Mary Richards

as divorced. Nevertheless, the series did address the subject in several episodes surrounding Lou Grant's divorce. Commenting on that situation Brooks said,

> We had Lou Grant separated from his wife, who is the last person who should do that. We had one show where they had a fight and you couldn't help but feel wonderful because the laugh on the show was that Lou didn't go home. Later we had a show where his wife, Edie, didn't come home, where she wanted to step out, to reflect on what was happening in society. We didn't concentrate on her; we concentrated on the guy left behind, sort of an old-fashioned guy hit by this.

The most memorable treatment of divorce by the two producers came in the 1976–77 season of *Rhoda* when they determined to have Rhoda and Joe divorce during the year. This was particularly startling because so much attention had been paid in the previous season to Rhoda's marriage. The decision for divorce altered the entire structure of the series, and focused attention on marital difficulties in a new and dramatic way. Commenting on the plan before it was implemented, Brooks noted in 1976, "If we were able to treat a separation in a marriage realistically and find the humor in that, then we have done something pretty spectacular."

The second primary issue that has been attached to Brooks and Burns is that of women's rights. Brooks insists, true to his avoidance of "issues," that he did not espouse women's rights in *Mary,* but his disclaimer is hardly convincing given the record of achievement on the show since 1970. The antics of Sue Ann Nevins regarding men were always cast as ridiculous, and Mary was constantly presented to the viewer as cutting through her sham and lack of sensitivity. Sue Ann was the stereotype of the woman fancying herself as sex object and a satirical representation of male conceptions of such objects. Georgette was the conforming woman, desiring a home and wifely responsibilities. Yet faced with Ted's insensitivity, she asserted her sense of worth and dignity as a woman, speaking volumes for women filling traditional roles of subservience to men, women victims of centuries of prejudice. Phyllis was the absurd advocate of liberation without understanding, faddish to a fault.

Mary, on the other hand, was both a symbol of the liberated woman and a reflection of the traditional "girl next door." She found herself struggling for equality against a backdrop of being a high-school cheerleader from a Protestant, picket-fence environment. Much of her working life was concerned with questions of responsibility, of equality, of power and control. But the complexity of her character is revealed by the fact that though she could demand equal pay from Lou, she consistently called him "Mr. Grant."

Mary's "home life" revolved around her relation with Rhoda Morgenstern in the early years of the show. The women, with their strikingly different personalities, were presented as clinging to one another as they experienced a new freedom. Rhoda, no less than Mary, came from a protected environment. Her home was New York and Jewish, complete with hovering, domineering parents who pressed her toward traditional behavior. The story of Mary and Rhoda was a statement on the struggle of two women to be themselves, to express their potential while remaining rather traditional in many of their values. The show was an expansive comment to men and women in the seventies about relationships and values relative to the entire movement for women's rights. Mary became angry when she discovered that she was paid less because she was a woman, and there was no doubt in the viewer's mind as to where the writer's sympathies lay. Brooks and Burns never sought to justify a conservative perspective on women in society. Further, they clearly stacked the cards for decency, freedom, justice, tolerance, and sexual freedom.

Mary was decent *and* sexually free, a wedding of two traits that made her a modern woman appealing to viewing women of all ages. Two episodes involving Mary and men come to mind. In the first, Mary became involved with an intellectual lightweight. Jay Sandrich, gifted director of most of the *Mary* episodes, comments:

> We did a show where Mary got involved with a ski instructor who was physically very attractive. He was not terribly bright. And the comedy came off the fact that Mary finally, after several dates, got into the position where she had to talk to him. And they really had nothing to talk about. His whole life was skiing. All Mary's friends were saying, "What are you getting out of the relationship? What can you possibly see in him other than the fact that he evidently was very good in bed?" So

Mary told him they should stop seeing each other. And he said, "Why?" She said she was using him, but he refused to accept that, saying he was having a wonderful time. And it was left that way. That was a sort of daring concept for *Mary* at that time, the idea that people can have relationships without having to have a lasting import.

In contrast, television had presented that perspective concerning men from its inception. But the portrayal of Mary in this role was a telling comment on equality.

Another example had Mary bringing home a date who quickly began to remove his clothes. Angered, Mary threw him out and then began to muse on the dating she had done in her life, literally thousands of hours of pointless chatter and sparring. It was an excellent commentary on the mating habits of Americans and, in particular, the futile position in which it places the woman. Both Brooks and Burns affirm that Mary Richards was "promiscuous" but her decency and integrity, her girl-next-door attitude, allowed her to rewrite the definition of "affair," causing it to be thought of as a "relationship."

Bridging the distance between these concerns for tradition and innovation, family and individuality, is one of Brooks and Burns's strongest contributions to the television world, the creation of a genuine surrogate family in the newsroom setting of the *Mary Tyler Moore Show*. The relations among Lou, Murray, Ted, and Mary progressed from narrowly defined professional interactions to deeply felt emotional ties. These people supported one another in ways usually reserved to families, and even in the clearly problematic male-female relations they behaved as family. At different times both Lou and Murray had "crushes" on Mary, only to discover that one doesn't profit from a crush on one's sister. Replacing romantic attraction is the deep sense of family reliability, and even in their arguments, in the times when they are estranged from one another, the working group remains familial in its anger. While they portray the peculiarities of individuals, the overarching theme of this show, and many others on which Brooks and Bruns have worked, is compassion for one another. Nowhere is this more evident than in the treatment of the Ted Baxter character. Indeed, Ted's foolishness and selfishness are employed creatively to make the opposite points. And Ted himself is never rejected.

He is loved, protected, and possibly even encouraged to express a deeper concern for wife, child, and friends. In the final episode of the *Mary* show, Mary Richards speaks to her colleagues and tells them they are her family. "What is a family anyway?" she asks. Then she answers her own question: family is "people who make you feel less alone and really loved." This, then, in the final message of the Brooks and Burns concern for character and the "day to day stuff." They have tried to make all of us feel less alone, more loved. They have chosen not to moralize, but to have the viewing audience make its own moral judgments against the backdrop of the best character development the producers can offer. Yet those characters carry the indelible stamp, the moral vision, of the creator's values and views.

After all the debate, Brooks is willing to admit that, with careful definition, "everything we do is social comment" in a real sense. In 1970 he and Burns were bold to suggest that Mary Richards might make it on her own. But they did not have her make it by "doing issues." In their view they must ask, "By what virtue are we experts on any issue there is except . . . on the people we write about?" Their shows were not about politics or power or patriotism or position; they were about people. For a decade that meant telling an enormous viewing public that people should be open and loving toward one another, even in the places where they worked. They chose to do this because of a desire on their part not to do *Father Knows Best* or *Beaver* kinds of comedy. To us those earlier series were about similar themes, but there is a significant difference. The difference is that Mary and her friends were set firmly within the fabric of a society based in our own time, our own world of experience. It was a unique quality that caused millions of Americans to have a love relationship with Mary Richards, and, oddly, may explain why the *Mary* show has never been popular in reruns. Americans lived with Mary, changed with her, and the world of the seventies is now history. Possibly that is the best evidence that Brooks and Burns *were* true to character and true to their own experience.

INTERVIEW WITH JAMES L. BROOKS
AND ALLAN BURNS

THE PRODUCER'S PERSONAL STYLE

Q. *Is the producer the creative center in television?*

BROOKS: The word producer has a special connotation for me. I think of it as an extension of writing. I never for a minute of my life think of myself as a producer when I wake up in the morning. I do think the definition of producer may be in the process of changing. There are very few pure producers. The kind of producer that I always wanted to work for as a writer was somebody who would feel a real sense of mission with a script and with a creative idea. They didn't exist and I think the void is being filled by the development of the writer-producer. In the days with MTM, MTM was small, especially in relation to what it is now. I had real control over my work as producer. And that is true now. I don't experience it any differently except that it was more personal when I worked for Grant. It is less personal now. I consider myself as now having to do part of the job that Grant did when I was with MTM. I wish he were here to do it still. I left MTM when its size precluded the luxury of intimacy in work.

BURNS: There is no argument, today at least, that the director is the whole ball of wax in motion pictures. In television the producer's authority is total; he has ultimate creative responsibility. It seems to me television directors are for the most part itinerant journeymen, some excellent, some not so good, who come in temporarily (with the exception of people like Jay Sandrich, whose involvement with our show was unique). Most directors don't stay with one show for a long time. There are, as I say, exceptions. As producers the creative overview of the show was ours and we kept it on course. It helps when you are a writer too. There is a greater problem in television in particular with free-lance writing. I think that a large percentage of writers in the

Writers' Guild are not very good writers; they've gotten in there because of a credit or two, and they have lived off that credit. Even with good writers—very few of them have exactly the concept of the series in their minds that the creators of the series do. We have in mind exactly who our characters are and what the thrust of the show should be. You have to do it on a day-to-day, hour-to-hour basis to really know your people. A writer who is a producer or a producer who is a writer has the advantage of being able to take these sometimes less than wonderful scripts, and rewrite them to suit the show's needs.

In a case like MTM or any show that is shot like that—the three-camera shows—like Garry Marshall does it, it is a constant process of rewriting. Free lance writers cannot afford to spend all their waking hours around the show. They may write the script and then just leave it with you while they go on to do another. But even our own scripts, the ones that Jim and I did, that Ed Weinberger and Stan Daniels did, or David Lloyd, even with those scripts, we did a great deal of rewriting based on the five days of rehearsal each week. It gives you a unique chance to make something work. The person who is there all day long rewriting and cutting and adding and watching rehearsals and rewriting off of those; and then being there for the actual filming; and then seeing what worked and what didn't and maybe going back and reshooting some scenes after the audience has left to improve it further; the person who has the ultimate authority of taking the finished film and cutting it and editing it and supervising the dubbing and the scoring: he is the producer. He is totally immersed in the show; one can't expect the director who is there of-and-on to shoulder that responsibility.

Q. *How do you function as a producer?*

BROOKS: I think a key function is to set priorities and to create the goals we are shooting for. The goal has always been good work. One of the best aspects of peer and public approval is that it frees you to attack your own work, with no energy wasted being on the defense.

BURNS: In TV you do not want someone as director who has his own vision of the show. Again, with writers you assume when you have a writer in to discuss a script that he or she is going to know your character. We had shocking examples of writers who wrote a show even like the *Mary Tyler Moore Show* with characters that didn't even resemble the real characters. They were going off on their own trips. You can't afford that because the audience expects a certain continuity and that it should stay within certain bounds, not that it should be constrictive, but within certain bounds, and if it goes outside of those you tend to confuse your audience and upset viewers. So you have to keep it going along a given path.

Q. *How much writing do you do?*

BROOKS: A lot. We have two rewrite nights a week which have always taken place. Our story conferences include a great number of individuals and it is in those meetings that we determine what exactly is going to happen in a given script—scene by scene—sometimes word to word.

Q. *What kind of autonomy do you possess as a producer?*

BROOKS: Television's experiment has been successful, its experiment with giving writers control of their work. We were given a blank check on *Rhoda* and the *Mary Tyler Moore Show* as well as on *Taxi* and *Lou Grant*. I think there are three, four, or five people who get that privilege in television. I don't keep track of that. But for me that freedom is part of the effort to create the atmosphere for good work. Competing with all the other pilots that are made to get on the air in a season is not an atmosphere that produces good work, it is one that produces doublethink and compromise—the line between producing and hustling becomes very blurred. It requires saying, "They'll like this and this will test better." It involves acceptance of a lowest common denominator, a certain unflattering view of the audience and a callousness.

If you are able to circumvent the process of formulas and testing you are able to focus on the work. It's harder to maintain quality if you must go through the standard pilot process. As a producer that is something you fight for. Right now [in May, 1980] I am fighting very hard to keep *Taxi* in the same time period it has been successful in [Tuesday, 9:30 P.M.]. ABC has chosen to move it and I think that will hurt the future and the quality of the show. That's the part of the job that Grant used to do.

BURNS: Grant Tinker never sought to impose his political views in the shows. I can think of no better executive than he. I've had numer-

ous opportunities to go into business for myself in TV and I turned
them all down. Why would I want to do that? The only reason to do
it is to make an awful lot of money and to have a sort of death wish
at the same time. While you are making all that money you have to
deal with all those other non-creative things and you clutter up your
mind with the business and all those "Can or can't we?" decisions.
When you have a Grant Tinker out there running interference for you
it relieves you of a lot of that. I can't tell you the amount of times on
Lou Grant where we've had problems with the network and instead of
calling them and getting all aggravated, I would call Grant and tell
him and he'd take care of it. And why would I want to trade that? He
was out there running interference in the best possible way.

MTM, though, has changed a lot. We were all friends in the early
days, but now there are so many faces I don't recognize. Even when
we had a lot of shows going, Dave Davis and Lorenzo Music, who
created the *Newhart* show, had been our producers on *Mary* the first
year and we had known them for a long time. They just sort of slid
over and did that series and then Tom Patchett and Jay Tarses came
in to produce after them and then they did *Tony Randall*. We were
very close with all of them. Then Ed Weinberger and Stan Daniel did
Phyllis. It was sort of like The Begats, very much that; interlocking
friendships over many years. I don't feel that anymore. MTM's bigger
than it was and the company seems to be more interested in doing
drama these days, out of necessity I think. There doesn't seem to be
a place right now for the kind of comedy we did.

Q. *Do actors have any voice in script content and other decisions?*

BROOKS: I think what would be the perfect situation is where nobody was aware of whether they were having a say or not, where the
work just got done. It's called ensemble. Usually when anybody is
keeping score it's not a healthy situation. Nor is it reasonable to expect
blind trust from the actors. If you go over to an actor and you say,
"Do it this way, it'll get a laugh," and it gets a laugh, the actor will
tend to listen to you next time. If you say do it this way and it'll get
a laugh and it doesn't get one, then you're going to find the actor
starting to want his own way. That's fair. But somebody does finally
have to be in charge or there is chaos.

Q. *You have worked with highly acclaimed directors like Jay San-drich. What is the relation between producer and director?*

BROOKS: Jay and I had a lot of fights later on. We always liked each other and I think we still like and respect each other a lot. In the early days there were distinctive roles we each played. Allan and I were in charge of the show and Jay represented the cast's thoughts. While we did communicate with the cast directly, it was usually through Jay. As the *Mary Tyler Moore Show* became more and more en-trenched and Jay became more and more successful, he found it diffi-cult to have producers possess the kind of authority we needed to have. It was never mean, never mean, just some OK blowups. Jay is the best director to come out of television. I think he is the best, Jay is the champ. There are no directors who do what he does.

Q. *How do you function with other members of the staff?*

BROOKS: When you start off you are basically producing the show and you are called executive producer. As you get into the second and third season you start backing away; I start backing away and doing other things. And then the line producers become more and more prominent. There are a lot of titles and I don't think you can tell anything from titles. In Hollywood, titles tend to mean different things to different people, and in different operations. Sometimes an execu-tive producer is someone who is getting paid off and you never see him; other times he is actually the person who runs the show day in and day out. One of the things you do on a series is that you work with people you think are good, and that goes back and forth. Now Allan and I were a definite team; that's not the case here at *Taxi*. Allan and I wrote together and we wrote head to head together. We were partners. Here the business is the source of partnership. Ed Weinber-ger and Stan Daniels have been writing partners historically and I op-erate more in my own area, as an individual.

BURNS: Jim and I tried to be everything to every show: a mistake, I think now. We would try to be at every reading, every rehearsal, every run-through, every show—even if it meant two or three on the same night [*Rhoda, Paul Sand in Friends and Lovers*]. It was a mess running between two shows shooting on the same night; I hated it. Every time I would go on the *Rhoda* stage it was like walking into a warm embrace, because everything was going right, people were laughing, the audience was reacting well, and the cast was clicking. I would hate to turn to go back to the Paul Sand show where the audience was sitting staring grimly at the cast, who were getting no laughs no matter how hard they worked. It was a real temptation to stay in the warm womb of the *Rhoda* show.

Jim and I were not a team at the beginning. We worked on *Room 222* together and liked each other but it was Tinker's idea to make us a team. I think that doing that kind of show, a three-camera show, is so demanding, that teams are almost a necessity; it's just tremendously hard to do them alone. There are notable exceptions, people who work alone, Garry Marshall is one, and Norman Lear is another, but they were both part of teams: Bud Yorkin and Lear, Jerry Belson and Marshall, at one time when they were first getting into it. Who knows, it may be Belson and Brooks one day. Oddly, Jim and I were signed, sealed, and delivered to do her show without ever having met Mary Tyler Moore. It was a scary prospect. If we had hated each other it would have been disastrous. But I guess Grant's judgment was that he knew her and he knew us and he figured we were going to get on. And we did.

Q. How do business partners exercise creative control? Who is in charge?

BROOKS: I think we each have different areas we care about. Ed Weinberger tends to be very involved with the business side, and the pure production side, and the running of below the line. He has gotten more and more involved with that. Stan Daniels attends most story conferences and he's always there on rewrite night and he gets involved musically. I tend to get most involved with the stories—rewrites and work on the stage where we decide what's not working and why. There has never been a time when I felt it necessary to convince them of my way of thinking creatively. We don't tend to fight. I don't know whether they have ever felt a problem, whether they defer to me or we all agree all of the time. I don't know, but things work well.

Q. Has your attention to movies affected your activities with television production?

BROOKS: During the production of *Starting Over,* I was necessarily away from the show, but even then the revised *Taxi* pages arrived regularly and we had two-hour phone conversations. The writing of *Starting Over* was done on a moonlighting basis.

My new script, *Terms of Endearment,* was written primarily during the hiatus of *Taxi* and it is being produced after eleven shows have been shot for this year [1982]. What happens, I think, is that *Taxi* saves my mind when you have to go through the excrutiatingly slow decision-making process of motion pictures.

Q. *You mention casting. Does the network interfere in casting?*

BROOKS: There have been instances where actors came and read for you four times for something they're very anxious about and then they have had to go across town and read for network people. We try not to do that.

At a key series of readings we will invite the network and say, "Come over here and sit in the room." Network people have done that. To me it is ludicrous to do a show and say I want John Smith to be the lead because I believe he's exactly what I had in mind, he is a person I think I can get it from, and then to have the network say, "No, no, you're going to get it from Paul Jones." I don't understand how I can stay under those circumstances. That hasn't happened to me, but if it did it would be the network saying that it put more stock in its creative judgment of casting than in mine. Then I think the network doesn't believe in you enough.

Again, we don't send in story outlines anymore because if you are writing and the network says your story is no good, well, nobody can give you a memo and tell you to write better. I mean, you tend to do your best and we try and be open to criticism. I think you are crazy if you do a series and you're not open to criticism because there is so much happening so fast that you necessarily miss a lot. So you want the criticism, but you cannot give away the authority. Remember, there are those producers who are terrible and whose creative judgments are poor, a result of so much being needed in television. And the network sometimes finds it necessary to deal with such people and to cast for them, but here you are dealing with some kind of feverish hunt for a sex symbol or a guy who will get thirteen-year-old girls crazy. When you are into that kind of guessing game anybody, producer or network, can play. However, I repeat, if you are trying to do a good piece of work, then it is different and the producer must retain the authority.

Q. *Does the audience have an effect on your writing and producing?*

BROOKS: We have a studio audience of about three hundred people who respond to the show as you are doing it. The audience tends to confirm what you know was good work, but in the fuzzy areas where you don't know, and you may be trying to shield yourself, the audience prevents you from shielding yourself too much. There are sure audience laughs and the things that are certain to make studio audiences laugh are usually the least imaginative things you can do. On *Rhoda* if we had Nancy Walker break into a tap dance, people would laugh and applaud and that's tempting for sure. But if we were able to treat a separation in a marriage realistically and find the humor in that, then we have done something pretty spectacular. It keeps you honest. There is no way to feel good after a show if the audience hasn't responded. However, I have managed to feel awful after the audience has been enthusiastic. It is one of my many hollow achievements.

Q. *Do you have a style?*

BROOKS: I'm not sure. People tend to interest me more than yarns and stories. I love comedy. There are some things I try not to do. I try not to make a moment serve the joke, I try to make the joke serve the moment. I try to stay true to the characters. If there was a style at MTM it was to give creative persons on the show absolute freedom and support to find and present their style—freedom to seek your best.

BURNS: I think that the difference between our style and Lear's, for instance, is that he probably would have made a big deal of Mary's sex life. He deals with controversy; we are subtler about it. We were more content to take on small issues, the day-to-day issues of living, of just getting through the day, of interpersonal relationships and heartbreak and disappointment and hopes and small dreams and big ones. We dealt with problems, the day-to-day stuff that ordinary people go through as opposed to big themes that Norman would take on: birth control and abortion. Our issues were the small ones. I find those frankly more interesting for myself. That's what I like about *Taxi*, for example, that's why I like *M*A*S*H*. Despite the fact that there is a large war going on, basically those are people just trying to get through the day.

CREATIVE CONTROL

Q. *What is creative clout?*

BROOKS: I think that all creative clout means is that you get listened to. What you say is still up to you. I don't like the idea of using every bit of success you've had as a club to beat the people at the network into submission. It doesn't work that way. The network executives are strong men and they are very sure of themselves. What I'm hoping, what I try and appeal to, is that something in them that cares about having some good shows on their networks. And given everything else, given their profits, given happy stockholders, given a good lead in the ratings race, given all that, there is also this little voice that would, as well, like someone on the commuter train to say, "Hey! I saw a show on your network the other night, it was terrific!" I try to appeal to that small voice when I can.

Q. *Do you have censorship problems with the network?*

BROOKS: Less and less. On certain episodes of *The Associates* we actually had a great deal of cooperation from ABC's broadcast standards.

Q. *What about pressure groups?*

BROOKS: I try not to let it play a part. I've never seen a group in this country espousing any cause that didn't want to get its hands on television. I think to experience the characters I do means they must take their places in society and some of them may become involved in one side of an issue. What I try and do is just be close to the character because the minute you start to be aware of the issue and the character you are on dangerous terrain. The moment you grind your own ax, I think, you hurt the work.

BURNS: Grant backed us the whole way. I remember once, early on in the *Mary* show, when someone at the network said, "We don't like that script," and Grant challenged them and said, "The boys want to do it, and creatively it's up to them, not you. Our deal says you've got to put it on unless it's offensive. You can't tell them themes that they can or can't do." He bailed us out any number of times.

SOCIAL RESPONSIBILITY AND EFFECTS

Q. *Do you seek to express a point of view in the series you create? Would that tend to "hurt the work"?*

BROOKS: Well, if somehow I want to express myself on the relationships with my father, that's right and proper, but if I want to say how all people my father's age should be treated, then I become a different kind of person, with a different kind of mission.

We did an episode of *The Associates* concerning network program practices and creative freedom. The big challenge of that script was not the political thoughts involved; the big challenge of that script was to show how a kind of lusty comedy that we love, we laugh at, gets watered down, still not bad, but it just doesn't have the spark. That was the big challenge of the episode, to show the segment after censorship and before. We talked a long time about that, but we never said to ourselves, "Let's do a show to change censorship on television," we never did it as a part of a power struggle. We did it because the script interested us. I don't think it's a narrow line either; it's what motivates us. You step over that line and you stop being a writer. I know many people like me, where the big problem is to remember who you are and not to get alienated by living and working in this community. There are very seductive forces at work to make you role play as a Hollywood producer. The labels and the fact that you are compensated very well tend to seduce you and I think it's really important to be at war against that.

Q. *You co-created* Lou Grant. *Is it not issue-oriented?*

BROOKS: Yes, as a matter of fact, I think you can mark it as becoming more and more issue oriented, and I think brilliantly so, but I was less and less involved as that was happening. If I were active with *Lou Grant* right now [1981] it would be less involved with issues, but I love what they are doing. It just happens to be what they are doing and they are doing it brilliantly. It's not my style. True, we did it at the beginning, but what we did was set rules forbidding the use of the term investigative reporter. We were not doing Woodward and Bernstein like everybody else was doing; we were going into a paper and finding out who these people are and trying to write them. That I was very much involved with. I am very proud of *Lou Grant* and I think the people who are contributing day in and day out should be enormously proud, because they are really giving the show what it's going to be historically, they are giving it right now. I'm glad of the seeds from which it started, the same search for character and the search for accuracy. When we went to visit cab drivers to create *Taxi* it was the same kind of thing we were doing when we went to a newspaper to research *Lou Grant*.

BURNS: In *Lou Grant* we are into larger issues because of the newspaper setting. Newspapers deal with large issues as well as small ones. I'm uncomfortable with *Lou Grant* sometimes because I think some of the subject matter leads us into polemic. I think our most successful shows are the ones that deal more with people and less with issues. *Lou Grant* has very much taken on the character of Gene Reynolds, who is executive producer. Gene, having come off of *M*A*S*H,* I think saw an opportunity to say some things he felt needed airing. When we all (Jim, Gene, and I) did *Room 222* together Gene would want to get into issues. Gene is a very concerned individual, more than I am on a day-to-day basis. Gene really pays his dues. He does a lot of research and goes to a lot of conferences and he especially wants to impart his knowledge to other people, to share it. *Lou* is a much more liberal show than *Mary* was. I don't think politically you could pinpoint the *Mary* show, though there was a conservative columnist who did a number on us trying to show that TV is in the hands of the liberals, but I think he picked the wrong show. The *Mary* show couldn't be accused of having a political bias, I don't think. Where I think you see it is in *Lou Grant,* but there is an attempt, and Gene is really scrupulous in this, to try to balance everything. He thinks we should always keep a point of view but that you should try to show the other side too. Nobody would deny Lou has a liberal slant, but then most newspapers have a liberal slant. Most reporters are liberal. Most management is not. So we try to show that, too.

Q. *The* Mary Tyler Moore Show *has been described as a pioneer in dealing with the rights of women. Were you addressing issues there?*

BROOKS: Well, that gets tricky, because part of the fun of doing the show was a chance to try out your ideas, a chance to put your values out there. And one of the dangers is that you become so self-indulgent that you're representing yourself and not the characters on the show. So you try, and there is nothing else you can do but call on your own experience.

When we first started *Mary* there were things we didn't want to do. We came from *Room 222* which had a certain amount of integrity and when we started *Mary* what we didn't want to do was *Father Knows Best*. We had had the experience of *Room 222* of trying to deal honestly with issues. We didn't want to say that American life was perfect, trouble free, that all it needed was a good hardy talk and there were no problems. Starting with Mary Tyler Moore who came from a problem free, though brilliant environment on the *Dick Van Dyke Show*, we started her off on the new show as somebody who was at the end of a bad love affair, which was horrific for the network at that time. We began with the character, Mary Richards, who believed *Father Knows Best*. She was brought up in middle America, had done everything right and had not been prepared for an adulthood where there would be these problems. Mary began to evolve almost immediately. I mean our timing was very fortunate, the way the women's movement started to evolve. So not only our ideas, but what was happening in society began to appear in the show. But we did not espouse women's rights, we sought to show a woman from Mary Richard's background being in a world where women's rights were being talked about and it was having an impact. It had an impact on Rhoda, but a far different one than on Mary, as it would.

We try not to get into right and wrong. I'm personally distrustful of anything political, so it was not an issue in our show, the conservative-liberal arguments. My guess would be that Lou Grant was a pretty conservative guy, but it's not an issue, it didn't come up. The women on *Mary* were disparate in how they reacted. We had a woman who had a running part in the show who wanted nothing else but a different man all the time, we had another woman who really wanted to get married very badly. We had a third woman who really felt enormously independent and we had Mary somewhere in the middle, asserting her independence but still needing people. The best thing about the show was that they all tended, in one way or another, no matter how absurd, to be love relationships. It's about people being interdependent, not independent. I mean, mostly that seems to be what we were doing although we never thought about it that way. I'm talking to you in a far more scholastic way than we ever talk, but when you talk about it, that is there.

BURNS: The concept for the show changed several times. It is hard coming up with concepts. I mean, I don't think the concept we eventually came up with sounds like a world-beater on the face of it. I think if we had not had Mary to begin with we never would have sold that idea to anyone. It's a very mild idea: a single girl working in a television newsroom in Minnesota doesn't sound too scintillating and it was not our initial concept. Our original idea, frankly, I thought was better than that, at least to get us going. It had been our observation, and not ours alone, that a divorce on TV was something that should be done. Up to then it hadn't been. Almost everybody in America is touched in one way or another by divorce. If not directly, by marriage, by friendships. Divorce is just a fact of life and we thought it was another of those things television was ignoring. It was as if a woman on TV either had to be half of a couple or a maiden lady of indeterminate years. You could go from the very young ones to the very middle-aged ones and none of them seem to have been sullied by a marriage bed or divorce. We thought it was damn well time to do it. We backed it up with lots of good reasons and Mary liked the idea. We did not have the TV newsroom concept at the time. We had her working at a newspaper as a stringer for a columnist. We were really centering on the idea of divorce as being something that was interesting. This was just on the cusp of the women's movement, it not having become really full-blown yet. We might not feel it necessary today to explain why a woman at age thirty-one is not married but at that time—curious isn't it how that would change now?—we thought it was necessary to explain. We didn't want to make her one of those girls like Doris Day who didn't seem to have any age. It seemed to us that it was important.

BROOKS: If we were innovative it was in subtler ways. Norman Lear just took on subjects that had never been taken on before; he had language that had never been uttered before on television. We had very little of that. It's hard to evaluate your own work because you are always aware of its shortcomings, but it is much easier to see *All in the Family* and appraise it. It's a marvellous accomplishment and it is very easy to stand in awe of it. I just love that show and I think it's really important. I think it made a great contribution. I believe the common ground for us with Lear is integrity. We try to have integrity toward what we are doing and, Lord knows, Norman Lear has that. Archie is a great American hero.

Q. *Will you define what you mean by integrity?*

BROOKS: We did a *Mary Tyler Moore Show* where Phyllis's brother started to date Rhoda. Phyllis was up in arms. It was Wednesday night when we did our rewrite and the show was not working. We said, what if we make the brother homosexual? We did and at the end we changed a few lines and the show turned out to be such a great statement for some kind of tolerance about gays and gay liberation simply because we never set out to write a gay man. We got a lot of compliments for that show we didn't deserve. We were simply doing a Wednesday night fix, but we were trying to remain true to character.

Q. *Have there been exceptions to your refusal to deal first with an issue?*

BROOKS: Yes, there have been exceptions. Somebody will say, "My God, you've been doing a lot of stuff about Lou Grant drinking and getting laughs off it, it's a little irresponsible," and we will tend to listen to that because it makes sense to us. The network will say, "Meet with zero population control, the population problem is enormous." If we could do any shows that would tend to respond to something like that we do make the exceptions.

Q. *How do you feel about television today* [1980]?

BROOKS: I think it's in a slump. I used to turn on television and see five shows that were great. I'd say, "We better really put ourselves out this week." You felt the right kind of competition. It was so hard to even imagine yourself as trying to be the best show on, but you always had to shoot for that after you watched a brilliant *All in the Family,* a brilliant *M*A*S*H.*

BURNS: Everything is cyclical. *Taxi* could have been done at MTM, and *The Associates* and maybe *Barney Miller.* The other kinds of shows that are popular comedies now don't seem to be those kind of shows, so by necessity Grant has made that switch to drama. Doing hour-long one-camera shows and half-hour three-camera shows is an entirely different way of working. One is conducive to the interplay of a family of players and producers and the writers' concept and the other is just the reverse. I seldom see the cast; I'm too busy rewriting and you don't go down and visit a stage very often except when you feel you should, because it's boring. One-camera shows are boring to hang around. You wait around for an hour just for the cameraman to light a scene. You have to be a director to love that. So it's not conducive to the same spirit. Enforced sociability went with the three-camera shows.

From 1971 to 1976 was a tremendously exciting time in television comedy. There was a great deal of competition. We felt a need to be better than Norman and his shows and we respected them and watched them and we watched *M*A*S*H* and we watched *Maude* and *All in the Family.* There was an enormous amount of respect that I think was mutual amongst the shows then. Even within our own company, the *Newhart Show* and *Rhoda,* there was a certain amount of competition that was really good for us all. We were always trying to do a little better show than the other guy. You didn't want to rub anybody's nose in it, but it was nice to feel like in any given week that you had a better show than they did.

Q. *Why has there been a change?*

BROOKS: I think as far as comedy is concerned, there are more alternative places to work. A lot of people have made the transition to movies, comedy is working in movies, it's doing a good business in movies, so it's harder for television to hold on to its best writers and actors. Acting is so important to it and more and more gifted, brilliant actors are resisting five-year contracts for series. Also television is in a ratings war. It was only three years ago that network people were making speeches saying that they didn't care about the rating race. Now it's news. You can't pick up a newspaper without knowing whether NBC, CBS, or ABC did better that week. There is a great emphasis on that. I don't know how many businesses have had that kind of attention paid to how they are faring with their competitors. And it's not healthy. But it's part of the times and it's OK.

To be specific, there is nothing I can come away with after watching *Real People* that sparks me. There is nothing I can come away with from the *Dukes of Hazzard* except to say, "Well-produced show."

They do the car chases real well, but that's a different kind of producer. I am not going to say, "How can we do a car chase like that next week?" But the great thing is that everything is changing and nobody has any idea how it's going to come out. Here in Los Angeles there are twenty channels to look at through cable plus several movie channels that compete with each other. There are people at conferences on television saying the words "soft ware" more often than any human being should say those words.

My main satisfaction comes from the few times I like my own work. There have been times when people have thought I should feel terrific when I was really depressed because I didn't believe the work was good. There have been other times the work was good but I felt bad that that opinion wasn't shared to the extent I would like it to be. But I prefer the latter.

Q. *Is the family regaining significance for the eighties? What about the soap-opera style?*

BROOKS: I don't know. I don't try and spot trends. I know there are times when it seems healthy for me to get in and do a show; where I feel like there is a new series I really want to do and the time feels right. I don't feel that time right now for me. Television is great. It is warm and when it's working that surrogate family we were talking about is not only on the screen, it's part of your life. There is something about coming in for five or six years and doing good work with the same people day in and day out—it's a terrific environment. It's like an idealized company town, you'd kill to have a regional theatre like that, where you had a wonderful group of actors and you did a play a week and you were able to get the right sets and do the right thing and you heard an audience reject it or accept it. It's a lovely way of existing, it's a terrific job. I'm sure I'll experience again certain kinds of ideas that are best developed in a series and I'll be back.

INTERVIEW WITH GRANT TINKER*

THE PRODUCER'S PERSONAL STYLE

[TINKER] Our biggest problem as producers is that we cannot get directly to the audience with what we choose to make, to let the audience decide. Occasionally we get through the maze, and a show will get out there, and the audience will make a judgment and they will watch it or they won't. It is unlike stage and the movies where, if you can raise the money, you can make whatever it is you are making and then the audience makes its judgment. We are obviously only going to get shows made that the three networks want us to make or order to be made. Our interests and theirs are not always the same. I spend most of my day, I think, battling with network people in an effort to keep them out of the business of our producers, that business being to produce the shows. I am not always successful. In fact the networks are the customers and as you well know they have the last word. My own attitude, which goes back to when I first worked for NBC, is that my job was simply to get my hands on the best creative people, help them in any way that they required, but not to try to legislate what they did or how they did it; just simply to get them into the tent and let them do their thing. People like Jay Sandrich or guys like Link and Levinson would be ideal. Link and Levinson are at a point where they probably brook very little interference. They do the things they want to do, and if Fred Silverman or somebody chooses to tell them how to do it, I think they would just go across the street and work for somebody else. MTM as a company is to some extent in that situation, but its very hard to shoot down the network. They divide and conquer the producers. There are a lot of us and only three of them. We all have to do business with them, or we don't do business at all. There are a lot of guys sitting in networks, some of whom are very bright

*The first three sections of this interview were done before Grant Tinker became president of NBC in 1981. The last section, ''The Current State of Television,'' was done afterwards.

people, trying like puppeteers to produce programs around town, or maybe they are sitting in New York trying to produce programs out here, indirectly, vicariously, second-hand, and it just doesn't work. The way to do a program is to order it from a qualified producer, in whom you have confidence, and then let him do it.

CREATIVE CONTROL

[TINKER] The network is less likely to mind your business in comedy. Sometimes they will say, "That story is a downer." They don't like you to get into tough stuff in comedy. Their conviction is that people want to be entertained and that they are tuning in to tune out and not to worry. I think that's a problem with *White Shadow*, which is about real and frequently unresolvable problems and situations.

The network is usually more reactive. When I was at NBC in the sixties we had a show on called *Mr. Novak* which was about a high-school teacher. Jack Neumann, whose show that was, came to me; I was in charge in Burbank at the time and he said he wanted to do a two-parter on VD, because there was sort of an epidemic, and he thought it could be very useful. I thought that was a terrific idea, and he wrote it. It never occurred to me to go ask somebody about it. Well, as it turned out, the continuity department, as we then called it, took a dim view of the idea, and I then got into a battle with them, and it got all the way back to New York to Walter Scott, who was then the executive vice president of the network. He called me up and I said, "Walter, let me come to New York. I'm going to talk you into it if I can." I actually got on an airplane and went to New York to try. Walter's attitude was, do it at ten o'clock as a documentary. I said, "Walter, it won't be seen by the people at whom it is aimed." He was superior to me, so he was going to win. His final argument was, "They are eating in Chicago." (The show played at 6:30 P.M. in Chicago.) He thought it was inappropriate for this very well-written two-parter to play, and we never did do it. Today we can do it. Maybe there is some hope, because the *White Shadow* plays at seven in Chicago and presumably they are still eating then.

There are some very bright people who work for networks who can be very constructive and very helpful, and then there are some others, who, because the networks are now so layered, so over-populated, are doing a lot of "making work." One of their favorite activities is supervising production companies. Sometimes you have to take a very hard position with the networks. The people we have, because they are like Link and Levinson, like Burns and Brooks and Gene Reynolds, are respected. They probably have a better chance to win those arguments than some people without their good credits. When they are losing, or about to lose, they invite me in to join them. It's not a sport exactly, but I'm getting pretty good at it, since I used to work at a network. It helps to know how to do that.

MTM was founded on writers, Burns and Brooks being the first two, and then others joined us later and those people became writer-producers. It's particularly important in three-camera comedy, which is evolutionary, from the Monday script read around the table till the Friday night we shoot it, that the people who are involved should all be writers. That's what they are doing all week rewriting the show, as things don't work, or they see they can improve.

I think there's a connection between how high you set your sights and the resultant programs, and I'm not talking taste so much as I am quality, if you will, of the shows. I think if you set your sights high enough, those problems that perturb Donald Wildmon and Jerry Falwell will largely go away, or be significantly reduced. I don't mean they won't have some problems—for instance, on Wildmon's hit list is *Hill Street Blues,* because he sees it as violent, and I guess, maybe, sexy. The reason that the Wildmons don't bother me, and that I don't think that they ever will become any kind of major factor in terms of influence, is because he's crazy to pick a show like *Hill Street.* It is a legitimate entry in the mix of network television; I think a rather responsibly made show with good values. So I think he's tilting at the wrong windmill there. If we all do *better* television, I think we will be much too tough a target for Wildmon or Falwell to hit very often.

Q. *From the perspective of 1980 has there been a significant change in television since the mid-seventies?*

The excitement of the mid-seventies and its shows, the work that excited the creative people, are casualties of a fierce high-decibel competition, a competition that has resulted in everybody kind of reaching desperately. It means networks reaching for the lowest common denominator programming. Shows of the quality of *Mary* no longer get started, and to the extent that they don't, the kinds of people who do that kind of good work have perhaps been lost to television. If you visited *Hill Street* and spent a little time hanging around the set, you would have a feeling of ''Boy, these people are really loving what they're doing.'' They have that same sense of excitement and pride that the people who did *Mary,* or Norman's people, had several years ago, because they know that they're doing something that is superior to most other television. I think our problem starts with everybody running around saying, ''Geez, *Three's Company* is working, so let's all do that'' or *Charlie's Angels,* or *Dukes of Hazzard.* I don't mean to denigrate them, because a lot of people obviously like to see those shows, and they should be able to do so, but unfortunately the people who have been buying shows in the last few years have wanted it all to look like that.

SOCIAL RESPONSIBILITY AND EFFECTS

[TINKER] The MTM style is set by a lot of people with whom I have been fortunate to be associated. I think of it as character comedy. In the case of *Lou Grant* and to a somewhat lesser extent *White Shadow* and *Hill Street,* it is character drama. You are telling a story, for sure. That's important, but the shows are peopled by characters who are credible and carefully developed, and whose interrelationships are valid and consistent. I don't think that is true of all television. But the kind of people to whom I am attracted, those creative people, do that kind of work. I'm not all that modest about it; I do occasionally confess to working here, but I don't confuse myself with Burns or Brooks, the people who actually get down there and do the work. I'm perfectly willing to accept the credit for going after guys like Jim and Allan. In fact I did marry them to each other and certain other people who have been here and are here now. They do a less superficial, less sizzly kind of program, more substance and less sizzle.

Serious issues make network people nervous. Where you are doing an out-and-out comedy, and you begin to edge over into stuff that's a little too real, maybe a little too down, even though that can make, in fact usually does make, a better episode, because you have something substantial to deal with, they worry about it not being funny enough or entertaining enough. They are concerned about offending people, because they tuned in to laugh and you dared to do something more serious, so the network will suggest we don't do that.

On *Lou Grant* we had a kind of Love Canal show, and the network made us put in a speech that one character makes, saying, "Well, not all chemical companies do this." Even though we were telling the story about a fictional chemical company that was polluting, consciously, and that seemed believable enough, the network didn't want to suggest that all chemical companies were that way. I guess that saves them a lot of grief.

We did an episode last year about nursing care, and there was an organization that started a letter-writing campaign not just to CBS, but to the sponsors. I got a lot of it here. And people do pay attention. In that case, even though in the body of the show there were the same "Not all nursing homes" kind of speeches, they don't hear those; they just see you doing a story about inadequate or bad care and they take offense at that. That's what I love about the *Lou Grant Show,* its topicality, the fact that more often than not what you see on Monday night was in the paper yesterday or will be tomorrow. I think they do really a remarkable job of staying current with what's going on. What we do is open up the mind a little bit. I think we shouldn't take a strong position, though I guess you can't not seem to be on the side of God and motherhood and what's right, but if we just get people thinking about things, talking to each other, I think then that's about all that you can expect to do. If you just do personal stuff, then it doesn't have any great value; if you just have Linda and Bobby and Ed relating to each other, I think that wouldn't last too long. I think the glue is that it's about something. The old shows were fun. I miss those days. I used to spend a lot of nights here doing those shows.

THE CURRENT STATE OF TELEVISION

[TINKER] I have thought about television programming in the eighties, and it's obvious that networks will be getting a slightly or perhaps significantly smaller *share* of the total audience as television fragments off into the new technologies and other viewing opportunities that exist. But in terms of that total viewer universe, I think that *absolutely* we will be as big as we are now, and, if I can believe the research I see, maybe even, as we look toward the end of the eighties, getting to a few *more* people. I'm not pessimistic, because I think that's a pretty big audience that's out there for us to attract, if indeed we have programming to attract it. I think our basic business will remain largely the same, that is, in all the main parts of entertainment programming. I see news and reality things, just to pick an umbrella word, as representing an ever growing proportion of what we do, which I happen to applaud. I mean, it excites me to think that, instead of just cloning another night-time serial, we will find a way to do more news magazines or more sports. I'm sort of caught up in the word "service," and I think that in the white hot competition that we've had over the last few years—to attract audiences—between the three networks, we've kind of lost sight of the fact that we are supposed to be a broadcasting service. I would love to see us get more over into the direction of supplying viewers with legitimate alternatives. Example: we are going to schedule the *NBC Magazine* dead against the *Dukes of Hazzard* on Friday nights. I see that as a really black and white choice, and I think that that's an appropriate place for us to put it in terms of offering the viewer a legitimate choice. I would like to see repeal of the Prime Time Access Rule. Personally I'm convinced that it's time to do an hour of network news in the evening. In short, I think, given the somewhat declining state of networking as we've known it, that it wouldn't be a bad time to improve our act by supplying more service, as opposed to just simply going out there every night or every day and in every hour to attract the most, the biggest audience. And I say that fully realizing that profitability and viability obviously are highest priorities.

Garry Marshall

Garry Marshall began his career in comedy by selling jokes to comedians Jack Paar, Joey Bishop, and Phil Foster. The Bishop connection resulted in a move to Los Angeles from New York and a full-time job writing comedy material. In the late fifties and sixties Marshall and his partner, Jerry Belson, wrote over one hundred episodes for such series as *The Danny Thomas Show, The Lucy Show,* and *The Dick Van Dyke Show.* In 1970 the two men developed their own comedy series, *The Odd Couple.* In January of 1974 Marshall brought *Happy Days* to television, and in 1976 it was the top-rated network program for the year. Working closely with several members of his family, Marshall produced *Laverne and Shirley, Mork and Mindy,* and *Joanie Loves Chachi.* His most recent addition to the prime-time schedule was *The New Odd Couple.*

Marshall, a graduate of Northwestern University, has also produced and written a broadway comedy and two motion pictures. A third film, *Young Doctors in Love,* released in 1982, was directed by him.

Marshall grew up in the Bronx and, after early stints as an amateur jazz musician and a newspaper copy boy, he found his career when he began to feed newspaper columnists funny lines which they used in the *New York Daily News.*

Garry Marshall has the reputation of being one of the three or four most successful television producers over the decade of the seventies, and a list of his popular shows—*The Odd Couple, Happy Days, Laverne and Shirley, Mork and Mindy*—creates immediate recognition among millions of viewers. Like many of his contemporaries, Marshall began as a writer for television, in his case working for Jack Paar on the *Tonight Show*. He became a free-lance writer and "reached a point where my free-lance writing was good enough for them [the network] to let me create my own show. Once I had my own show, I became a producer by hiring myself as a producer." This off-the-cuff summary of his career is typical of the man who has presided over the comedy revival at ABC during its most impressive ratings gains in TV history. And while his New York street language masks a well-educated and literate alumnus of Northwestern University, Marshall has no apparent ambition to extract himself from commercial television in order to achieve some "higher" form of dramatic art. Indeed, his style has served him well.

How does Marshall think of a television producer? He is direct and descriptive.

> Television is a producer's medium. Feature movies are a director's medium, and the theatre is a writer's medium. There are exceptions, but in general these cliches are true. I feel the key to a television show is the "writer-producer." There are other people in television, called "producers," but they are not writer-producers. The screen credits only read "producers," so it's very hard to determine who was the technical and production producer and who the writer-producer. There is a big difference. Finally there is an executive producer who is the supervisor of the whole show and in most cases he is a writing executive producer. Norman Lear is now an executive producer; I'm an executive producer. The semantics are a little tricky.

Garry Marshall the policeman, albeit benevolent, is an apt description when one observes him course through the sound stages at Paramount from show to show during the long working days of August and September. He is not an office executive, and the very facilities he uses make this point. No elaborate system of assistants separates

Marshall from the day to day activities. Indeed, when he wishes to be an "office person" he physically moves across town to a quiet retreat in Studio City. He extends his control into all areas of programming, but it is creative control that excites him. While asserting that "with a series, after five years together you are like a family," nevertheless he remains that "last stop." And it is in the exercise of that creative authority that one sometimes perceives Marshall's need to restrict the range of creativity of others in the family, particularly directors.

It is true that the words "committee" and "team" fall freely from his lips, but Marshall recognizes that someone has to be in charge and there is little doubt that he exercises that responsibility.

Unlike many of his contemporaries, Marshall has apparently had little brush with censorship problems. In our discussions he failed to develop any consistent theory on the subject. Clearly he is opposed to censorship in principle and he resists it in his own way, "mumbling a lot," as he says. Yet when he suggests in the interview that television have a czar modeled on the commissioner of the National Football League, there lurk some serious questions about forms of control.

The Marshall imprint is never far from the surface in his three most recent hits. In assessing that imprint he talked of two characteristics of his own creativity.

> Love and surprise! Comedy has to be done by somebody you love because you don't laugh at people you hate. Love is very important and surprise is the other key. You have to be able to surprise the audience. A loving person surprises them and they laugh. It is the true art form because you can't fake laughter. It's a spontaneous response.

This definition of comedy largely determines the range of people Marshall will employ and sets the standard for his shows. He gets his people in what he terms "the tight arena." His comedy is gentle, often nostalgic, and he has his own ideas about each of the successes he has produced. *Laverne and Shirley* explores "physical comedy." *The Odd Couple* was "sophisticated comedy." *Mork and Mindy* is "far out comedy, off the wall, a little crazy because I have an actor who can do that." To Marshall all the shows "have the same style in a sense."

Garry Marshall

They have compassion plus some human quality in them. After the comedy comes the human comedy between people, their relationships. All of my shows usually have high crazy comedy moments and at the end, warmth. It's a style I have done that has been successful for me.

This style, which he also refers to at times as showing people "being nice," is dependent in part on a sense of removal from contemporary life. Marshall thinks of *Mork and Mindy* as a costume piece, related in some ways to *The Waltons* or to *Little House on the Prairie*. In *Happy Days* and *Laverne and Shirley* that distance is created by the strong sense of nostalgia that envelops each production. Both shows were originally positioned in the fifties and have moved into the sixties. They have struck a responsive chord with the public by playing on the past, at times almost satirizing it, while incorporating traditional views. The mix is not accidental.

Leave It to Beaver, Father Knows Best were about nice men saying, "Be nice." Can't do that anymore; nobody listens. Now I got a guy with a leather jacket and black boots who says, "I can beat you up. I can ride a bike better than you, I do a lot of things better than you, and I get girls, and I'm kind of a rebel, but, also, be nice." It's the same message, only it's coming from a more modern voice. Now Mork, the man running around in red pajamas from outer space, is also being nice, but he's not just a plain fellow. He's exciting. It's a voice, it's the same voice as *Leave It to Beaver*, only it's done in a much more dynamic and appealing way now, because the times have changed.

Of course what Marshall means by saying the guy is "kind of a rebel" is that the threat and power of a James Dean are absent from the Fonz. His own power is much more pleasant, more delightfully domestic. Framed as a member of the working class, Fonzie is thoroughly imbued with the values of middle-class America. It is quite legitimate for him to admonish children in the same words used by Jim Anderson, for they espouse the same world-view. If their behaviors appear to be different it ultimately comes down to a matter of surfaces. Marshall is clear in his intention: same message, different rhetorical strategy.

The difference does lie, of course, in the fact that *Beaver* and *Father Knows Best* were themselves nostalgic accounts, portraying family life as it was idealized from the youth of people who looked back to pre-World War II America. For both those earlier series the time was incidental. It was presumed that times had not really changed, and perhaps *should* not change. The picket-fence existence of the Cleavers and the Andersons was the present looking *back,* to verities clearly a part of traditional American family life. Thus, while cast in the language and dress of the fifties, each show tended to have a time-less quality, a half-hour morality playlet.

If, as we suspect, the late fifties were not complacent, quiet times, but a watershed for changing mores in American multi-cultures, this may explain how Marshall can utilize the same time period as *Beaver* when he looks *forward,* for neither *Happy Days* nor *Laverne and Shirley* is actually a part of the fifties. For *Beaver* it was a rare show that engaged some "issue" in society and the viewer of that era seemingly found no such need for issue-oriented series.* In contrast, Marshall's episodes bristle with references to the life-style of the period, but the time-frame is used primarily as a backdrop.

> I set *Happy Days* in the fifties because of the kids; to take away the kids' anxieites. *Happy Days* took place in the past. There were no drugs and the world was calmer, less anxious. Paul Klein, an executive, says that it's called "least objectionable programming." That's kind of negative; it sounds bland. You can look at it like that. But I feel that if a person isn't anxious, he will listen to you. I put it in the fifties where it's socially accepted. Richie says the girl wouldn't go bed with him. Everybody says, "Fine." Today they're a little suspicious, so that's why we set it in the fifties.

Taking Marshall at his word, his underlying motivation is to pro-claim a message about teenagers and parents and the problems of growing up in the world of the 1980's. Desiring the message to be heard, he removed immediate causes of anxiety—drugs and sex—and set his shows in a time known first-hand only by the parents of today.

---

*The continued popularity of series like *Beaver* and *Andy Griffith* among teen-agers who watch reruns is at least a suggestion that such a need is not per-ceived as total even in the eighties.

His thinking suggests this line: Teenagers are anxious about growing up and always have been. Parents are anxious about current conditions under which teenagers are being reared, as *they* always have been. Thus, by turning to the fifties, the parents' anxieties are relieved and the teenagers' anxieties can be translated into common experiences that might allow them to "get the message" that it's all right to avoid some of the problematic areas related to contemporary youth experience. To the criticism that his approach might actually avoid the rugged world faced by modern teens and parents, Marshall replies, "It has never changed. Nobody was born cool with girls; no girls were born cool with boys. It's the same thing. It's the same dialogue. There may be other factors today, but it's the same core. We're still there."

Marshall is particularly conscious of the desirable consequences, in these situations, of having children and parents watch television together. Obviously, one clear value is an increase in the size of the program's audience. But one gets the distinct feeling that there is more here than a concern for ratings. Marshall's conversation is laced with references to teenage problems and parental concern. One significant ingredient for the parents watching Marshall shows is their ability to identify with the times being portrayed, remembering that they went through similar experiences and came out reasonably well. The parent becomes an instant authority for children who may ask, "What was it really like in the fifties?" Of all the writer-producers of the seventies Marshall stands out as the single example whose focus was, and has remained, the child. The blend he developed made the series he produced genuine "family" shows.

It is difficult to deny that Marshall intends to convey traditional values, as he understands them, when he is doing comedy television. As he puts it, "I deal with what society's images are and then try to change it. Now sometimes I'm wrong on society's images, but I really work very hard at investigating it." When Marshall speaks of these images he speaks freely in terms of those things that are "morally right," "righteous kinds of things," "basic values," "right values in our society." He is less than expansive, as one might expect, when requested to define these terms. An examination of his shows, however, offers strong clues to the most concrete versions, and the concrete goes beyond his often-cited desire to present "nice" people doing "nice" things.

He is promoting the nuclear family, God-fearing offspring, stable neighborhoods, sexual abstinence outside of marriage (we never really know what goes on with Fonzie and the girls), marital fidelity, the competitive free-enterprise system, the fundamental value of education, parental authority, justice, law, freedom. This partial list of "nice" things excludes what Marshall perceives as the Lear issues— current, changing values related to specific social issues. By this he means questions concerning abortion, drugs, sexual freedom, busing, welfare, medical ethics. It seems to be a case of making a distinction between social comment and underlying values, unchanging values as Marshall sees them. He is not critical of Lear ("He speaks to the adults, I speak to the children.") but he does not choose to explore the specific relationships that might exist between the two categories, asking, for example, what the nature of "freedom" and "law" have to do with "abortion."

All of Marshall's values have an honored tradition and are drawn from common American experiences of decades past. That the experiences were not equally or commonly shared among social groups does not obviate the quality of the values or the desirability of holding to them. Even the pseudo-cynicism of *The Odd Couple* has disappeared in the newer series. In *Mork and Mindy* the message is actually spelled out in the tag as Mork speaks to Orson on Ork about human traits of compassion, love, jealousy, competition, loneliness, and prejudice. A homily a week, fit—as Marshall affirms—for some Los Angeles pulpits, is reminiscent of *The Loretta Young Show* of the fifties. It is interesting that Miss Young's remarks at the close were as pointed as Mork's and that she too was in costume—the swirling dress that keyed each dramatic entrance. It may not be simple to make the clear distinction Marshall attempts between personal and social ethics, but it is a common American phenomenon. One is reminded of President Eisenhower, who responded to the racial violence of the late fifties— the fifties of *Happy Days* and *Laverne and Shirley*—with a plea to be nice and get right in the heart.

This is not to belittle Marshall's efforts, but to place them in perspective in the history of ethical theory. He is responding to current crises by dealing almost exclusively with individual morality. Lacking is the biting criticism of the system one frequently spots in Lear productions, or in Larry Gelbart's work. Likewise, the gentle comedy of MTM explores the impact of society on the lives of individuals far more aggressively than does Marshall. Hence it may be appropriate to compare *Happy Days* with *Beaver*, *Mork and Mindy* with *Loretta Young*, and *Laverne and Shirley* with *The Life of Riley*.

It may be that his shows are Marshall's way of suggesting that even if one cannot return to the simpler times, the verities of those days can still apply in the more complex society we experience. In this regard, he is closer to *The Waltons* and even to *Gunsmoke* than he is to many of his contemporaries in the field of comedy. None of this should suggest that Marshall is naive. It is rather that he understands the dynamics of the world he works in with far less skepticism than many of his peers, and is able to find ways to express his personal perspective without conflict.

INTERVIEW WITH GARRY MARSHALL

THE PRODUCER'S PERSONAL STYLE

[MARSHALL] Television is a producer's medium. Feature movies are a director's medium, and the theatre is a writer's medium. There are exceptions, but in general these clichés are true. I feel the key to a television show is the "writer-producer." There are other people in television, called "producers," but they are not writer-producers. The screen credits only read "producers," so it's very hard to determine who was the technical and production producer and who the writer-producer. There is a big difference. Finally there is an executive producer who is the supervisor of the whole show and in most cases he is a writing executive producer. Norman Lear is now an executive producer; I'm an executive producer. The semantics are a little tricky. On the *Odd Couple*, I was, at first, the writer-producer. Later I became the executive producer. As a writer-producer I did every aspect of that show. I was actually working every day with the show, and I hired a couple of other producers to help me out. These days, I can't work on a day-to-day basis with any show. Instead, I supervise all my shows as executive producer. Consequently, the producer under me has much more of an input into the show. On *Odd Couple,* I pretty much dictated. Now I can't quite dictate. It's more of a sharing process with the producers who are running each show for me. In the past, I did everything all the way myself. Now I can't do it all myself. That's where the problem comes. Norman used to do it himself. Then, like me, he supervised. Now he has quit even supervising, and he put in another fellow to do this job.

Many of the people working with Norman, particularly writers, were unhappy because he put in a businessman as an executive producer. The writers are not used to working with a businessman. They're used to working with another writer of some sort. So they had a problem.

This movement to businessmen as producers and executive producers is happening now. It seems like there's an old guard of writer-producers, who have become over-worked by the networks. They are pressed by the networks to do too many shows. When they *do* too much, they become tired. They start to move out, like Larry Gelbart, Lear, and myself. During the interim, businessmen come in to run it for a while until a new guard of writer-producers rise up and kind of take over for a while, then they get tired and . . . The businessmen are stopgaps. It's only temporary, until the next shift of Norman Lears and Garry Marshalls, and Larry Gelbarts, and Danny Arnolds, and Jim Brooks come up.

Besides being artistic and cultural, theatre, film, and television are all businesses. Television is the biggest, and thus becomes the least artistic and the least cultural. That's the biggest difference as I see it. When you have a big business, there are more compromises to make. Also, another difference between television and the other two is that you have to roll it out every week. A TV series is a weekly process. I have done 114 *Odd Couples,* 200 *Happy Days,* and 100 *Laverne and Shirleys.* That's a different kind of work than doing one play, and then a year later doing another, or one movie, and two years later another movie. Since you have to do it every week, you can't perfect it as much as you would like to. I would say the difference between the three is mostly one word, *time.* You get the most time with theatre, the next would be the movies, and the least amount of time allowed is in television. This affects quality. Instead of trying for a top level every time, you try to keep the bottom level out of the sewer. Seriously, I don't think we have ever put a terrible episode on the air. I would never do that because I have my name on it. We all have a certain pride in our series, but when you are rolling out that many, there're going to be some we gently refer to as "weak" shows. We also have medium shows, and we have excellent shows. We actually have a grading system: A, B, C, and D. We try to keep all of the D's off the air. We re-shoot them if we have to. We often do that. The unfortunate part is that sometimes the critics only see the C episodes. But that's the way life goes. Most of the C episodes, oddly enough, in any series, are the first few. You don't get a series really cooking until about thirteen weeks.

Q. *Can you describe the various components of producing?*

Most television production is broken down into above the line and below the line. The above the line groups are the writers, producers, directors, and actors. Below the line are the cameramen and technical crew. I myself am now working above the line as a creator and executive producer. That means I create the show, and then I'm the last stop before all of the major decisions are made. I personally work with two partners, Tom Miller and Eddie Milkis, who are also executive producers. They do most of my shows with me.

I work very closely with the creative staff of each show. I've kind of become the policeman and the supervisor. I create most of the initial story areas. I work closely with the producers and writers. I hand-pick most of them, so it's easier for me to work with them. They are mostly people I have brought in, or people who have started with me in some other capacity and worked their way up.

In a sense, I could say I have four shows on the air right now. I think 80 percent of the producers working with me right now started with me on the *Odd Couple* series as junior writers. We developed writer-producers on that show, which ran for five years. In my particular company, Henderson Productions, which is under the Paramount banner, one of my partners is my father who moved out from New York. He is my co-executive producer, working mostly with below the line technical staff. However, I know all of the cameramen personally and all of the sound men, so I usually know when something is wrong. I work close enough so that I know what every person is doing and if somebody is not doing the job quite right. Often with below the line people, I try to make them care about their jobs and contribute more. Specific example: wardrobe people, on some shows they do the costumes and that's it. Somebody tells them at the beginning of a series, "This is the style," and that's it. I don't like to work that way, because I feel that you can score in every area. So at my run-through, even when I'm not there, before each scene in a rehearsal, the wardrobe people come out with the costumes, hold them on hangers, and show what each person is wearing. The actors and the writers can actually see what the characters will be wearing. Traditionally, you never see the wardrobe until the night of the show, and then it's too late to make comments on it, or use it in a creative sense. Some of our best jokes have come off of wardrobe. The writer saw it two days before and will make a joke about a loud sportsjacket. Another thing I do with below the line people, which I don't know if other producers do, is I try to make them join in creatively. Everybody can make a comment on the show. I listen to all of the comments. I try to have my producers, directors, and writers listen to all of the comments. We don't use them all, but I do like an atmosphere in which any given person can contribute. With a hit series, you're all together for years. You are like a family. Some of our better jokes have come from cameramen.

Directors in series television are a very different breed from directors in other forms of show business. I think a lot of any piece of entertainment is "made" in the post-production stages, through editing, sound, dubbing, or whatever. In television the director usually directs the show, and then leaves without doing the post-production. He leaves and goes to the next job, or he finishes one show and has to go to the next one. Very rarely can he get into much post-production. The Directors' Guild has a rule that states that the director must get first cut. Most of my directors don't have time to get a first cut in television.

If a director is famous for doing his thing by editing, and putting pieces of film together, and it's all in his head, that's the kind of director I don't hire. The medium does not lend itself to that kind of a man. Personal self-indulgent visions are an aspect of directing that isn't needed in a TV series, since it's a committee business, done in a limited time period. If a director is going to do more than one episode or direct all of my episodes, I look for a mature person who can run a set, handle actors and crew, and create a nice atmosphere on the set. You need a person who almost projects a father image. This can also be a woman, it doesn't matter.

We have women directors too. They have to take charge of the situation. Sometimes a director can be very eccentric and crazy, and a genius, and all of that, but there's no time for that in television. The director has to be the more mature member of the staff, in order to take care of the actors. I look for somebody who can take charge and run a peaceful place, because it's *every* week. Sometimes the director says, "I want to do my job perfectly," then the others can't do their jobs even near-perfectly, because the director has taken too much *time* doing his. You see, it's a team effort in television.

I like directors who can get what they have to do done within a schedule, so everybody else can have a shot at doing their job at a reasonable hour. A producer, or executive producer, must know every man's job. If he doesn't, it leads to hassles. He also should know every person's job so that he can fix it. My own directing made me know all of the problems, so that when new directors come in, they can't fool me about why something can't be done. I know whether he can do something, or whether he can't. A lot of what I do on the set now, as the executive producer, is to come down on the stage and combine my writing and directing talents in fixing a show.

I happen to love actors. Maybe that's why I like the business so much. No matter what happens, they are the ones who are out there, and I try to work with love and understanding of their problems. The first thing I do is to tell the actors that if they have a scene they can't do comfortably, I will stay up all night trying to re-write it, or spend hours trying to direct them in order to make them comfortable.

However, if an actor says, "My dressing room doesn't have a lamp in it, or I have no phone, or why don't I have a car picking me up?" I don't talk to them about it. I will just say I don't deal with this type of thing. Paramount Studio executives do that. That's put in very clear at the beginning. I only deal with the creative side of a show. Many producers have to deal with both sides and that's sometimes a problem. When Norman Lear was directing Redd Foxx, they would discuss the script and at the same time discuss the fact that Redd didn't have a window in his dressing room. I think that muddles the creative relationship.

When a cast gets a little sluggish that's another case when the executive producer comes in. You have to make some changes. There are various things you can do as producers to hype up a cast that is kind of walking through it. You bring in a guest star and suddenly the whole cast rises and they start to come up. You bring in good actors, who will kick the cast up and challenge them. Sometimes you bring in a guest director. The other thing is to have your writers start to stretch your actors and directors. Give them harder things to do, and take them to unknown ground. That usually challenges and wakes them up.

I try to do my best to supervise all my shows. The best way I can do it is to get in at the beginning. That's why most of the basic story areas, and the initial stories, I try to do myself. Then they are executed by others. Another way I can keep control is by spending a lot of time lecturing and teaching the people who work for me, but still giving them leeway. I don't want to cut off anyone's creativity. In many cases I have to make the final decision, but I certainly listen very closely to my staff. You can't inspire people by telling them to just do it *your* way. They have to win some battles too. That has really nothing to do with entertainment or television; it's just the ability to be an executive in any field. Somebody once said the executive part of the executive producer is as important as the producer part. You have to inspire your people to work. That is the whole trick.

If I read a script from the guys on my staff and they don't have the characters right, I yell. From the beginning, I try to see if they understand the characters. I look for an episode that gives us reasons to do the show. Usually the reasons are: it's exciting, it's a great bravura piece for one of the performers, it's a story that isn't just silly, it has a plot or point or a moral, or it sounds a little fresh. I will take a switch on something that's old, as long as it's a fresh switch. The important thing is that there must be reasons to do the show, not just because it's a story that "works." That's what I try to teach my producers. Don't just take a story that works; there has to be a reason to do it. Why are we doing this show? The reason could be because there's a classic scene for Penny and Cindy or highlights for some of the other characters. I often ask if it is in the realm of our production rules. You can't go over budget. When you look at a script, you look for something that is organic to the series, and makes it special, and the writer has some knowledge of what we are doing on this series. Often they have little knowledge of what you are trying to do, unless you tell them. You inform them of the budget so they don't write "Four hundred camels wander through the scene."

I'm an artist in a business, and since television is the biggest business it's harder to be an artist. In some episodes we reach what I think are excellent quality shows where I feel our artistic hopes are rewarded. But we don't manage to do it every week. Thus I'm an artist as often as I can be. I have to be a craftsman, too. The craftsman is the stopgap—he doesn't let it get really bad. On the weeks when you don't have time for the art, your craft has to keep it up to a certain quality. It's very hard to get something perfect on television, but I think that many of the episodes, and often scenes from some of the episodes I have done, have been perfect.

CREATIVE CONTROL

[MARSHALL] When the network puts on pressure, it's not so bad for me. If the network says we want a gang of twenty hoodlums in the show, I tell them about Fonzie. They want a gang, so I say, "No, there's no gang, I can do one man that's a gang, and it'll be fun. I'll write it, you'll be so excited and you'll love it." Norman did that, too. A businessman can't do that. A businessman can be very talented but he doesn't write. He goes back to four writers and says, "The network wants a gang," and then he goes home. And then the writers stare at each other. That's what the problem is. I'm not just saying writers are wonderful people. I'm saying their creative force is always better in dealing with the networks than the business force, because the business force can't do anything about it and then it falls to the writers. The writers may not be competent yet. I'm not being egotistical; I mean, they just don't have the years of creative experience. Creative clout is much stronger than business clout, much more important.

It's just that the creative guys are eccentric. They don't sit still too well. The networks probably prefer the businessman. They can reason with a creative man, but a creative guy won't take orders. A businessman will take orders, not because he's a weak human being or anything like that, but because it's his job to take orders.

What the networks like best of all is someone like Lee Rich, who is a creative businessman, or Grant Tinker. They're both good, and understand writers. They're businessmen, but they have a way with writers. They can't really tell the writer what to do, but they guide them and they empathize. If I were writing for Lee, and I said, "Lee, go back to the network and tell them that it doesn't work this way," then he'd understand and go back and take a stand.

I seem to have less trouble with networks than other producers and creators. Mostly I guess because I mumble. I don't like head-on confrontations and a lot of fighting and yelling—that's just not my style of life. I mumble a lot, go and do what I want, and then I show it to them and most of the time they see it's okay and say, "Go." My confrontations with them really have to do with other areas. Sometimes they bother you with casting; they're wrong. I think it unfair that a network is casting a person *you* are going to work with for five years. Other network battles are about scheduling shows and sometimes censorship. I have found that if you argue with theory you get nowhere. You have to *show* them. ABC had a theory that *Happy Days* must have a *gang* of hoodlums from the other side of the tracks. I said, "Well, we'll see," and then gave them just Fonzie, alone. They said, "Where's the gang?" and I said, "You don't need a gang. This man is good enough, he's symbolic." They watched and agreed. The same with *Mork and Mindy;* I say that a Martian lands here. They say, "It sounds silly." I mumble. I make it. They see Robin Williams. They say, "Fine." Every year they told me the *Odd Couple* was really about two homosexuals. Their research kept saying that, and they wanted a lot of girls around. I kept mumbling.

If you are the boss, you have to develop a working style with networks and with studios. I know that some of the other executive producers are great at yelling, they scare people and that's terrific for them. They probably don't get ulcers. But I don't get ulcers, either. I have found network people unreasonable sometimes and sometimes even silly, but I have never found them to be totally crazy. Networks always have a reason for what they do. People do not say things to me just to hear themselves talk. Once I know the reason, I usually deal with that and appease it in some way. I think the problem with producers and networks is that producers who have not been down the pike and had experience tend to take the network literally. You can't take them literally. It's the old phrase, "Don't do as I say, do as I mean." Oddly enough, that phrase makes a lot of sense to me. I usually try to do what they mean, not what they say. If I did what they said, I would be selling shoes. Most of them aren't writers or directors, so they don't say things in your terms, so you have to figure out what they *are* saying and do it yourself.

SOCIAL RESPONSIBILITY AND EFFECTS

Q. *In your series do you have some point of view, something you are trying to say?*

I think each creator's series, if you do more than one, have a certain vision, or a certain point of view or approach. My shows are entertainment with an occasional social comment. *Mork and Mindy* comments more than the others, but the others have some social commentary. But mostly my shows are just entertaining. They don't have any weighty message other than what is moral, or what are right values in our society. It's basic values, there's no big trick. I think Norman keeps up with more of the changing values. I pretty much stick to basic values of the family unit, I mean, nothing startlingly new, but just wrapped in a package that will get through to people, especially kids.

So that's why my shows are selling in Europe. I asked Europeans why *Happy Days* is selling, for instance, around the world. It's not violent, it has no car chases, which they love. Why? They all told me when I was in Europe, "We love it because it's morally right." It's moral, it's a moral show. And that's mostly what I do. Everything in it is sound, all sound, righteous kinds of things. Not that I'm a preacher or anything, but it's done in an entertaining form. You may say, "I know that," and say it's not a sophisticated enough message for me, but you can't deny the message is right.

Most parents say to me, "I love *Happy Days*." We give the illusion that the show is for children, but it's for adults, too. The adults pick up on it and that's how we get hits. We can't get a hit with just kids. Adults like morals, a mass message, "Be nice to each other." That's one basic message in all my shows. I think the morals are basically the same as in other shows, only they're a little more real, I think. *Leave It to Beaver, Father Knows Best,* were about nice men saying, "Be nice." Can't do that anymore, nobody listens. Now I got a guy with a leather jacket and black boots who says, "I can beat you up, I can ride a bike better than you, I do a lot of things better than you, and I get girls, and I'm kind of a rebel, but, also, be nice." It's the same message, only it's coming from a more modern voice. Now Mork, the man running around in red pajamas from outer space, is also being nice, but he's not just a plain fellow. He's exciting. It's a voice, it's the same voice as *Leave It to Beaver,* only it's done in a much more dynamic and appealing way now, because the times have changed. *Eight Is Enough* is basically doing *Father Knows Best* but doing it with a more real feeling for the times. I think you can also do it that way; they're very successful with it. It's been equally successful with the costumes. *The Waltons* was a costume show. *Little House on the Prairie* is a costume. *Mork and Mindy* is in a costume. We found a larger audience, and more attention is paid to a show if it's packaged in a dynamic way. Yet it's basically the same message, "Be nice to each other. Don't hate."

I set *Happy Days* in the fifties because of the kids; to take away the kids' anxieties. *Happy Days* took place in the past. There were no drugs and the world was calmer, less anxious. Paul Klein, an executive, says that it's called "least objectionable programming." That's kind of negative, it sounds bland. You can look at it like that. But I feel that if a person isn't anxious, he will listen to you. I put it in the fifties where it's socially accepted. Richie says the girl wouldn't go to bed with him. Everybody says, "Fine." Today they're a little suspicious, so that's why we set it in the fifties.

Growing up has never changed. Nobody was born cool. No girls were born cool with boys. It's the same thing. Richie was nervous saying to the girl, "Let's go to Inspiration Point." In the eighties we really can't relate to that, but maybe we're still nervous saying to the girl, "I got grass in the car, let's go smoke a joint." It's this *young* thing basically. So the parents can relax when we show Richie and Potsy and everybody running around. They know that Richie's not going to pull out a needle any minute, they won't have to turn the set off, so that's what the networks call "least objectionable." I call it less anxiety, because if you don't have anxiety, you may listen to the message.

Sometimes it doesn't get through; sometimes it does. Norman has probably gone the farthest with it in situation comedy, and he got some negative reaction. We still try certain social messages but we don't do abortion or rape. That is a little out of line with our characters. But, then, we do child abuse and alcoholism. *Mork and Mindy's* doing a lot. We did geriatrics and now Mork's series is doing a whole shot at the oil companies. *Happy Days* does more on human behavior. *Happy Days* does "How does it affect me?" Because sitcoms reach so many people, we might as well try to put some issues in them. So we'll stretch once in awhile and do social issues. Even though sometimes it's called silly, it's really not so silly.

The most clear-cut comments are Mork's soliloquy at the end, which was designed just for that reason, to say it head-on. It scared the network. They don't understand the ice cream theory. If you give them ice cream, they'll listen. They said, "You can't do that, nobody will listen." But it's become probably the most popular part of the show because Mork comes out in a red suit and at the end of his comments he'll go, "Na-no, na-no," and that's that. The audience will listen to what he has to say. And it is not hard sell, I feel, coming from him. It would be very offensive to me to have Fred MacMurray stand in front of the camera in a tie and a coat and say social comments. You take it from Pogo better than from a man in a suit. I deal with what society's negative images are, and then try to change them to be positive. Now, sometimes maybe I'm wrong on society's images, but I really work very hard at investigating it. The tag on *Mork* is almost like the sermon of the week. But it doesn't *look* like that. It's very cleverly disguised to look like something else, but that's what it is. There is a place for entertainment with just the nice message, but if everybody wanted to do it, it wouldn't work. But I'm doing it and doing it fine, and if somebody else does it better, then I won't do it anymore. But, while it's rolling, I think I have to be open for more shows to come out of existing shows. Then we do spin-offs.

I feel my shows play on two levels, one for the kids and one for the adults. So that's one thing we're doing. Another thing we're doing is dealing with the handicapped. I always felt that when a person is handicapped they don't get less talented. They can't do everything but they don't lose their talent. I'm trying to show that on *Happy Days*. Instead of hiring an actor to sit in a wheelchair, I went and spent time, and sent my people all over the place, to find some handicapped people who were interested in acting, who wanted to be actors and were not afraid to compete with Robert Redford because they're in a wheelchair. So we'll write a show for them.

My shows hit so many people. We average twenty-three million, so I feel an obligation to say something in the shows; not heavy messages, but just get some things across. There are a lot of people watching. We do minor little things like having Fonzie get a library card so all children will get a library card and the Library Association uses our film to show kids in school rather than the film they had. From that level we go to much deeper levels with social problems. I get a lot of flack from the network in that area. And in that area I'm not totally free, but I'm winning. The network would rather just make it a totally lighthearted comedy because they think anything meaningful, or strong commentary, will hurt the show's ratings. I don't feel that way. The ratings have never gone down when we did a serious episode. It's a fight. When I am reaching so many people, I feel I should be saying something good, not just entertaining and getting laughs. I don't mean to be pretentious, because our messages are pretty basic. I have said that Norman Lear is working on the adults and I'm working on the children. I like to catch the kids and maybe give them some values right at the beginning. Most of our mail and our accolades on *Happy Days* and *Laverne and Shirley* have been in that area. *Mork and Mindy* seems to be one of those shows that crosses all bounds and gets things across to everybody. I can't seem to get this through to the networks sometimes. If twenty-three million people are watching you, you should give them something besides entertainment. The network doesn't always feel that way. They feel if you just entertain the audience it won't go away. Most of my shows are designed to make people feel good.

In *Laverne and Shirley,* I think I have figured a way to do low comedy and the best kind of physical comedy. In the early days of television nobody else did that except Lucy, and I have managed to do what I set out to do with Penny and Cindy. With *Happy Days,* I showed that there could be a family show that children watch, that adults can also watch with them without falling asleep. I have children. I can watch *Happy Days* with them without falling asleep. I think you can have a hit series without sex and violence. I have. I was very happy that I could break some ground with *Mork and Mindy*. Networks said you can't do *Saturday Night Live* humor or satirical humor at eight o'clock. I said you could, with the right actor. We're doing it with a man named Robin Williams.

Q. *What is the standard by which you judge the content of the shows?*

I think if I enjoy it, a lot of people will. I can enjoy many different things. Sometimes our intellectual community has these great dreams of what is going on, but you have to understand what is really going on. The working man isn't going to go to plays every week. Who can afford it? You can't go out and see all of the cultural things that are being done, so they are brought to you on television. I also believe in reading, and we push that on *Happy Days*. We do some cultural things on *Happy Days*. We brought on Leslie Brown from *Turning Point* and we exposed our audience to ballet. *Happy Days* draws twenty-five million people. You can't go on the air and say, "Watch the ballet," but we can expose people to it. You expose people to things they can't see, possibly because of where they are, or where they work, or because they're sick, or often because they can't afford it. I don't sit home and watch television every single night, because of where I live. I have enough money to buy a ticket and go to the movies or theatre, or ballet or even opera. Many people can't.

Television is probably the most powerful thing in the country. It's the medium that reaches the most people, so to me it is the most powerful. I think my shows can do a lot of good in the country, especially with kids. The drawback is that since my shows are successful, they make money, and then other people start to copy my shows, and you get the same kind of shows all over TV. In that sense, my shows would contribute to making TV a vast wasteland. If I do what I do and Norman does what he does and everybody does their separate thing, then that's very healthy. It's the lesser craftsman or artist who just copies who will turn it into a wasteland, not the guys who are really trying to get their styles across.

I think television does a lot of good, but like anything else, it is misused, half misused by the public and half by the networks. I certainly feel that when the networks put great shows opposite each other or put in too many commercials, then they are misusing the medium of TV. But so is the parent who doesn't want to talk to his child, and instead tells him to go shut up and watch TV. The parent is then also misusing this medium. How we use it is up to us.

Q. *Will you give us a critique of your own work?*

Actually, I sleep very well. I think I am doing something that is positive in a negative world. It would be easier for me to say I'm a cynic, because I can pronounce the "cynic" very well. The word I don't pronounce very well is "sentimentalist." It's a hard word for me to say. I feel I am a sentimentalist in the tradition of Norman Rockwell. I also like Aesop's Fables a lot. I think there is a place for that and that's what I do. I know the definition of "artist" is not necessarily "cynic." I think there is room for a sentimental and positive approach, to balance off the negative approaches. I was once watching TV and I heard on the news that your car was going to blow up because you may have a defective Pinto. They showed a lot of shots of cars blowing up and facts about people being killed. I was very glad when *Happy Days* came on. And I don't even own a Pinto.

Love and surprise! Comedy has to be done by somebody you love because you don't laugh at people you hate. Love is very important and surprise is the other key. You have to be able to surprise the audience. A loving person surprises them and they laugh. It is the true art form because you can't fake laughter. It's a spontaneous response.

Q. *Will you make some precise distinctions for us respecting your series?*

When I first start a series I usually "set" it. You have to set it with the actors and tell them what type of things we are going to do. There are some discussions and disagreements, but we work it all out. Each show has a base that everybody follows. In other words, the base of *Laverne and Shirley* is survival. People with nothing going for them, no education, no money, no class, still survive. The basic core of *Happy Days* is growing up, and the pain of growing up. The core of *Mork and Mindy* is social comedy. The naiveté of a new man on Earth and his outlook on everything in our society is the heart of it. The staff and the actors are told this very clearly and if their contributions are within the bounds that I set, then it's all right, I don't have to even be there a lot. Mostly Tom Miller and Eddie Milkis and I set the style for the shows. Most of my shows are done because I'm examining some aspect of comedy. On *Laverne and Shirley* I was examining physical comedy, on *Happy Days* it was straight, family, warm, relationship comedy, and the *Odd Couple* I was doing sophisticated comedy. In *Mork and Mindy* I am examining far-out comedy, off the wall, a little crazy, because I have an actor who can do that. However, all of them have the same style in one sense. They have compassion plus some human quality in them. After the comedy comes the human comedy between people, their relationships. All of my shows usually have high crazy comedy moments and at the end, warmth. It's a style I have done that has been successful for me.

Q. *Will you discuss your perspective on commercial television? What do you see for the future?*

Seventy-five percent of the negative things you hear about television are sour grapes from guys who couldn't sell their show, you know, so, sure, why are they going to be thrilled? The network shot down their show.

I think there are a lot of things wrong with the system, but it's just so complicated to fix, because it has to do with time and money and everything, so people keep asking me, "Well, how do we fix the whole thing?" and I'll give you my theory, which I told PBS.

Television is finally being accepted in the country now as an intense competition, that's what you keep hearing about. It's really becoming a competition; you can see it in the airways. It's just been traditional in our society that when anything becomes an intense competition, suddenly we are bright enough to say, "What is the name of this field we're all competing in? Let's have an overview of this field." In other words, comparing this to football—I'm always comparing things to football—in football they had all these teams. They were playing, everybody was nice enough. Suddenly it got immensely competitive because it suddenly became big money. Who's got the biggest crowds and television rights, and all that? As soon as it got intensely competitive, they made a Commissioner of Football, a man who oversees it all, and "for the good of the game" became a philosophy.

In television we don't have anybody up there saying, "for the good of the game." It's all fragmented. And it's not healthy when the competition gets so intense with nobody with an overview. Television needs a commissioner, not an FCC guy who doesn't know what's happening, because he doesn't know the business. They got a sports man to do sports. They need a television man to say something is for the good of television, so that there is a rule. There are no rules now, and no rules, in intense competition is not healthy. So, I'm looking at a total overview of what's wrong with television, rather than to get into why everybody can't sell their pilot. What is really wrong with it is that there is no one to whom you can say, "This is not ethical folks." I mean even the advertising community—who's worse than the advertising community?—they have an advertising council that says, "You can't say that this will cure your throat problems if it's not true." They have rules. Nobody in television states rules. We haven't any council or commissioner. All TV cares about is how many minutes of commercials you get on. I mean, all that is important, but we're supposed to live in a world of ethics. Somebody's got to say you can't move a show on one night and throw it up against another. Somebody's got to say it's not for the public interest to run *Elvis Presley* against *Gone with the Wind,* not good, folks. In the AFL and NFL, football leagues had the sense not to run the two games at the same hour. There was one in the morning, one at night, and I mean, they *got together* to do this. It doesn't seem to be something that takes a genius to do. It just takes somebody to say it. We need a commissioner.

Another problem in TV is the policy of going with people who have "track records." That means creators who have sold shows before that were hits. There have to be more executives at the networks who will say, "Let's put on Joe Smith's pilot, he has no track record but that show is good." If they do that, I think the public will get the true variety of programming. The track record thing isn't good for the public interest, either. I have three shows on; the networks want more. The three series are different but I'm still doing my own style. There seems to be room for shows in other styles. I might make a better show than Joe Smith, but the point is, why do four of mine, why not do a couple of his? I think that is best for the public interest. The networks have *recently* been buying shows from mostly five people: Aaron Spelling, Lee Rich, Grant Tinker, Norman Lear, and myself. They should buy from other people. If not, there's still hope because somewhere there is a kid sitting, maybe you, saying, I'm going to become one of those five people. By then I hope I will be doing something else.

Index

ABC, 4, 6–7, 15, 61, 84, 174, 176, 210, 216, 231, 245
action-adventure series, 47, 97, 109, 119. *See also specific titles*
actors and acting, TV, 60, 88–89, 96, 98, 105, 119, 142, 169, 211, 222, 242, 243
Adams, Nick, 82
advertising and advertisers, 12–13, 20, 109–10, 166, 253. *See also* commercials; sponsors
AFTRA, 7
Alda, Alan, 4, 14, 17
Alfred Hitchcock Show, The, 128
All in the Family, 4, 7, 11, 16, 109, 173, 174, 176, 177, 178, 179, 180, 182, 183, 184, 187, 188, 194, 197, 220–21
All That Glitters, 42, 173
American Medical Association (AMA), 66, 88, 190, 202
America 2Night, 173
Amos, John, 180, 185, 186
Andy Griffith Show, The, 26, 28, 174, 235
anti-violence campaign, 65–66, 97, 119, 126. *See also* violence on TV
Apple's Way, 154, 159–60

Arnaz, Desi, 57
Arness, James, 97, 100–101, 113, 117, 118
Arthur, Beatrice, 188
Asner, Ed, 65, 126, 228
Associates, The, 196, 216, 217
audience, TV, 53, 109, 137, 138, 164, 185, 224, 228–29
effect on TV production, 11, 215; mass, 20, 42, 165
producer's conception of, 64, 89–90, 143, 166, 192, 210, 215

Balding, Rebecca, 65
Barnaby Jones, 46, 56, 63, 64, 67
Barney Miller, 9, 126–27, 223
Baxters, The, 173, 181
Beach Patrol, 170–71
Belson, Jerry, 213, 230
Ben Casey, 65, 176
Benjamin, Walter, 37, 45
Beverly Hillbillies, The, 26, 27–28, 29, 174
Bishop, Joey, 230
Black Saddle, 128
Blake, Amanda, 111–12, 115
Bob Newhart Show, The, 4, 7, 201
Bonanza, 109

Borgnine, Ernest, 83
Brando, Marlon, 60
Bridges, Jeff, 149
Bridges, Lloyd, 105
Brodkin, Herb, 59, 73
Brooks, James L. (Jim), 4, 5, 6, 43, 196, 200–207, 208–23 (interview), 226
Brown, Les, 7
Brown, Leslie, 250
Bruce, Lenny, 232
Buck Rogers in the 25th Century, 96, 97, 101–2, 121, 122–24, 126, 127
Burns, Allan, 4, 6, 7, 43, 196–97, 198, 200–207, 208–23 (interview), 226
Burr, Raymond, 83

cable TV, 3, 7, 33, 43, 72, 127
Cannon, 46, 56, 67
Cantor, Muriel, 35, 36, 44
Capra, Frank, 115
Carey, James, 22, 24, 25, 44
Carol Burnett Show, The, 176
Carr, John Dixon, 140
Carter, Jimmy, 29
Carter, Virginia, 150, 180–81
Case of Rape, A, 153
Caulfield, Holden, 140
Cawelti, John, 38, 45
CBS, 4, 5, 6, 7, 15, 29, 65, 66, 110, 113, 154, 164, 165, 167, 173, 174, 187, 188, 189, 198, 200, 203, 228
censors and censorship, 7, 10, 13, 14, 165, 166, 189–90, 217, 232
Centennial, 116
Chain of Command, 148
Chamberlain, Richard, 83
characters and characterization in TV shows, 40, 64, 76, 80, 90, 159, 160–61, 172, 203, 216, 243
Charlotte's Web, 154
Chayevsky, Paddy, 130, 135, 138, 145, 148, 152

Cimarron Strip, 122
Class of '65, 67
Clements, Cal, 117–18, 122
Colgate Comedy Hour, 173
Columbo, 4, 16, 43, 128, 129, 132, 133, 136, 141, 146, 148, 150, 151
comedy, TV, 5, 7, 42, 176, 182, 222, 225, 226, 232, 234, 249, 251, 252
    See also specific comedy series titles
    production of, 10–11; series, 4, 39, 192, 195
    situation, 152, 248
commercials, 9, 20, 90. *See also* advertising and advertisers; sponsors
Congressional Black Caucus, 189
Copolla, Francis, 72
Corby, Ellen, 28, 163, 169, 171
Crane, Stephen, 51, 55
Crisis at Central High, 128–29, 132
Curtis, Ken, 115

Dallas, 30, 106, 160, 164
Dan August, 46
Daniels, Stan, 209, 211, 212, 213
Danny Thomas Show, The, 230
Davis, Dave, 211
Day, Doris, 220
Dean, James, 234
Defenders, The, 65, 116
Desilu, 46
Desilu-Westinghouse Playhouse, 57, 96, 116
DeLoach, Cartha, 70
detective and crime detection drama, 43, 129, 136, 137. *See also* specific titles
Dick Van Dyke Show, The, 230
Diff'rent Strokes, 182
directors, TV, 35–36, 59–60, 84, 104–6, 145–46, 162, 208, 209, 212, 241–42, 243
Directors' Guild of America, 162, 241

Doc, 4
Dr. Kildare, 16, 74, 82, 86, 88, 91, 128
Double Indemnity, 74
dramas, social and socially oriented, 132, 134–36, 138, 141, 152
Dukes of Hazard, The, 26, 222–23, 229
Dunaway, Faye, 83
Dynasty, 164

Eastwood, Clint, 64
Eight Is Enough, 247
Eisenhower, Dwight, 237
Eleventh, Hour, The, 82
Ellery Queen, 128, 129, 136
Embassy Communications, 150, 173
Execution of Private Slovak, The, 128, 129, 141, 143, 145

Fagan, Jack, 118
Falcon Crest, 154, 160–61, 163–64
Falk, Peter, 128, 133
Falwell, Jerry, 226
Family, 156, 169
family, as portrayed in television, 103, 154, 156, 160, 168–70, 185, 186, 236
Family Viewing Time (FVT), 6, 177
Fantasy Island, 25
Father Knows Best, 5, 86, 178, 207, 219, 234–35, 247
FBI, The, 46, 47, 52, 53–54, 56, 66, 69–71
Federal Communications Commission (FCC), 6, 17, 166, 252
Fernwood Forever, 173
Firecreek, 96
"Fires of Ignorance, The," 119, 120–21, 126
Fiske, John, 31, 44
Flamingo Road, 164
Flanders, Ed, 191
Ford, John, 51, 61

Ford Star Review, 173
Foster, Phil, 250
Four Star Television, 128
Foxx, Redd, 242
Friendly, Ed, 111
Fugitive, The, xii, 46, 47, 53, 54, 56, 61–62, 71, 79, 128

Gable, Clark, 60
Geer, Will, 28, 159, 163
Gelbart, Larry, 4, 38–39, 41, 42, 237, 239
Gerbner, George, 151
Get Smart, 196
Goldberg, Leonard, 15
"Golden Years" of television, 5, 12–13, 116, 152
Goldman, William, 150
Good Times, 4, 173, 180, 183, 184, 185–86, 193
Goodyear TV Playhouse, 185
Green Acres, 26
Greene, Graham, 141
Gunsmoke, xii, 4, 74, 96, 97, 98, 100, 106, 109, 110, 111–13, 118–19, 121–22, 126, 158, 238
Gun, The, 142, 143, 145, 146

Haley, Alex, 181
Hamner, Earl, 4, 42, 154–61, 161–72 (interview)
Happy Days, xii, 16, 230, 231, 234, 235, 239, 245, 246, 247, 248, 249, 250, 251, 252
Harris, Susan, 18
Hartley, John, 31, 44
Hartman, David, 86, 95
Hawkes, Howard, 51–52
He and She, 196
Hello, Larry, 182
Hemmingway, Ernest, 51, 55
Henderson Productions, 240
Hill, Arthur, 95
Hill Street Blues, 7, 109, 226, 227

Hirsch, Paul, 26, 44
Hitchcock, Alfred, 139, 143, 145
Holbrook, Hal, 15
Holocaust, 147
Homecoming, The, 154–55
homosexuals and homosexuality as
  portrayed on TV, 81, 127, 129,
  135, 142, 152, 176, 221, 245
Hoover, J. Edgar, 69–70
Horn, Alan, 182
Hot l Baltimore, 173
How the West Was Won, 96, 97, 98,
  100, 102, 116–18, 120, 122

idealism and idealization in TV, 47,
  51–52, 54–56, 63, 79, 80, 88,
  92, 136, 156
I Love Lucy, 177
Invaders, The, 46, 53

James at 15, 67
Jane Wyman Show, The, 57
Jankowski, Gene, 188–89
Jeffersons, The, 4, 176, 183, 184
Joanie Loves Chachi, 230
Johnny Ringo, 128
Johnson, Lyndon, 29

Katzman, Leonard, 106
Kelsey, Linda, 65, 228
Kennedy, John F., 97, 135
Kennedy, Robert F., 135
King, Martin Luther, Jr., 135
King, Paul, 122
Klein, Paul, 247
Klugman, Jack, 176
Knebel, Fletcher, 83
Knots Landing, 29–30, 31
Kraft Television Theater, 116

Land of the Giants, 102
Laugh-In, 111

Laverne and Shirley, 230, 231, 232,
  234, 235, 239, 249, 251, 252
Leachman, Cloris, 6
Leacock, Phillip, 121–22
Lear, Norman, 59, 73, 107, 173–82,
  183–95 (interview).
  and CBS, 7, 15
  his influence, 10–11, 140, 220–21
  his method of production, 213,
  215, 239, 242, 244
  his series, 4, 16, 152, 197, 249,
  253; his style, 42, 135, 165,
  201–2, 237, 244, 248, 249
Learned, Michael, 163
Leave It to Beaver, 5, 169, 174, 178,
  207, 234–35, 247
Lee, Joanna, 165
Leonard, Bert, 73
Leonard, Sheldon, 15
Levinson, Richard, 4, 15, 16, 43, 59,
  73, 128–39, 139–53 (inter-
  view), 224
Lewis, Jerry, 173
Life of Riley, 238
Link, William, 4, 15, 16, 43, 59, 73,
  128–39, 139–53 (interview), 224
Little House on the Prarie, 234, 241
Little Women, 74, 83
Lloyd, David, 209
Lombardi, Vince, 83
Loretta Young Show, The, 237, 238
Lorimar Productions, 16, 30, 154,
  160, 161
Lou Grant, 7, 65, 196, 201, 202,
  210, 211, 217–18, 227, 228
Love American Style, 196
Love Boat, 25
Lucas Tanner, 74, 86
Lucy Show, The, 230

MacMurray, Fred, 248
McCallum, David, 94
McCarthy, Joseph, 140
McCloud, 129, 136
McDonald, Norman, 115

McNeeley, Jerry, 83
Magnum, P.I., 29, 66
Malden, Karl, 60
Mama, 174, 178
Man from U.N.C.L.E., The, 74, 82, 89–90, 91, 93–94, 128
Manhunt, 46
Mannix, 67, 129, 151
Mantley, John, 4, 42, 96–104, 104–27 (interview), 183
Marcus Welby, M.D., 4, 16, 74, 78, 79, 82, 84, 86–87, 88, 89, 92–93
Marshall, Garry, 4, 11–12, 15, 16, 43, 183, 198, 209, 213, 230–37, 238–53 (interview)
Marshall, Penny, 243, 249
Martin, Dean, 173
Martin, Quinn, 4, 15, 16, 42, 46–56, 56–73 (interview), 75, 76, 78–80, 136
Mary Hartman, Mary Hartman, 42, 173, 182, 183, 184, 195
Mary Tyler Moore Show, The, 4, 6, 152, 174, 196, 197, 201, 202, 203, 204–7, 209, 210, 211, 212, 218–20, 221
M*A*S*H, 4, 7, 38–39, 126, 215, 218
Matinee Theatre, 154
Maude, 4, 7, 173, 176, 180–81, 183, 184, 188
Mayer, L. B., 57
medical shows, 75, 92. *See also specific titles*
Medical Story, 87, 88
melodrama and melodramatists in TV, 48, 50, 75, 76, 78, 80, 174
Meston, John, 115
Metro-Goldwyn-Mayer (MGM), 16, 82
Miles, Vera, 69
Milkis, Eddie, 240, 251–52
Miller, Tom, 240, 251–52
minorities in the TV industry, role of, xvi–xvii

Mr. Dugan, 188–89
Mr. Novak, 225
Moore, Mary Tyler, 6, 198, 200, 219
Moore, Tom, 69
Moral Majority, 66
Mork and Mindy, 230, 231, 232, 234, 237, 245, 246, 248, 249, 250, 251, 252
Morris, Frank, 145–46
Most Wanted, 46, 66
movies, made for TV, 9–10, 130. *See also specific titles*
MTM, 4, 5, 6, 7, 11, 16, 65, 182, 196, 197–98, 200–201, 203, 208, 211, 215, 224, 226, 227, 237
Munsters, The, 196
Murder by Natural Causes, 15, 128, 141, 145–46, 147
Music, Lorenzo, 211
mysteries, TV, 132–33, 134, 139, 140, 141, 143
My Sweet Charlie, 128, 129, 141, 146, 151, 152

Name of the Game, 82, 93
National Association of Broadcasters (NAB), 189
National Education Association (NEA), 119, 120
NBC, 13, 16, 38, 97, 182, 197, 198, 201, 224, 225
NBC Magazine, 229
New Breed, The, 46
New Odd Couple, The, 230
networks, 3, 13–14, 15, 134, 164, 190, 194, 216, 225, 227–28, 249. *See also* ABC; CBS; NBC
and anti-violence campaign, 66, 67
and casting, 10, 86, 214
and programming, 8, 9, 108, 116, 117, 166
and creative control, 58, 109, 110, 149
their relationship to producers and

networks (*continued*)
    production, 111, 112–13, 114,
    148, 165, 166–67, 224, 244–46
Neumann, Jack, 225
Newhart, 201, 211
Newman, Paul, 60, 148
Nicholson, Jack, 60
Nielsen ratings, xii, 4, 46, 182. *See
    also* ratings

O'Connell, David, 83, 95
Odd Couple, The, 230, 231, 232,
    237, 238, 239, 240, 245, 252
Olivier, Laurence, 148
One Day at a Time, 4, 173, 183, 184
One Step Beyond, 167
Owen Marshall, Counselor-at-Law,
    74, 78, 83, 92

Paar, Jack, 230, 231
Palmerstown, U.S.A., 173, 181
Paramount Pictures, 74, 231, 240
Parent-Teachers Association (PTA),
    66, 120, 190, 202
Patchett, Tom, 211
Paul Sand in Friend and Lovers, 196,
    212–13
People for the American Way, 173,
    181–82
Petticoat Junction, 26
Philco TV Playhouse, 185
Phyllis, 4, 5, 6, 211
Playhouse 90, 13, 116, 185
Poe, Edgar Allen, 134
Pope John XXIII, 83
Portraits, 83
Prescription Murder, 128
Presley, Elvis, 253
Price, Arthur, 198
Prime Time Access Rule, 229
producers, 32, 33, 83–85, 95. *See
    also specific producers*
    as creative artists, 12, 17–18, 107,
    132, 183

    their creative control, 35, 65–69,
    85–91, 107–18, 147–50, 165–
    68, 182, 186–91, 200, 216,
    225–27, 244–46
    independent, 7, 8, 13–15
    their social responsibility and ef-
    fect, 69–70, 91–95, 118–27,
    150–53, 168–72, 191–95, 217–
    23, 227–28, 246–53
Producers' Caucus, 177
Public Broadcasting System (PBS), 3,
    252

QM Productions, 15, 46
Queen, Ellery, 140

ratings, 11, 20, 108, 109, 113, 148,
    194, 222, 249. *See also* Nielsen
    ratings
Ravage, John, 35–36, 45
realism in TV shows, 51, 78, 134
Real McCoys, The, 26
Real People, 222
Rebel, The, 74, 82
Redford, Robert, 60, 249
Rehearsal for Murder, 129, 141
Reynolds, Gene, 218, 226
Rhoda, 4, 7, 196, 204, 210, 212–13,
    215
Rich, Lee, 16, 162, 245, 253
Roddenberry, Gene, vii, 8
Rogues, The, 128
Room 222, 196, 198, 203, 213, 218,
    219
Roots, 147
Ross, Katheryn, 15
Rozsa, Miklos, 139
Ryan's Four, 74

St. Elsewhere, 7
Sahlins, Marshall, 32–33, 44
Salinger, J. D., 40, 139

Sandrich, Jay, vii, 18, 205, 208, 212, 224
Sanford and Son, 173
Sartre, Jean Paul, 140
Saturday Night Live, 250
science fiction in TV, 101–2, 123, 125
Scott, George C., 88
Scott, Walter, 225
Screen Actors' Guild, 7
Seiden, M. H., 35, 44
Selleck, Tom, 66
77 Sunset Strip, 69, 128
Shea, Jack, 18
Sheen, Martin, 149
Shepard, Sam, 142
Sikes, Don, 122
Silverman, Fred, 38–39, 66, 67–68, 122, 224
Silverstone, Roger, 23, 44
Simmons, Ed, 173
Simmons, Norbert, xvi
$64,000 Question, 110
Slattery's People, 128
Sloan, 67–68
Smothers Brothers, the, 178
Smothers Brothers Show, The, 196
Snow Birch, 96
SOAP, 6
Sontag, David, vii, 12, 13, 14
Spelling, Aaron, xvi, 15, 179, 253
Spencer's Mountain, 154, 155
sponsors, 13, 109, 110. *See also* advertising and advertisers; commercials
Stack, Robert, 60, 82
Stanton, Frank, 13
Starsky and Hutch, 151
Starting Over, 196, 213, 214
Star Trek, 97, 102, 123
Stein, Ben, 151
Stephens, John, 106
Stewart, James, 69
Stone, Milburn, 111, 112, 115, 119
Story of Esther, The, 84
Storyteller, The, 128, 137, 142, 146, 147

Streets of San Francisco, The, 16, 46, 47, 52, 53, 56, 59, 61–62, 63, 64, 66, 67
Streisand, Barbra, 130
Studio One, 116
studios. *See specific studios*
Sugarfoot, 128
Supreme Court of the United States, 190–91
Susskind, David, 173
Swafford, Tom, 5

Take Your Best Shot, 129, 132, 142
Tales of the Unexpected, 46
Tandem/TAT, 4, 6, 7, 173, 179, 182
Tarses, Jay, 211
Taxi, 196, 210, 213–14, 215, 218
television
    and American culture, 18–34
    and creativity, 34–44
    future of, 72–73
    political functions and attitudes of, 19, 21, 47, 55, 71–72, 79, 151–52
    producer's medium, 3–18, 57, 106–7, 238–39
    white male dominance of, xvi–xvii
Tenafly, 128, 129
That Certain Summer, 128, 129, 141
That Was The Week That Was, 178
Theater Guild of America, 154
Thomas, Danny, 4, 15, 173
Thomas, Richard, 28, 159, 163
Three's Company, 227
Till Death Do Us Part, 174
Tinker, Grant, 8, 43, 196–207, 213, 224–29 (interview), 245, 253
    his method of producing, 11, 210–11
    as president of MTM, 4, 16, 65, 208, 216
Today, 13, 154
Tonight Show, 13, 231
Truman, Harry, 83, 191
Turner, Victor, 23, 24, 44, 45

Twelve O'Clock High, 46, 52
Twentieth Century Fox, 4, 16, 197, 198
27th Day, The, 123
Twilight Zone, 167
Tyson, Cicely, 119

United Artists, 187
United States, 38–41
Universal Studios, 16, 74, 82, 85, 122, 128, 129, 132, 144
Untouchables, The, 46, 47, 52, 57, 66, 67, 96, 98, 119

Vanished, 83
Vaughan, Robert, 83, 94
Verne, Jules, 139
Victor, David, 4, 16, 42, 74–82, 82–95 (interview)
violence on TV, 6, 47, 50–51, 66–67, 103, 137, 150, 151, 166, 178, 189–90, 202. *See also* anti-violence campaign

Waite, Ralph, 172
Walden, Robert, 228
Walker, Nancy, 215
Waltons, The, 26, 28–29, 30, 31, 109, 154, 155, 156, 158–59, 161, 162, 163, 164, 165–66, 168–69, 171
Wanted: Dead or Alive, 128
Warner, Jack, 51, 69
Warner Brothers, 16, 69

Warren, Charles Marquis, 115
Weaver, Dennis, 115
Weaver, Pat, 13
Webb, Jack, xvi
Weinberger, Ed, 209, 211, 212, 213
Wells, Orson, 133, 146
westerns, TV, 97, 100, 101, 102–4, 116, 118, 120, 125. *See also specific titles*
White Shadow, The, 201, 225, 227
Wildmon, Donald, 226
Wild, Wild West, The, 96, 97, 121, 122
Williams, Cindy, 243, 249
Williams, Robin, 245, 250
Windsor, Duke and Duchess of, 83
Woman in White, 74
women in the TV industry, influence of, xvi–xvii
Wood, Robert, 6, 165, 174, 176
Wrathful Man, The, 96
writer-producer, 15, 86, 130, 144, 147, 179, 182, 183, 203, 208, 226, 231, 238, 239
writers and writing, TV, 58, 155, 165, 208–9, 240, 243, 244
Writers' Guild of America, 147, 209

Yorkin, Bud, 173, 174, 179, 213
Young, Robert, 78, 84, 86, 91
Your Show of Shows, 116

Zimbalist, Efrem, Jr., 70
Zukor, George, 51